RightStart™ MATHEMATICS

by Joan A. Cotter, Ph.D.
with Tracy Mittleider, MSEd

LEVEL B LESSONS
Second Edition

A Activities for Learning, Inc.

A special thank you to Kathleen Cotter Lawler for all her work on the preparation of this manual.

Note: Rather than use the designations, Kindergarten, First Grade, ect., to indicate a grade, levels are used. Level A is kindergarten, Level B is first grade, and so forth.

Copyright © 2013 by Activities for Learning, Inc.

All rights reserved. No part of this publication may be reproduced, stored in a retrieval system, or transmitted, in any form or by any means, electronic, mechanical, photocopying, recording, or otherwise, without written permission of Activities for Learning, Inc.

The publisher hereby grants permission to reproduce the appendix for a single family's use only.

Printed in the United States of America

www.RightStartMath.com

For more information: info@RightStartMath.com
Supplies may be ordered from: www.RightStartMath.com

Activities for Learning, Inc.
321 Hill Street
Hazelton, ND 58544-0468
United States of America
888-775-6284 or 701-782-2000
701-782-2007 fax

ISBN 978-1-931980-62-3

January 2019

RightStart™ Mathematics Objectives for Level B

	Quarter 1	Quarter 2	Quarter 3	Quarter 4

Numeration
- Can recognize quantities 1 to 10 without counting
- Can enter and recognize quantities to 100 on the abacus
- Knows even numbers and odd numbers
- Can identify even/odd numbers to 120
- Can count by 2s, 5s, 10s

Place Value
- Knows 37 as 3-ten 7
- Knows traditional names: e.g., 18 as eighteen as well as 1-ten 8
- Can trade 10 ones for 1 ten — Q1: N/A
- Can trade 10 tens for 1 hundred — Q1: N/A
- Can trade 10 hundreds for 1 thousand — Q1: N/A
- Can write and read 4-digit numbers — Q1: N/A

Addition
- Understands addition as combining parts to form a whole
- Knows number facts to 18 — Q1: N/A, Q2: N/A
- Can add 2-digit numbers mentally — Q1: N/A
- Can add 4-digit numbers — Q1: N/A, Q2: N/A

Subtraction
- Understands subtraction as missing addends — Q1: N/A, Q2: N/A
- Understands subtraction as partitioning — Q1: N/A, Q2: N/A
- Knows subtraction facts up to 10 — Q1: N/A, Q2: N/A

Problem Solving
- Can solve word problems
- Perseveres in solving problems

Geometry
- Knows parallel and perpendicular lines
- Knows square is a special rectangle
- Knows lines of symmetry — Q1: N/A, Q2: N/A, Q3: N/A
- Composes shapes from existing shapes — Q1: N/A
- Knows names of special quadrilaterals — Q1: N/A, Q2: N/A, Q3: N/A

Measurement
- Can measure to one half of a centimeter — Q1: N/A, Q2: N/A, Q3: N/A
- Can measure to one half of an inch — Q1: N/A, Q2: N/A, Q3: N/A
- Can measure around a shape — Q1: N/A, Q2: N/A, Q3: N/A

Fractions
- Can partition into halves and fourths — Q1: N/A, Q2: N/A, Q3: N/A
- Knows that one fourth is also called a quarter — Q1: N/A, Q2: N/A, Q3: N/A
- Knows unit fractions up to tenths — Q1: N/A, Q2: N/A, Q3: N/A

Time
- Knows days of the week and months of the year — Q1: N/A
- Can tell and write time in hours & half hours on analog & digital clocks — Q1: N/A, Q2: N/A
- Can tell time to five-minute intervals — Q1: N/A, Q2: N/A

Money
- Knows name and value of penny, nickel, dime, and quarter — Q1: N/A, Q2: N/A, Q3: N/A
- Can determine the value of three coins — Q1: N/A, Q2: N/A, Q3: N/A

Calculator
- Can add and subtract whole numbers — Q1: N/A, Q2: N/A, Q3: N/A

Materials Needed That Are Not Included the RS2 Math Set

Occasionally within the lessons materials list you will see items in bold that are not included in the RS2 Math Set. Below is a list of the items that will be needed to teach those lessons.

Lessons 3, 4, 7, 9, 14, 15 – Large calendar with 12 months
Lessons 14, 57, 101, 102 – Scissors
Lessons 14, 57, 58, 101 – Glue
Lesson 24 – Children's Scissors
Lesson 24 – Construction paper
Lesson 25 – Pencils of unequal length
Lessons 31, 46, 97, 105 – Crayons
Lessons 34, 109 – Opaque bag
Lessons 55, 107, 130 – Sheets of paper
Lesson 98 – Books with at least 50 numbered pages
Lessons 99, 117 – Sticky notes
Lesson 103 – Four identical transparent containers with straight sides
Lesson 103 – A pitcher of water, preferably colored with food coloring to make it more visible
Lesson 106 – Business card
Lesson 109 – A ball, a funnel, a cylindrical can
Lesson 111 – Book about pyramids
Lesson 126 – Four-inch (10 cm) paper cups, and two rubber bands
Lesson 126 – Objects for weighing

How This Program Was Developed

We have been hearing for years that Japanese students do better than U.S. students in math in Japan. The Asian students are ahead by the middle of first grade. And the gap widens every year thereafter.

Many explanations have been given, including less diversity and a longer school year. Japanese students attend school 240 days a year.

A third explanation given is that the Asian public values and supports education more than we do. A first grade teacher has the same status as a university professor. If a student falls behind, the family, not the school, helps the child or hires a tutor. Students often attend after-school classes.

A fourth explanation involves the philosophy of learning. Asians and Europeans believe anyone can learn mathematics or even play the violin. It is not a matter of talent, but of good teaching and hard work.

Although these explanations are valid, I decided to take a careful look at how mathematics is taught in Japanese first grades. Japan has a national curriculum, so there is little variation among teachers.

I found some important differences. One of these is the way the Asians name their numbers. In English we count ten, eleven, twelve, thirteen, and so on, which doesn't give the child a clue about tens and ones. But in Asian languages, one counts by saying ten-1, ten-2, ten-3 for the teens, and 2-ten 1, 2-ten 2, and 2-ten 3 for the twenties.

Still another difference is their criteria for manipulatives. Americans think the more the better. Asians prefer very few, but insist that they be imaginable, that is, visualizable. That is one reason they do not use colored rods. You can imagine the one and the three, but try imagining a brown eight—the quantity eight, not the color. It cannot be done without grouping.

Another important difference is the emphasis on non-counting strategies for computation. Japanese children are discouraged from counting; rather they are taught to see quantities in groups of fives and tens.

For example, when an American child wants to know 9 + 4, most likely the child will start with 9 and count up 4. In contrast, the Asian child will think that if he takes 1 from the 4 and puts it with the 9, then he will have 10 and 3, or 13. Unfortunately, very few American first-graders at the end of the year even know that 10 + 3 is 13.

I decided to conduct research using some of these ideas in two similar first grade classrooms. The control group studied math in the traditional workbook-based manner. The other class used the lesson plans I developed. The children used that special number naming for three months.

They also used a special abacus I designed, based on fives and tens. I asked 5-year-old Stan how much is 11 + 6. Then I asked him how he knew. He replied, "I have the abacus in my mind."

The children were working with thousands by the sixth week. They figured out how to add 4-digit numbers on paper after learning how on the abacus.

Every child in the experimental class, including those enrolled in special education classes, could add numbers like 9 + 4, by changing it to 10 + 3.

I asked the children to explain what the 6 and 2 mean in the number 26. Ninety-three percent of the children in the experimental group explained it correctly while only 50% of third graders did so in another study.

I gave the children some base ten rods (none of them had seen them before) that looked like ones and tens and asked them to make 48. Then I asked them to subtract 14. The children in the control group counted 14 ones, while the experimental class removed 1 ten and 4 ones. This indicated that they saw 14 as 1 ten and 4 ones and not as 14 ones. This view of numbers is vital to understanding algorithms, or procedures, for doing arithmetic.

I asked the experimental class to mentally add 64 + 20, which only 52% of nine-year-olds on the 1986 National test did correctly; 56% of those in the experimental class could do it.

Since children often confuse columns when taught traditionally, I wrote 2304 + 86 = horizontally and asked them to find the sum any way they liked. Fifty-six percent did so correctly, including one child who did it in his head.

The following year I revised the lesson plans and both first grade classes used these methods. I am delighted to report that on a national standardized test, both classes scored at the 98th percentile.

Joan A. Cotter, Ph.D.

Some General Thoughts on Teaching Mathematics

1. Only five percent of mathematics should be learned by rote; 95 percent should be understood.

2. Real learning builds on what the child already knows. Rote teaching ignores it.

3. Contrary to the common myth, "young children can think both concretely and abstractly. Development is not a kind of inevitable unfolding in which one simply waits until a child is cognitively 'ready.'" —*Foundations for Success* NMAP

4. What is developmentally appropriate is not a simple function of age or grade, but rather is largely contingent on prior opportunities to learn." —Duschl & others

5. Understanding a new model is easier if you have made one yourself. So, a child needs to construct a graph before attempting to read a ready-made graph.

6. Good manipulatives cause confusion at first. If a new manipulative makes perfect sense at first sight, it is not needed. Trying to understand and relate it to previous knowledge is what leads to greater learning. —Richard Behr & others.

7. According to Arthur Baroody, "Teaching mathematics is essentially a process of translating mathematics into a form children can comprehend, providing experiences that enable children to discover relationships and construct meanings, and creating opportunities to develop and exercise mathematical reasoning."

8. Lauren Resnick says, "Good mathematics learners expect to be able to make sense out of rules they are taught, and they apply some energy and time to the task of making sense. By contrast, those less adept in mathematics try to memorize and apply the rules that are taught, but do not attempt to relate these rules to what they know about mathematics at a more intuitive level."

9. Mindy Holte puts learning the facts in proper perspective when she says, "In our concern about the memorization of math facts or solving problems, we must not forget that the root of mathematical study is the creation of mental pictures in the imagination and manipulating those images and relationships using the power of reason and logic." She also emphasizes the ability to imagine or visualize, an important skill in mathematics and other areas.

10. The only students who like flash cards are those who do not need them.

11. Mathematics is not a solitary pursuit. According to Richard Skemp, solitary math on paper is like reading music, rather than listening to it: "Mathematics, like music, needs to be expressed in physical actions and human interactions before its symbols can evoke the silent patterns of mathematical ideas (like musical notes), simultaneous relationships (like harmonies) and expositions or proofs (like melodies)."

12. "More than most other school subjects, mathematics offers special opportunities for children to learn the power of thought as distinct from the power of authority. This is a very important lesson to learn, an essential step in the emergence of independent thinking." —*Everybody Counts*

13. The role of the teacher is to encourage thinking by asking questions, not giving answers. Once you give an answer, thinking usually stops.
14. Putting thoughts into words helps the learning process.
15. Help the children realize that it is their responsibility to ask questions when they do not understand. Do not settle for "I don't get it."
16. The difference between a novice and an expert is that an expert catches errors much more quickly. A violinist adjusts pitch so quickly that the audience does not hear it.
17. Europeans and Asians believe learning occurs not because of ability, but primarily because of effort. In the ability model of learning, errors are a sign of failure. In the effort model, errors are natural. In Japanese classrooms, the teachers discuss errors with the whole class.
18. For teaching vocabulary, be sure either the word or the concept is known. For example, if a child is familiar with six-sided figures, we can give him the word, hexagon. Or, if he has heard the word, multiply, we can tell him what it means. It is difficult to learn a new concept and the term simultaneously.
19. Introduce new concepts globally before details. This lets the children know where they are headed.
20. Informal mathematics should precede paper and pencil work. Long before a child learns how to add fractions with unlike denominators, she should be able to add one half and one fourth mentally.
21. Some pairs of concepts are easier to remember if one of them is thought of as dominant. Then the non-dominant concept is simply the other one. For example, if even is dominant over odd, an odd number is one that is not even.
22. Worksheets should also make the child think. Therefore, they should not be a large collection of similar exercises, but should present a variety. In RightStart™ Mathematics, they are designed to be done independently.
23. Keep math time enjoyable. We store our emotional state along with what we have learned. A person who dislikes math will avoid it and a child under stress stops learning. If a lesson is too hard, stop and play a game. Try the lesson again later.
24. In Japan students spend more time on fewer problems. Teachers do not concern themselves with attention spans as is done in the U.S.
25. In Japan the goal of the math lesson is that the student has understood a concept, not necessarily has done something (a worksheet).
26. The calendar must show the entire month, so the children can plan ahead. The days passed can be crossed out or the current day circled.
27. A real mathematical problem is one in which the procedures to find the answer are not obvious. It is like a puzzle, needing trial and error. Emphasize the satisfaction of solving problems and like puzzles, of not giving away the solution to others.

RightStart™ Mathematics

Ten major characteristics make this research-based program effective:

1. Refers to quantities of up to 5 as a group; discourages counting individually. Uses fingers and tally sticks to show quantities up to 10; teaches quantities 6 to 10 as 5 plus a quantity, for example 6 = 5 + 1.

2. Avoids counting procedures for finding sums and differences. Teaches five- and ten-based strategies for the facts that are both visual and visualizable.

3. Employs games, not flash cards, for practice.

4. Once quantities 1 to 10 are known, proceeds to 10 as a unit. Temporarily uses the "math way" of naming numbers; for example, "1 ten-1" (or "ten-1") for eleven, "1-ten 2" for twelve, "2-ten" for twenty, and "2-ten 5" for twenty-five.

5. Uses expanded notation (overlapping) place-value cards for recording tens and ones; the ones card is placed on the zero of the tens card. Encourages a child to read numbers starting at the left and not backward by starting at the ones.

6. Proceeds rapidly to hundreds and thousands using manipulatives and place-value cards. Provides opportunities for trading between ones and tens, tens and hundreds, and hundreds and thousands with manipulatives.

7. Teaches mental computation. Investigates informal solutions, often through story problems, before learning procedures.

8. Teaches four-digit addition on the abacus, letting the child discover the paper and pencil algorithm.

9. Introduces fractions with a linear visual model, including all fractions from 1/2 to 1/10. "Pies" are not used initially because they cannot show fractions greater than 1. Later, the tenths will become the basis for decimals.

10. Teaches short division (where only the answer is written down) for single-digit divisors, before long division.

Second Edition

Many changes have occurred since the first RightStart™ lessons were begun in 1994. First, mathematics is used more widely in many fields, for example, architecture, science, technology, and medicine. Today, many careers require math beyond basic arithmetic. Second, research has given us new insights into how children learn mathematics. Third, kindergarten has become much more academic, and fourth, most children are tested to ensure their preparedness for the next step.

This second edition is updated to reflect new research and applications. Topics within each level are always taught with the most appropriate method using the best approach with the child and teacher in mind.

Daily Lessons

Objectives. The objectives outline the purpose and goal of the lesson. Some possibilities are to introduce, to build, to learn a term, to practice, or to review.

Materials. The Math Set of manipulatives includes the specially crafted items needed to teach RightStart™ Mathematics. Occasionally, common objects such as scissors will be needed. These items are indicated by boldface type.

Warm-up. The warm-up time is the time for quick review, memory work, and sometimes an introduction to the day's topics. The dry erase board makes an ideal slate for quick responses.

Activities. The Activities for Teaching section is the heart of the lesson; it starts on the left page and continues to the right page. These are the instructions for teaching the lesson. The expected answers from the child are given in square brackets.

Establish with the children some indication when you want a quick response and when you want a more thoughtful response. Research shows that the quiet time for thoughtful response should be about three seconds. Avoid talking during this quiet time; resist the temptation to rephrase the question. This quiet time gives the slower child time to think and the quicker child time to think more deeply.

Encourage the child to develop persistence and perseverance. Avoid giving hints or explanations too quickly. Children tend to stop thinking once they hear the answer.

Explanations. Special background notes for the teacher are given in Explanations.

Worksheets. The worksheets are designed to give the children a chance to think about and to practice the day's lesson. The children are to do them independently. Some lessons, especially in the early levels, have no worksheet.

Games. Games, not worksheets or flash cards, provide practice. The games, found in the *Math Card Games* book, can be played as many times as necessary until proficiency or memorization takes place. They are as important to learning math as books are to reading. The *Math Card Games* book also includes extra games for the child needing more help, and some more challenging games for the advanced child.

In conclusion. Each lesson ends with a short summary called, "In conclusion," where the child answers a few short questions based on the day's learning.

Number of lessons. Generally, each lesson is to be done in one day and each manual, in one school year. Complete each manual before going on to the next level.

Comments. We really want to hear how this program is working. Please let us know any improvements and suggestions that you may have.

Joan A. Cotter, Ph.D.
info@RightStartMath.com
www.RightStartMath.com

Level B: Table of Contents

Lesson 1	Initial Assessment
Lesson 2	Review Subitizing 1 to 5
Lesson 3	Review Subitizing 6 and 7 & the AL Abacus
Lesson 4	Review Subitizing Quantities 8 to 10
Lesson 5	Review Partitioning with Part-Whole Circle Sets
Lesson 6	Review Partitioning Ten
Lesson 7	Review Go to the Dump
Lesson 8	Review Introducing the Math Balance
Lesson 9	Review Writing Addition Equations
Lesson 10	Review Tens on the Abacus
Lesson 11	Review Tens and Ones
Lesson 12	Adding One
Lesson 13	More Adding One
Lesson 14	Evens and Odds
Lesson 15	Even Numbers Plus 2
Lesson 16	Odd Numbers Plus 2
Lesson 17	The Doubles 1 to 5
Lesson 18	The Doubles 6 to 10
Lesson 19	Practicing the Doubles
Lesson 20	The Commutative Property
Lesson 21	Applying the Commutative Property
Lesson 22	Solving "Add To" Problems
Lesson 23	Quadrilaterals
Lesson 24	Building Rectangles
Lesson 25	Triangles with Right Angles
Lesson 26	Adding Ten to a Number
Lesson 27	Adding Ones and Adding Tens
Lesson 28	Introducing Hundreds
Lesson 29	Numbers 100 to 120
Lesson 30	More Hundreds
Lesson 31	Enrichment Working with 100s and 1000s
Lesson 32	Two-Fives Strategy
Lesson 33	More Two-Fives Strategy
Lesson 34	Adding Five to a Number
Lesson 35	Partitioning 5, 10, and 15

Level B: Table of Contents

Lesson 36	Corners™ Exercise without Scoring
Lesson 37	Corners™ Exercise with Scoring
Lesson 38	Basic Corners™ Game
Lesson 39	Solving "Combine" Problems
Lesson 40	Sums Equal to 11
Lesson 41	Review
Lesson 42	Assessment 1
Lesson 43	Making Rectangles with Tangrams
Lesson 44	Continuing Patterns
Lesson 45	Continuing Patterns with Geoboards
Lesson 46	Designs with Diagonals
Lesson 47	The Greater Than Symbol
Lesson 48	Adding 9 to a Number
Lesson 49	Adding 8 to a Number
Lesson 50	Two-Fives Strategy Practice
Lesson 51	Adding 8s and 9s Practice
Lesson 52	Thousands
Lesson 53	Base-Ten Picture Cards
Lesson 54	Trading with Base-10 Cards
Lesson 55	Adding with Base-10 Cards
Lesson 56	More Adding with Base-10 Cards
Lesson 57	Enrichment Cotter Tens Fractal—Prep
Lesson 58	Enrichment Cotter Tens Fractal
Lesson 59	Adding Even Numbers Practice
Lesson 60	Adding up to 10 and up to 15
Lesson 61	Adding Several Numbers
Lesson 62	Solving Problems with Three Addends
Lesson 63	Introducing Side 2 of the Abacus
Lesson 64	Bead Trading
Lesson 65	Adding 2-Digit Numbers and Tens
Lesson 66	Corners™ Game
Lesson 67	Mentally Adding 2-Digit Numbers
Lesson 68	Long Chain Solitaire
Lesson 69	Addition Bingo Game
Lesson 70	Days in a Year Problem

LEVEL B: TABLE OF CONTENTS

Lesson 71	Adding 1, 10, and 100
Lesson 72	Adding 4-Digit Numbers
Lesson 73	Continuing the Pattern
Lesson 74	Review
Lesson 75	Review Games
Lesson 76	Assessment 2
Lesson 77	Hours on a Clock
Lesson 78	Hours and Half-Hours
Lesson 79	Minutes on the Clock
Lesson 80	More Minutes on the Clock
Lesson 81	Hours and Minutes
Lesson 82	Adding 4-Digit Numbers on Paper
Lesson 83	Enrichment Adding Very Large Numbers
Lesson 84	Solving "Take From" Problems
Lesson 85	Ten Minus a Number
Lesson 86	Subtraction as the Missing Addend
Lesson 87	Subtracting by Going Back
Lesson 88	Subtracting Consecutive Numbers
Lesson 89	Subtracting from 9 and 11
Lesson 90	Subtracting with Doubles and Near Doubles
Lesson 91	Subtracting by Taking All from Ten
Lesson 92	Subtracting by Taking Part from Ten
Lesson 93	Finding the Difference
Lesson 94	Solving Compare Problems
Lesson 95	Addition and Subtraction Equations
Lesson 96	Continuing Patterns in the Hundreds
Lesson 97	Higher Even and Odd Numbers
Lesson 98	Pages in Books and Reading Years
Lesson 99	Greater Than or Less Than Symbols
Lesson 100	Introducing Area
Lesson 101	Halves and Fourths
Lesson 102	Fourths and Quarters
Lesson 103	Finding Quarter Parts
Lesson 104	Measuring with Centimeters
Lesson 105	Graphing

Level B: Table of Contents

Lesson 106	Measuring with Inches
Lesson 107	Paper Measuring Problems
Lesson 108	Making Rectangles with Tiles
Lesson 109	Geometry Solids
Lesson 110	Building with Cubes
Lesson 111	Mentally Adding with Sums over 100
Lesson 112	Pennies, Nickels, and Dimes
Lesson 113	Coin Problems
Lesson 114	Choosing Coins
Lesson 115	Counting Money with Quarters
Lesson 116	Using the Fewest Coins
Lesson 117	Making Change
Lesson 118	Adding with a Calculator
Lesson 119	Introducing Multiplication as Arrays
Lesson 120	Multiplication as Repeated Addition
Lesson 121	More Calculator Activities
Lesson 122	Introducing Division
Lesson 123	Beginning Fractions
Lesson 124	Unit Fractions
Lesson 125	Fractions of Twelve and Eight
Lesson 126	Comparing Fractions by Weighing
Lesson 127	Lines of Symmetry
Lesson 128	Finding Symmetry
Lesson 129	Tangram and Geoboard Figures
Lesson 130	Enrichment Introducing Angles
Lesson 131	Number and Operations in Base-10 Review
Lesson 132	Number and Operations in Base-10 Games
Lesson 133	Number and Operations in Base-10 Assessment
Lesson 134	Operations & Algebraic Thinking Review
Lesson 135	Operations & Algebraic Thinking Games
Lesson 136	Operations & Algebraic Thinking Assessment
Lesson 137	Measurement and Data Review and Games
Lesson 138	Measurement and Data Assessment
Lesson 139	Geometry Review and Games
Lesson 140	Geometry Assessment

Lesson 1: Initial Assessment

OBJECTIVES:
1. Review or assess for understanding

MATERIALS:
1. Checklist (Appendix p. 1)
2. Worksheet 1, Initial Assessment
3. AL Abacus
4. *Yellow is the Sun* book

ACTIVITIES FOR TEACHING:	EXPLANATIONS:
Assessment 1. Use the checklist to record the child's responses.	IMPORTANT NOTE TO TEACHER:
Questions 1–3. Ask the child to show the following numbers with her fingers: 2, 5, 7.	If the child is new to the RightStart Mathematics™ curriculum, skip this lesson and continue with the Review Lessons.
Questions 4–6. Ask the child to say the following numbers without counting as you enter them on the abacus: 3, 6, 9.	If the child has done RightStart Mathematics™ Level A, complete this assessment. If the child gets at least 15 questions correct, you may skip the following review lessons. If the child scores less than 15 correct answers, complete the following review lessons.
Questions 7–11. Have the child take out Worksheet 1 from the front of her workbook. Have her show all the ways to partition 10 using the part-whole circle sets. Answers shown below.	Use the checklist to track the child's progress.

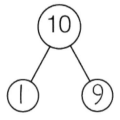
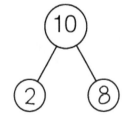
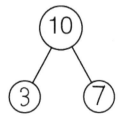
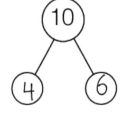
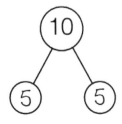

ACTIVITIES FOR TEACHING:

EXPLANATIONS:

Questions 12–14. Have the child complete the addition problems listed on the worksheet. Answers are shown below.

$4 + 3 = 7$ $3 + 6 = 9$ $4 + 5 = 9$

Questions 15–20. Ask the child the enter the following numbers on the abacus: 8-ten 6, 92, 5-ten 3, 47, 1-ten 8, and 12.

Name	Can show with fingers			Can recognize on the Abacus			Can enter on the Abacus					
	2	5	7	3	6	9	8-ten 6	92	5-ten 3	47	1-ten 8	12

In conclusion. Read the *Yellow is the Sun* book.

© Activities for Learning, Inc. 2013

REVIEW LESSON 2: SUBITIZING 1 TO 5

OBJECTIVES:
1. To start learning "Yellow is the Sun"
2. To subitize quantities 1 to 5
3. To learn to use tally sticks

MATERIALS:
1. "Yellow is the Sun" music (Appendix p. 2) or the "Yellow is the Sun" CD
2. *Yellow is the Sun* book
3. 1" x 1" colored tiles
4. Tally sticks

ACTIVITIES FOR TEACHING:	EXPLANATIONS:
Warm-up. Teach the following song and ask the child to show the correct fingers at the appropriate words. **Yellow is the Sun** Yellow is the sun. This is only one. (Raise one finger on the left hand.) Why is the sky so blue? Let me show you two. (Raise two fingers on the left hand.) Salty is the sea. One more and it's three. (Raise three fingers on the left hand.) Hear the thunder roar. Here's the mighty four. (Raise four fingers on the left hand.) Ducks will swim and dive. My whole hand makes five. (Raise five fingers on the left.) Yellow is the sun. Six is five and one. (5 fingers on left hand; 1 on right.) Why is the sky so blue? Seven is five and two. (5 fingers on left hand; 2 on right.) Salty is the sea. Eight is five and three. (5 fingers on left hand; 3 on right.) Hear the thunder roar. Nine is five and four. (5 fingers on left hand; 4 on right.) Ducks will swim and dive. Ten is five and five. (5 fingers on left hand; 5 on right.)	The first half of these RightStart™ Mathematics lessons refers to the child as a female and the second half refers to the child as a male.
Identifying small quantities. Tell the child that a scientist, Dr. Karen Wynn, discovered that babies 5 months old could tell the difference between groups of one, two, and three objects. If the child is interested, tell her how she did her research. Dr. Wynn found that most babies will look at something new for a longer time than something that they have seen before. She showed the baby one teddy bear. Then she covered the teddy bear with a screen that hid the bear. Next she showed the baby another teddy bear and put it behind the screen. When she removed the screen, the baby saw two teddy bears.	The article by K. Wynn, "Addition and Subtraction by Human Infants" was published August 27, 1992 in Nature, Vol. 358, p. 749-750.

RightStart™ Mathematics Level B Second Edition © Activities for Learning, Inc. 2013

ACTIVITIES FOR TEACHING:	EXPLANATIONS:

The baby didn't look very long because the baby expected to see two teddy bears.

Dr. Wynn did the experiment again, but this time she tricked the baby. Without the baby seeing, she put an extra teddy bear behind the screen. When the screen was removed, the baby saw three teddy bears. The baby looked much longer, trying to figure out where the extra bear came from.

By timing how long the babies looked, Dr. Wynn discovered that babies could tell the difference between one, two, or three teddy bears. Other researchers found many babies a year old could tell the difference up to four teddy bears.

Showing quantities 1 to 5. Tell the child to use her left hand for the following activity. Ask her to show 2 with her fingers. Tell her it makes no difference which fingers she uses. Repeat for 3, 4, 5, and 1. Explain that naming quantities or amounts without counting is called *subitizing*.

Because reading proceeds from left to right, the left hand is used for quantities 1 to 5.

Most children have been taught to express their age up to 5 years with fingers, so it should be easy for her to show fingers representing quantities 1 to 5.

Comparing 5 with 4. Show a group with five tiles and another group with four tiles. Ask: Which group has a middle, 5 or 4? [5]

Five has a middle.   Four does not have a middle.

Subitizing (SOO bih tighz ing) is perceiving at a glance the number of items without counting.

If necessary, demonstrate how to find a middle as follows:

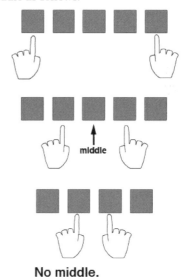

No middle.

Tell her: Show 5 with your left hand; show 4 with your right hand. Ask: Which number has a middle? [5]

 Five has a middle.   Four does not have a middle.

Naming quantities 1 to 5. Hold up 3 fingers on your right hand (if you are facing the child). Ask her to show the quantity with her fingers and to say its name, three. Repeat for 1–5. Ask her to do it as fast as she can.

Tally sticks. Show the child how to make numbers 1–4 with the tally sticks. Leave about an inch (2.5 cm) between sticks. To make 5, lay the fifth stick horizontally across the other four as shown below.

 Three.   Five.

In conclusion. Ask the child to show 3 with her fingers. Now ask her to show 4. Hold up 5 with your hand and have her name the quantity.

Conclusions may be a summary of the day's lesson or an expansion of the lesson to challenge higher level thinking.

© Activities for Learning, Inc. 2013

Review Lesson 3: Subitizing 6 and 7 & the AL Abacus

OBJECTIVES:
1. To continue to learn "Yellow is the Sun"
2. To review the days of the week
3. To subitize quantities 1–7 by grouping in 5s

MATERIALS:
1. Music for "Yellow is the Sun" (Appendix p. 2)
2. *Yellow is the Sun* book
3. **Large calendar showing one month***
4. Tally sticks
5. Tiles
6. AL Abacus

ACTIVITIES FOR TEACHING:

Warm-up. Show the child 2 with your fingers and ask the her to name the quantity. Now show 4 on your fingers. Ask the child to name the quantity. Repeat with 3 and 5.

Play or sing the "Yellow is the Sun" song for the child. Play or sing it again and have her sing along. Ask her to show the correct fingers at the appropriate words. (The words are in the previous lesson.)

Read the book, *Yellow is the Sun,* to the child.

Days of the week. On a large calendar, point to each column as you say the days of the week. Then using the tune of "Twinkle, Twinkle Little Star," sing the days of the week with these words:

Days of the Week
Sunday, Monday, Tuesday, too.
Wednesday, Thursday—this I knew.
Friday, Saturday that's the end.
Now let's say those days again!
Sunday, Monday, Tuesday, Wednesday, Thursday,
Friday, Saturday!

EXPLANATIONS:

*An item listed in bold face is not part of the RightStart™ materials and will likely be found around the house.

RightStart™ Mathematics Level B Second Edition © Activities for Learning, Inc. 2013

ACTIVITIES FOR TEACHING:	EXPLANATIONS:

The quantities 6 and 7. Ask the child to show 6 with her fingers. Then ask her to make 6 with tally sticks as shown below.

Showing 6.

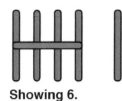
Showing 6.

Be sure the child uses her left hand for five and her right hand for amounts over five.

Repeat the above activities for 7.

Practice with her to construct quantities from 1–7 using the tally sticks. They should only change the quantity to reflect the new number, not start from scratch.

Naming quantities is part of the 5 percent of mathematics that needs to be memorized.

Quantities with tiles. Ask the child to take 10 tiles, 5 of two different colors. Ask her to construct 6 as shown below. Repeat with 7.

Six.

Seven.

Introducing the AL Abacus. Tell the child to place her abacus flat with the wires horizontal and the logo on the top. Tell her to clear the abacus by lifting the left edge so the beads fall to the right side near the logo.

Ask her to enter 3 on the abacus by sliding 3 beads on the top wire to the left edge. Now ask her to clear the abacus and to enter 6. See the figure below. Repeat for 7.

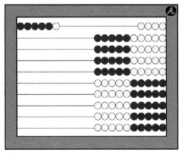
Six.

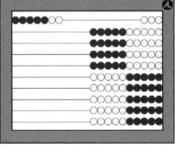
Seven.

The beads must be moved together as a unit, not one by one.

In conclusion. Ask the child to construct various quantities with the tiles grouped in fives and on her abacus. She need not clear the previous number before making the new number. Encourage those who can to work quickly, using numbers from 1 to 7 in random order.

Not all children respond well to answering quickly. For some it creates stress which interferes with learning.

© Activities for Learning, Inc. 2013

Review Lesson 4: Subitizing Quantities 8 to 10

OBJECTIVES:
1. To review the months
2. To subitize quantities 1–10 by grouping in 5s

MATERIALS:
1. **Calendar with 12 months, one per page**
2. *Yellow is the Sun* book
3. Music for "Yellow is the Sun" (Appendix p. 2)
4. Tally sticks
5. Tiles
6. AL Abacus

ACTIVITIES FOR TEACHING:

Warm-up. Ask the child to show the various quantities 1–7 with her fingers.

Show the child 7 with your fingers and ask her to name the quantity. [7] Repeat with other quantities 1–6.

Using the tune of "Twinkle, Twinkle Little Star," sing the days of the week with these words:

Days of the Week
Sunday, Monday, Tuesday, too.
Wednesday, Thursday—this I knew.
Friday, Saturday that's the end.
Now let's say those days again!
Sunday, Monday, Tuesday, Wednesday, Thursday,
Friday, Saturday!

Teach the child the new song, "The Months." Sing it to the tune of "Michael Finnegan." Turn to each month on the calendar as it is sung.

The Months
January, February, March, and April,
May, June, July, and August,
September, October, November, December.
These are the months of the year.

Read the book *Yellow is the Sun* to the child.

Sing *Yellow is the Sun* from a previous lesson. Tell the child to show the correct fingers at the appropriate words.

Quantities 8–10 with fingers. Show the child how to show 8 with her fingers as shown below. Then ask her to show 8 with her fingers. Repeat for 9 and 10.

Showing 8.   Showing 10.

EXPLANATIONS:

ACTIVITIES FOR TEACHING:	EXPLANATIONS:

Quantities 8–10 with tally sticks. Tell the child to construct 8 with tally sticks. See the left figure below. Then tell her to construct 9. Next ask her to construct 10. See the right figure below.

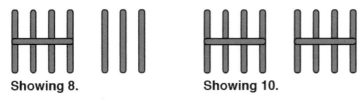

Showing 8.   Showing 10.

Usually, eight is the most difficult quantity for a child to recognize.

Ask: What makes 10 a special number? [all the fingers, two groups of five]

For practice, ask her to use the tally sticks to construct quantities 6–10, concentrating especially on 8–10.

Ask: Can you think of an easy way to remember 9? [all but 1]

Naming quantities is part of the 5 percent of mathematics that needs to be memorized.

Quantities 8–10 with tiles. Ask the child to take 10 tiles, 5 each of 2 different colors. Ask her to construct 8, shown below. Also ask her to construct 9 and 10. Then give her random numbers to construct.

 Eight.

Quantities 8–10 with the abacus. Ask the child to enter 8 on the abacus. See the left figure below. Repeat for 10 then 9.

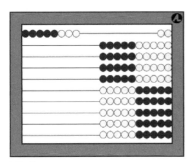 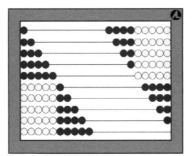

Eight.   The stairs.

It is vitally important that the child enter these quantities without counting.

The stairs. Ask the child to build the stairs by entering 1 on the first wire, 2 on the second wire, and so forth. See the right figure above. Ask her to read the quantities from top to bottom. [1, 2, 3, . . . , 10] Ask her to point to 8, to 10, to 6, to 9, and other quantities.

In conclusion. With the stairs on the abacus, ask the child to find 5. Then ask her to find the other 5. [on the right side of the abacus] Ask: Can you find both 2s? Repeat for other quantities at random.

For a child having difficulty constructing the stairs, use the following method:

Tell the child to enter 1 on the first wire.

Tell the child to copy what is on the first wire and enter it on the next wire. [1] Then tell the child to add one more. [2]

For the next wire, copy what is above and add one more. [3]

Continue for remaining wires.

It is important to see the group on the right as well as the left.

© Activities for Learning, Inc. 2013

Review Lesson 5: Partitioning with Part-Whole Circle Sets

OBJECTIVES:
1. To identify the whole and its parts

MATERIALS:
1. Dry erase board
2. Tally sticks
3. AL Abacus
4. Worksheet 2, Partitioning with Part-Whole Circle Sets

ACTIVITIES FOR TEACHING:

EXPLANATIONS:

Warm-up. Show a number with your fingers. Ask the child to say that number. Show a different number for the child to identify. Continue until all numbers 1 to 10 are named.

Sing "Days of the Week."

Play the Comes After game. Ask: What day comes after Tuesday? [Wednesday] What comes after Friday? [Saturday] What day comes after Sunday? [Monday]

Sing "The Months" and "Yellow is the Sun" songs.

Part-whole circle sets. Draw a part-whole circle set on the dry erase board as shown below. Explain that the larger circle is the whole and the smaller circles are the parts.

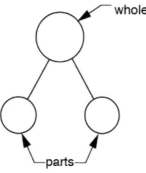

Ask the child to construct 5 with tally sticks. Then ask her to partition (take apart) the 5. Ask: What is the whole amount? [5] Write 5 in the whole-circle. Ask: If one of the parts is 4, what is the other part? [1] Write the parts in the part-circles as shown below on the right.

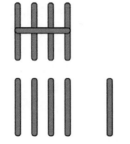
Partitioning 5 into 4 and 1.

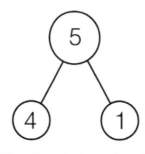
Writing the whole and parts.

RightStart™ Mathematics Level B Second Edition © Activities for Learning, Inc. 2013

ACTIVITIES FOR TEACHING:

Ask the child for another way to partition, or break, the 5. Tell the child to change the part-numbers to show a new part. [3 & 2, 2 & 3, 1 & 4, 0 & 5] Continue asking until they cannot find any more ways. The "0" partitions may not occur to her; if so, ignore it.

Partitioning 5 on the abacus. Tell the child to enter 5 on the abacus. Then ask her to partition it into 3 and 2. Pointing to the whole-circle, ask: What is the whole? [5] Write 5 in the whole-circle. What are the parts? [3 & 2] Write the parts in the part-circles.

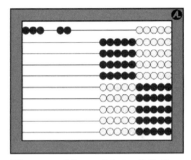
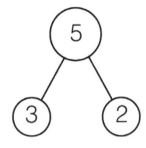

Five partitioned into 3 & 2.

Draw another circle set; write 5 in the whole-circle and 4 in the left part-circle. Ask the child to find the missing part by using the abacus. [1] Write it in the other part-circle.

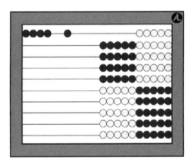
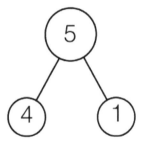

Finding the missing part.

Worksheet 2. For this worksheet, tell the child to use her abacus to find the missing numbers. The answers are below:

```
3    2    3
4    2    2
1    5    3
0    4    3
```

In conclusion. Let the child find more examples of partitioning a number and writing the results in a part-whole circle set.

EXPLANATIONS:

Review Lesson 6: Partitioning Ten

OBJECTIVES:
1. To learn the meaning of the word *plus*
2. To partition 10
3. To practice the 10s facts

MATERIALS:
1. Tally sticks
2. AL Abacus
3. Dry erase board
4. *Math Card Games* book,* A2

ACTIVITIES FOR TEACHING:

Warm-up. Play the Comes After game. Ask: What comes after 2, [3] 5, [6] 9? [10] Now tell the child that you are going to change the game slightly. Ask: How much is 2 books and 1 more book? [3 books] How much is 6 crayons and 1 more crayon? [7 crayons] How much is 9 balls and 1 more ball? [10 balls]

Plus. Tell the child that the game will change once again. Say: We are going to use a math word that means *and*. It is *plus.* Ask: What is 3 shoes plus 1 shoe? [4 shoes] What is 7 apples plus 1 apple? [8 apples] What is 1 plus 1? [2] Invite her to think of similar questions to share.

Partitioning 10 with tally sticks. Tell the child that today we will partition 10. Ask her to build a 10 with the tally sticks. Ask her to partition the 10 by moving a stick to the right and naming the partitioning. Say: 10 is 9 plus . . . . [1] Move another stick over and again ask her to continue. Say: 10 is . . . . [8 + 2] Continue to 10 is 0 plus 10.

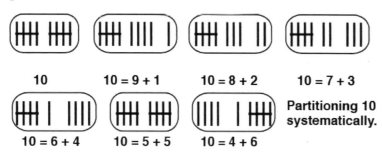

Partitioning 10 systematically.

Partitioning 10 on the abacus. Enter 10 on the abacus; move 1 bead a short distance to the right, as shown on the next page. Ask her to say the partitioning. [10 is 9 + 1] Continue to 0 and 10.

EXPLANATIONS:

*The Fifth Edition of the *Math Card Games* book is needed for this manual.

The book is arranged in chapters as follows:
1. Number Sense (N)
2. Addition (A)
3. Clocks (C)
4. Multiplication (P)
5. Money (M)
6. Subtraction (S)
7. Division (D)
8. Fractions (F)

The games are numbered sequentially within each chapter. For example, A2 is the second game in the Addition chapter and N3 is the third game in the previous chapter, Number Sense.

Within each chapter the games get progressively harder.

The facts totaling 10 are essential for learning facts over 10, so this mastery is an important goal.

ACTIVITIES FOR TEACHING:

EXPLANATIONS:

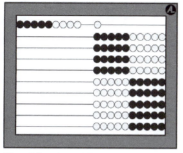 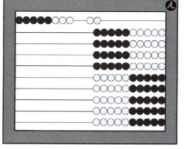

Partitioning 10 into 9 + 1.   Partitioning 10 into 8 + 2.

Part-whole. Draw several part-whole circle sets with 10 as the whole. Write a number in one of each of the part circles and ask the child to find the other part.

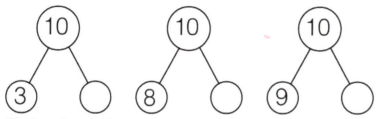

Finding the missing parts that make 10.

Show how to use the abacus to find the missing part. For example, to find the other part when the whole is 10 and the first part is 3, enter 10 on the abacus. Then move to the right a short distance all but 3 beads, as shown. The part is then seen as 7.

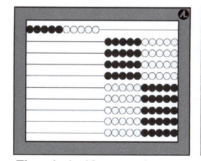 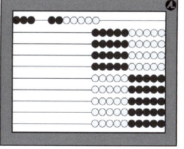

The whole 10 entered.   One of the parts, 3, is separated to find the other part, 7.

Find the Tens Memory game. Play Find the Tens Memory in the *Math Card Games* book, A2.

In conclusion. Ask: If you have 8, how many more will you need to make 10? [2] If you have 6, how many more will you need to make 10? [4]

Review Lesson 7: Go to the Dump

OBJECTIVES:
1. To review and practice the 10s facts

MATERIALS:
1. **Calendar**
2. AL Abacus
3. Dry erase board
4. *Math Card Games* book, A3

ACTIVITIES FOR TEACHING:

Warm-up. Sing the "Days of the Week." Ask: What day comes after Tuesday? [Wednesday] What day comes after Saturday? [Sunday] What day comes after Monday? [Tuesday]

Using a calendar, ask: What is today's date? What will the date be one week from today? What will the date be one week from Wednesday? If necessary, explain that *date* means the number of days in a month. What will the date be one week from Sunday?

Sing "The Months" from a previous lesson.

Sing "Yellow is the Sun."

Using the abacus, ask the child to count by 2s by moving over 2 beads at a time and reading the results. [2, 4, 6, 8, 10] Then ask her to remove 2 beads at a time and read the results. [10, 8, 6, 4, 2, 0]

Ask the child to partition 5. [1 + 4, 2 + 3, 3 + 2, 4 + 1] Continue until all options are named.

Partitioning 10. Enter 10 on the abacus. Ask the child to recite the partitioning of 10. Move over 1 bead at a time while they say the corresponding facts: 10 is 9 + 1, 10 is 8 + 2, and so on.

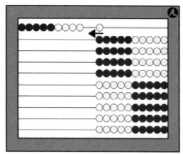

10 = 9 + 1.

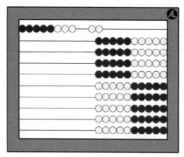

10 = 8 + 2.

EXPLANATIONS:

It is very important that the child enter and read quantities on the abacus without any counting.

ACTIVITIES FOR TEACHING:	EXPLANATIONS:
Game preparation. Ask: If you have 9, how many more will you need to make 10? Tell the child to enter 9 on the abacus and see what they need to move over to make 10. [1] See the left figure on bottom of the previous page.	
Ask: If you have 3, how many more will you need to make 10? [7] If you have 4, how many more will you need to make 10? [6]	
Ask: What do you need with 8 to make 10? [2] Draw a part-whole circle set with 10 as the whole and 8 as a part. Have the child write the missing part.	Discourage any counting on fingers.
Draw more part-whole circle sets with 10 being the whole. Write various numbers in one part and have the child find the missing part.	
Go to the Dump. Play Go to the Dump found in the *Math Card Games* book, A3.	
In conclusion. Ask: What are the ways to partition 10? [9 + 1, 8 + 2, 7 + 3, 6 + 4, 5 + 5, so on]	

© Activities for Learning, Inc. 2013

REVIEW LESSON 8: INTRODUCING THE MATH BALANCE

OBJECTIVES:
1. To introduce the math balance
2. To discuss the term *double*

MATERIALS:
1. Math balance and weights
2. *Math Card Games* book, A3
3. AL Abacus

ACTIVITIES FOR TEACHING:	EXPLANATIONS:
Warm-up. Ask the child to say the names of the days of the week. Then play the Comes Before game with the days of the week. Ask: What day comes before Saturday? [Friday] What day comes before Tuesday? [Monday] What day comes before Thursday? [Wednesday] Sing "The Months" from a previous lesson. Sing or recite "Yellow is the Sun." **Math balance.** Present the math balance (shown below.) Give the child two weights and ask her to make it balance. Avoid giving hints. 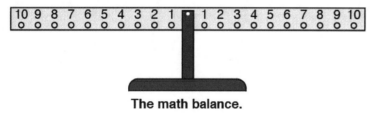 **The math balance.** Remove the two weights. Ask her to find another way to make it balance. 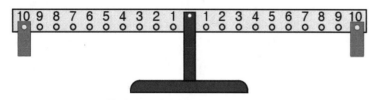 **Balanced with two weights.** Next give the child three weights and ask her to make it balance. Ask: Why does it balance? One possibility is shown on the next page.	After the math balance is assembled, check to be sure it is level. If necessary, adjust it by moving the little white weights under the yellow beam. All the weights are the same; ignore the number embossed on them. An interesting note: for a person's first attempt, many children choose the 10s, while adults usually choose low numbers. The white peg in the center is not a solution.

RightStart™ Mathematics Level B Second Edition © Activities for Learning, Inc. 2013

ACTIVITIES FOR TEACHING:

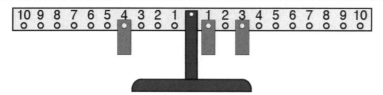

Balancing with three weights. [4 is 1 + 3]

Partitioning 5. Tell the child: Let's partition 5. Ask the child to enter a weight on the left 5. Then give two weights to make it balance. See the figure below for one solution.

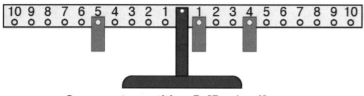

One way to partition 5. [5 = 1 + 4]

Comment by saying: So 5 balances 1 and 4. Why is that? [5 is 1 plus 4.] Ask: Is there another place to put the two weights on the right? [2 and 3] Ask: What does it show now? [5 is 2 + 3]

Partitioning 6. Tell the child to partition 6. If necessary, prompt the child to move the left 5 weight to the left 6. Then ask her to make it balance and to say the equations. [6 is 1 + 5, 6 is 2 + 4, 6 is 3 + 3]

Express delight at the two 3s and say: Six has a *double*. See the figure below.

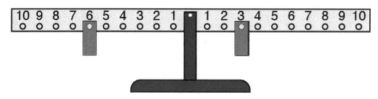

Six has a double, 3 and 3.

Go to the Dump game. Play Go to the Dump found in the *Math Card Games* book, A3. Have the child use the abacus.

More partitioning. Ask the child to partition 10 and to name the equations. If she is interested, she can partition 7, 8, or 9.

In conclusion. Say: Name the ways to partition 5 on the math balance. [1 + 4 and 2 + 3]

EXPLANATIONS:

Flash cards are not a good way to drill the number facts. The only people who like flash cards are those who do not need them. Many adults today, because they could not respond fast enough to flash cards or time tests, became convinced as child that they have no math "ability." These people often develop math anxiety.

Another problem with flash cards is the false impression they give that mathematics is a subject that doesn't require thinking, or that it is just a tidy collection of "facts" that everyone must memorize.

Flash cards are abstract; they require associating a symbol with two other symbols. On the other hand, a child familiar with the abacus thinks about the concrete beads when asked for a fact.

The theory behind flash cards, going back to 1910, is based on the erroneous concept that a person learns these facts by associating a third symbol with two symbols. For example, if you see 8 and 7, you think 15. Brain research now tells us our brains do not work well that way. Rather, it is more natural to use a strategy. In this case they might take 2 from the 7, combine it with the 8 and change it into 10 and 5, or 15.

Also, even if the child did memorize 8, 7, 15, a few years later, the hapless child is expected to memorize 8, 7, 56. Many children find this very difficult.

Facts practice should always provide a strategy for the learner to figure out a forgotten answer. The AL Abacus provides a good way through visual representation, based on 5s and 10s. A 5-year-old was asked how much is 11 and 6. After he said 17 without counting, he was asked how he knew. He replied with a grin, "I have the abacus in my mind."

Another reason to provide the abacus is to discourage counting. Counting is slow, unreliable, and habit forming. Those adding by counting dots on numerals are still counting dots decades later, although now in it might be in her head.

Review Lesson 9: Writing Addition Equations

OBJECTIVES:
1. To review the symbols "=" and "+"
2. To understand the terms *equation* and *equal*
3. To write addition equations

MATERIALS:
1. **Calendar**
2. AL Abacus
3. Math journal, which is found in the back of the child's worksheets
4. Worksheet 3, Writing Addition Equations

ACTIVITIES FOR TEACHING:	EXPLANATIONS:
Warm-up. Sing the "Days of the Week." Ask: What day comes after Sunday? [Monday] What day comes after Saturday? [Sunday]	
Using a calendar, ask: What will the date be a week from today?	
Sing "The Months" and sing "Yellow is the Sun" from a previous lesson.	
With the help of the abacus, ask the child to recite the partitioning of 10: 10 is 1 + 9, 10 is 2 + 8 and so forth. Leave the abacus with 10 partitioned into 9 and 1.	
Writing "=" and "+." Tell the child that today she will review writing, "10 equals 9 plus 1." Ask the child to write 10 in her math journal.	
10	
Next explain that the equals sign, written with two (parallel) lines that are the same length, tells us that it means "the same as." The equal sign has been used for hundreds of years.	
10 =	A child who sees equal signs only near the end of an equation may develop a misconception that the equal sign means do something, rather than that the two sides are equal, or the same. Therefore, the emphasis here is on equations that start, for example, with "10 =."
Ask: What do we write next in ten equals nine plus one? [nine] Ask the child to write the 9.	
10 = 9	
Write the plus sign. Ask her what it means. [add or and]	
10 = 9 +	
Again ask what is next. [1] Ask the child to write the 1.	
10 = 9 + 1	
See example on the next page.	

ACTIVITIES FOR TEACHING:	EXPLANATIONS:

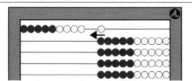 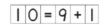

Writing the equation, 10 = 9 + 1.

Writing equations. Ask the child to write more equations in her math journal. Move over another bead and ask the child to write that equation in her math journal. [10 = 8 + 2]

Tell her that only one number or sign goes into each box. See the example below. Ask the child to continue with the abacus and write the remaining equations in her math journal.

1	0	=	9	+	1	
1	0	=	8	+	2	
1	0	=	7	+	3	
1	0	=	6	+	4	
1	0	=	5	+	5	
1	0	=	4	+	6	
1	0	=	3	+	7	
1	0	=	2	+	8	
1	0	=	1	+	9	
1	0	=	0	+	1	0

Writing the "10s" equations in the math journal.

Worksheet 3. Give the child the worksheet. Folding the sheet in half may be helpful for the child. Work with her to complete the left half. Encourage her to complete the right half by herself.

The equations to be written are as follows:

    10 = 6 + 4   8 = 5 + 3
    10 = 3 + 7   4 = 2 + 2
    5 = 3 + 2   7 = 6 + 1
    5 = 1 + 4   6 = 5 + 1

In conclusion. Ask the child to make the stairs on the abacus. Ask her to point to the equation on the abacus as you read it aloud. [10 = 9 + 1, 10 = 8 + 2 and 10 = 7 + 3] Ask: What is the total number of beads on each wire? [10]

An expression such as 2 + 2 = 4 is properly call an equation—the word equation comes from the word *equal*. The term "number sentence," which sometimes is used, makes no sense grammatically or mathematically and should be avoided. Engineers and scientists do not talk about number sentences.

A sentence is a group of words making a complete thought or sentence may refer to a punishment. Some children have thought that writing a number sentence meant spelling out the numbers.

However, some older tests still use "number sentence." If the child will be taking such a test, tell her that the person who wrote the test may use the incorrect words "number sentence" instead of equation.

© Activities for Learning, Inc. 2013

Review Lesson 10: Tens on the Abacus

OBJECTIVES:
1. To experience 10 as an entity
2. To learn the term *ones*
3. To realize the similarity between partitioning ones and partitioning tens

MATERIALS:
1. AL Abacus
2. Place-value cards
3. *Math Card Games* book, N43 Level 1

ACTIVITIES FOR TEACHING:

Warm-up. Sing "The Months" from a previous lesson. Play the Comes After game with the months. Ask: What month comes after February? [March] What month comes after June? [July] What month comes after October? [November]

Ask the child to name the partitions of 10. [10 & 0, 9 & 1, 8 & 2, 7 & 3, 6 & 4, 5 & 5, 4 & 6, 3 & 7, 2 & 8, 1 & 9, 0 & 10]

Tens on the abacus. Ask the child to enter 10 on her abacus. Then ask her to enter another 10 on the second wire. See the left figure below. Tell her there are two names for this amount: its regular name is *twenty* and its math name is *2-ten*.

Ask her to enter another 2-ten. How much do you have now? Ask her to give both names. [forty, 4-ten]

Ask the child to enter another twenty. How much do you have now? [sixty, 6-ten] See the right figure below. How can you tell it is 6-ten by looking? Make sure they see that the color changes after 5-ten. Ask her to enter 10-ten.

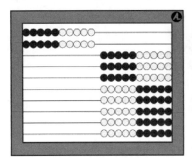 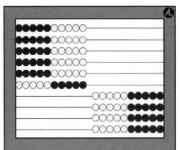

The abacus with 2-ten (twenty) entered.   The abacus with 6-ten (sixty) entered.

Practicing naming quantities. Enter various tens on the abacus and ask the child to name the quantities both the regular way and the math way. Especially emphasize the tens greater than 5-ten.

EXPLANATIONS:

Research shows that the *math way* of number naming greatly helps English-speaking children acquire the concept of place value.

It is more difficult for a child to see the beads change color after 5-ten than to see the beads change color after 5.

ACTIVITIES FOR TEACHING:	EXPLANATIONS:

Place-value cards. With 2-ten entered, show the child the place-value card "20" and tell her this is how we record, or write, 2-ten; point to the "2" while saying "two" and to the "0" while saying "ten." See the left figure below.

Relating the words to the digits.

Repeat for 3-ten; point to the individual digits of the "30" while the child reads it as "3-ten." Repeat for other tens up to 10-ten. For 10-ten point to the 10 on the left while saying "ten" and to the 0 while saying "ten" as shown above in the right figure.

Partitioning 10-ten. Tell the child that we will partition 10-ten. On the abacus, first enter 10-ten; to partition 1 part, offset it slightly from the edge as shown below. Ask the child to say it: 10-ten = 9-ten + 1-ten. Move over another 10 and say: 10-ten = 8-ten + 2-ten. Continue to 10-ten = 0-ten + 10-ten.

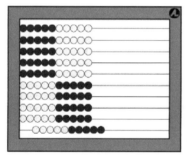

Partitioning 10-ten into 9-ten and 1-ten.

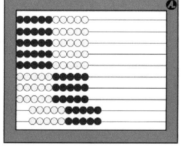

Partitioning 10-ten into 8-ten and 2-ten.

Ones. Enter 3-ten on the abacus and ask: What is its math name? [3-ten] Now enter 3 and ask: What do we call it? [three] Tell the child that sometimes we call it 3 *ones*. Explain that each bead is called a one, so 3 beads are 3 ones. Ask her to enter 2 ones, 2 tens, 8 ones, and 8 tens.

Can You Find game. Play the Can You Find game Level 1 found in the *Math Card Games* book, N43. Use both names when asking for quantities.

In conclusion. Tell the child to keep track on her abacus while finding all the different ways to partition 10-ten into groups of tens. [11 different groups]

It is important that the child identify a "ten" by noting that 1 digit follows it. This allows her to read numbers from left to right, the normal order. Later it will help her see 120 as 12 tens.

Thinking of numbers in columns hampers a full understanding of place value. That model requires first looking at the ones and then proceeding to the left, that is, reading numbers backward.

© Activities for Learning, Inc. 2013

Review Lesson 11: Tens and Ones

OBJECTIVES:
1. To combine tens and ones

MATERIALS:
1. AL Abacus
2. Place-value cards
3. *Math Card Games* book, N43
4. Worksheet 4, Tens and Ones

ACTIVITIES FOR TEACHING:

Warm-up. Ask the child to enter quantities on her abacus, such as 3-ten, 8, and 10-ten. Show various place-value cards and ask her to enter those quantities.

Ask the child to start with 3-ten and to count by ones to 9-ten 9. [3-ten, 3-ten 1, 3-ten 2, . . . , 9-ten 9]

Combining tens and ones. Tell the child to enter 3-ten on her abacus. Ask: What is its regular name? [thirty] Now tell her to enter 6 ones on the fourth wire. See the left figure below. Tell her: Its math name is 3-ten 6 and its regular name is thirty-six.

Tell her to add 2 more ones. Ask: What are the names for this amount? [3-ten 8, thirty-eight]

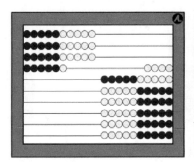 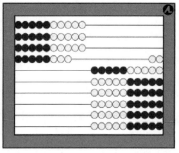

3-ten 6 (thirty-six) entered.   3-ten 8 (thirty-eight) entered.

Tell the child to enter other quantities, such as 7-ten 5, sixty-one, 4-ten 8, and twenty-nine.

Naming quantities. Enter various quantities on the abacus for the child to name, using both the math name and the regular name.

EXPLANATIONS:

ACTIVITIES FOR TEACHING:	EXPLANATIONS:

Writing tens and ones. Explain that we will use the place-value cards to compose numbers. Enter 3-ten 2 on the abacus. Ask: What is its math name? [3-ten 2] Show her the place-value cards for 3-ten and 2 and ask for the math names. [3-ten, 2] Demonstrate stacking the 2-card on top of the 3-ten card as shown below. Again ask her to read it. [3-ten 2]

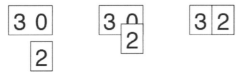

Composing 3-ten 2 by stacking the 3-ten card and 2 card.

Practice. Enter 1-ten 6 on the abacus and ask the child to find and stack the matching place-value cards. Also ask her to give both names. [1-ten 6 or ten 6, sixteen] Repeat with other quantities.

Enter a quantity on the abacus. Then have the child make the corresponding number with place-value cards. Verify that they have used the correct cards.

Show ten 2 (1-ten 2) with place-value cards; ask the child to read it and to enter it on the abacus. If the child is not quite sure, present the cards stacked, but wait a few seconds and separate them.

Repeat for 40 + 9 (4-ten + 9) [49] and for 10 + 7 (1-ten + 7). [17]

Can You Find game. Play the Can You Find game found in the *Math Card Games* book, N43 Level 1.

Worksheet 4. To provide practice in adding tens and ones, give her the worksheet. She may need an abacus and the place-value cards. The solutions for the worksheet are below:

        60 + 7 = **67**
        30 + 3 = **33**
        50 + 6 = **56**
        10 + 2 = **12**
        90 + 4 = **94**
        78 = 70 + **8**
        21 = 20 + **1**
        63 = 60 + **3**
        89 = 80 + **9**
        45 = **40 + 5**

In conclusion. Ask the child: How much is 10 + 5? [1-ten 5, fifteen] What is 1-ten 5 plus 2? [1-ten 7, seventeen]

© Activities for Learning, Inc. 2013

Lesson 12: Adding One

OBJECTIVES:
1. To review "Yellow is the Sun"
2. To add 1 to numbers from 1 to 99 on the AL Abacus
3. To explore using the math balance

MATERIALS:
1. Music for "Yellow is the Sun" (Appendix p. 2)
2. *Yellow is the Sun* book
3. AL Abacus
4. Math balance and weights

ACTIVITIES FOR TEACHING:

Warm up. Sing the following song and ask the child to show the correct fingers at the appropriate words.

Yellow is the Sun

Yellow is the sun.
This is only one. (Raise one finger.)

Why is the sky so blue?
Let me show you two. (Raise two fingers.)

Salty is the sea.
One more and it's three. (Raise three fingers.)

Hear the thunder roar.
Here's the mighty four. (Raise four fingers.)

Ducks will swim and dive.
My whole hand makes five. (Raise five fingers.)

Read the book *Yellow is the Sun* to the child.

Adding 1 on the abacus. Tell the child to enter 8 on her abacus. See the left figure below. Next tell her to add 1 more and say how much it is. [9] Repeat for 2-ten 8. [2-ten 9] See the right figure below.

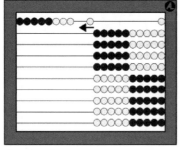 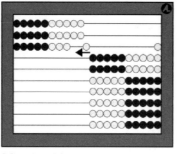

8 + 1 = 9.   28 + 1 = 29.

Continue with 47, [48] 95, [96] and 56. [57]

Ask the child if she is ready for some harder adding 1s: What is 4-ten 9 plus 1? [5-ten] What is 2-ten 9 plus 1? [3-ten] What is 79 plus 1? [80] What is 9-ten 9 plus 1? [one hundred]

EXPLANATIONS:

The first half of these RightStart™ Mathematics lessons refer to the child as a female and the second half of the lessons refer to the child as a male.

Research shows that the math way of number naming greatly helps children understand place value. The math way states the value of number. Both forms of number naming, the regular way and the math way, will be used for a while. For example, 37 is called 3-ten 7, 85 is 8-ten 5, and 13 is 1-ten 3 (or ten 3).

Some children may benefit from initially thinking of the answer and then verifying it with an abacus.

ACTIVITIES FOR TEACHING:

Adding 1 with the math balance. On the math balance enter weights on the left 8 and left 1. Give the child one weight and ask her to make it balance. See the figure below. Ask the child to state the equation. [8 + 1 = 9]

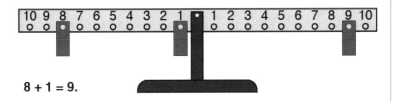

8 + 1 = 9.

Enter weights on both 10s and both 7s. See the figure below. Ask the child to state the equation using either way of number naming or a mixture of both. [17 = 17]

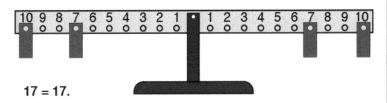

17 = 17.

Add 1 to the left side and ask the child to make it balance by moving only one weight on the right side. See the figure below. Tell the child to say the equation both ways. [1-ten 7 plus 1 equals 1-ten 8, 17 + 1 = 18]

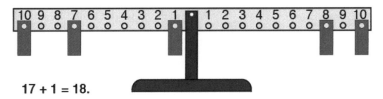

17 + 1 = 18.

Add another 1 on the left side. Ask the child to make it balance by moving only one weight on the right side. Repeat once more. See the figures below.

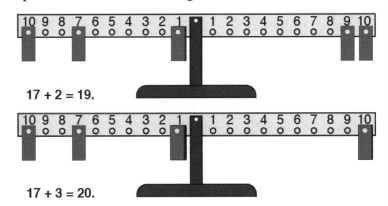

17 + 2 = 19.

17 + 3 = 20.

In conclusion. Ask: What is 14 + 1? [15] When you count, what number comes after 14? [15] What is 49 + 1? [50] When you count, what number comes after 49? [50]

© Activities for Learning, Inc. 2013

EXPLANATIONS:

Understanding that $n = n$ is also an equation is a difficult concept for most children. Here it is briefly introduced.

Lesson 13: More Adding One

OBJECTIVES:
1. To practice adding 1 to a number
2. To understand that repeatedly adding 1 results in counting

MATERIALS:
1. *Math Card Games* book,* N43
2. Place-value cards
3. AL Abacus

ACTIVITIES FOR TEACHING:

Warm up. Sing "Yellow is the Sun."

Using the tune of "Twinkle, Twinkle Little Star," sing the days of the week with these words:

Days of the Week
Sunday, Monday, Tuesday, too.
Wednesday, Thursday—this I knew.
Friday, Saturday that's the end.
Now let's say those days again!
Sunday, Monday, Tuesday, Wednesday, Thursday,
Friday, Saturday!

Play the Comes After game using the days of the week. Ask: What day comes after Tuesday? [Wednesday] What day comes after Friday? [Saturday] What day comes after Wednesday? [Thursday]

Can You Find game. Play the Can You Find game found in the *Math Card Games* book, N43. Use all levels. This game provides practice for the child in composing numbers up to 100.

Can You Find Plus One game. This harder version of Can You Find from the *Math Card Games* book, N43, asks the child to find one more than the number you say.

Below are suggested numbers you say; the numbers in brackets are the place-value cards the child picks up, overlaps, and sets aside. All the cards will be picked up at the conclusion of the game. See figure on the next page.

Can you find 6 + 1?	[7]
Can you find 4-ten 2 + 1?	[40 & 3]
Can you find 9-ten 7 + 1?	[90 & 8]
Can you find 2-ten 5 + 1?	[20 & 6]
Can you find 29 + 1?	[30]
Can you find 88 + 1?	[80 & 9]
Can you find 74 + 1?	[70 & 5]
Can you find 13 + 1?	[10 & 4]
Can you find 50 + 1?	[50 & 1]
Can you find 61 + 1?	[60 & 2]

EXPLANATIONS:

*The Fifth Edition of the *Math Card Games* book is needed for this manual.

The book is arranged in chapters as follows:
1. Number Sense (N)
2. Addition (A)
3. Clocks (C)
4. Multiplication (P)
5. Money (M)
6. Subtraction (S)
7. Division (D)
8. Fractions (F)

The games are numbered sequentially within each chapter. For example, A2 is the second game in the Addition chapter and N3 is the third game in the previous chapter, Number Sense.

Within each chapter the games get progressively harder.

ACTIVITIES FOR TEACHING:	EXPLANATIONS:

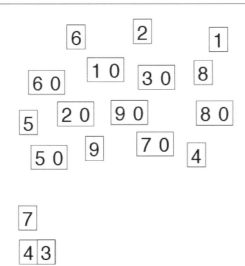

Can You Find Plus One game in progress.

Repeatedly adding 1 on the abacus. Ask the child to enter 10 on her abacus. Then ask her to add 1 and to say the quantity using the math way. [1-ten 1] Ask her to add another 1 and again say the quantity. [1-ten 2] See the figures below.

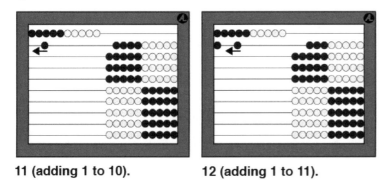

11 (adding 1 to 10).   12 (adding 1 to 11).

Continue to 4-ten.

Repeat the activity, but use the regular number names.

In conclusion. Tell the child to start with 70 and to add 1. [71] Tell her to add 1 again. [72] Ask her to continue until she reaches 80. Ask: What is another name for what you are doing? [counting]

Lesson 14: Evens and Odds

OBJECTIVES:
1. To review quantities 1–10
2. To work with even and odd numbers

MATERIALS:
1. **Calendar showing the current month***
2. AL Abacus
3. Tiles
4. Worksheet 5, Evens and Odds
5. **Scissors and glue**

ACTIVITIES FOR TEACHING:

Warm-up. Ask the child to say the days of the week. Ask: What day is today? Find it on the calendar. What date is today?

Tell the child to start with 80 and to add 1. [81] Tell her to add 1 again. [82] Ask her to continue until she reaches 90. Ask: What is another name for what you are doing? [counting]

Ask the child to build the stairs on her abacus. Enter 1 on the first wire, 2 on the next wire and so forth. See the figure below.

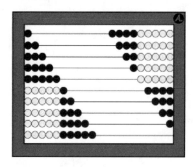

Stairs on the abacus.

Ask her to point to 3 on her abacus. Repeat for other quantities.

Point to 6 and ask her to name it. [6] Repeat for other quantities.

Evens with the tiles. Ask the child to lay out 8 tiles in groups of two in a column. See the left figure below. Then tell her to touch each pair proceeding from top to bottom. See the right picture. Then say: Eight is an *even* number. Repeat for 6 tiles.

Eight in the even-odd pattern.

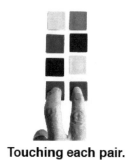

Touching each pair.

EXPLANATIONS:

*An item listed in bold face is not part of the RightStart™ materials.

Some children may find it interesting to observe that the word "even" has an even number of letters and even number of syllables, while the word "odd" has an odd number of letters and an odd number of syllables.

RightStart™ Mathematics Level B Second Edition © Activities for Learning, Inc. 2013

ACTIVITIES FOR TEACHING:	EXPLANATIONS:

Odds with the tiles. Ask the child to repeat the previous activity for 7 tiles. See the figure below. This time when they touch each pair, she will end with one finger dangling. Tell her: This is an *odd* number. Ask her to repeat for 5.

Seven in the even-odd pattern.   Finger left dangling.

Evens or odds. Tell her to lay out 4 tiles and ask: Is it even or odd? [even] Repeat for 9. [odd]

Ask her to start with 2 tiles, then make and name the even numbers to ten. [2, 4, 6, 8, 10]

Then ask her to start with 1, then make and name the odd numbers to ten. [1, 3, 5, 7, 9]

Even stairs. Tell her to build the even stairs. Enter 2 on the first wire and 4 on the second wire. Continue to 10. See the left figure below.

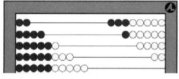
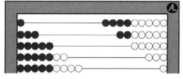

The even stairs.   The odd stairs.

Odd stairs. Ask her to say the odd numbers. Then ask her to build the odd stairs. See the right figure above.

Ask if she sees any interesting patterns with the light-colored beads. [The light-colored beads are odd on the even stairs and even on the odd stairs.]

Worksheet 5. Give the child the worksheet. Explain that she is to cut on the heavy lines. Next she joins the patterns by gluing the 5 to the tab before the 6. Finally, she glues the correct even or odd tag on the lines.

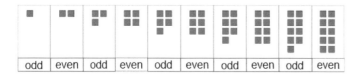

Some children may prefer to write the words, "even" or "odd" rather than glue in place.

In conclusion. Ask her to name the even numbers. [2, 4, 6, 8, 10] Ask her to name the odd numbers. [1, 3, 5, 7, 9] What pattern do you see? [They alternate, or take turns.]

© Activities for Learning, Inc. 2013

Lesson 15: Even Numbers Plus 2

OBJECTIVES:
1. To count by twos by repeatedly adding 2
2. To add two to even numbers

MATERIALS:
1. **Calendar showing the current month**
2. AL Abacus

ACTIVITIES FOR TEACHING:

Warm-up. Ask the child to say the days of the week. Ask: What day comes after Sunday? [Monday] What day comes after Saturday? [Sunday] What day is today? Find it on the calendar. What date is today?

Ask the child to name the even numbers. [2, 4, 6, 8, 10] Ask her to name the odd numbers. [1, 3, 5, 7, 9]

Ask the child to build the stairs on her abacus. Enter 1 on the first wire, 2 on the next wire and so forth. Ask: How many beads are on the fourth wire? [4] How many beads are on the sixth wire? [6] How many beads on the second wire? [2] See figure below.

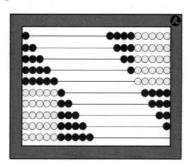

Stairs on the abacus.

Adding ones on the stairs. Tell the child to make the stairs on her abacus. Then tell her to add 1 to the 3. See the left figure below. Ask: What do you see? What row does it look like? [the next row]

Repeat by asking her to add 1 to the 8. See the right figure below. What row is it the same as? [the next row]

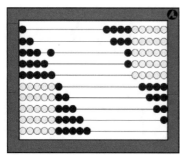 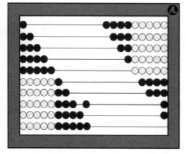

3 + 1 same as next row (4).   8 + 1 same as next row (9).

EXPLANATIONS:

ACTIVITIES FOR TEACHING:	EXPLANATIONS:

Adding twos on the stairs. Ask the child to count by 2s to 10. [2, 4, 6, . . . , 10] Now tell the child to construct the even stairs on the abacus. Next tell her to add 2 to the first row. See the left figure below. Ask her to say the equation. [2 + 2 = 4]

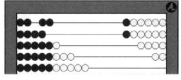 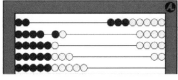

2 + 2 same as next row (4).   4 + 2 same as next row (6).

Ask her to add 2 to the next row and say the equation. [4 + 2 = 6] Repeat for 6 + 2 and 8 + 2.

Adding 2s on the abacus. Ask the child to clear her abacus. Ask: What quantity is entered? [0] Now ask her to add 2 to 0 and say the equation. [0 + 2 = 2] Ask her to add another 2 and say the equation. [2 + 2 = 4] See the figures below. Continue to 18 + 2 = 20.

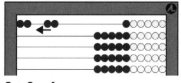 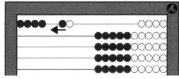

2 + 2 = 4.   4 + 2 = 6.

Adding 2 with the 2s patterns. Tell the child to turn her abacus sideways and enter 2 on the right two wires. Tell her: Add 2 and say the equation. [2 + 2 = 4] See the first two figures below. Enter 2 more saying. [4 + 2 = 6]

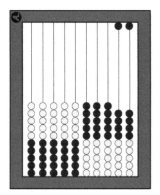 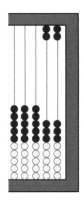 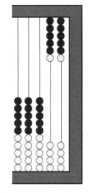

Entering 2.   Adding more 2s.

It makes no difference if the logo is at the upper left or the lower right.

Quantities are entered when they are moved up.

In the third figure, there are 10 blue beads, making the quantity entered easily seen as 1-ten 2.

Continue with 6 + 2 and 8 + 2. For adding 10 + 2, use the math way of numbers naming 10 + 2 = 1-ten 2. Continue to 2-ten.

In conclusion. Ask: What is 2 + 2? [4] What is 2 + 4? [6] What is 2 + 6? [8] What is 2 + 8? [10] What is 2 + 10? [12] What is 2 + 12? [14]

© Activities for Learning, Inc. 2013

Lesson 16: Odd Numbers Plus 2

OBJECTIVES:
1. To count by twos by repeatedly adding 2
2. To add two to odd numbers

MATERIALS:
1. AL Abacus

ACTIVITIES FOR TEACHING:

Warm-up. Ask the child to put to 3 on her abacus. Repeat for other quantities from 1-10.

Put 6 on the abacus and point to it and ask her to name it. [6] Repeat for other quantities from 1-10.

Start at 34 and repeatedly add ones on the abacus; stop at 87. [34, 35, 36, . . . , 87]

Ask the child to build the stairs on her abacus. Ask: How many beads are on the fifth wire? [5] How many beads are on the seventh wire? [7] How many beads on the first wire? [1] How many beads on the eighth wire? [8]

Ask: What is 2 + 12? [14] What is 2 + 10? [12] What is 2 + 8? [10] What is 2 + 6? [8] What is 2 + 4? [6] What is 2 + 2? [4]

Adding two with odd numbers. Tell the child to enter 1. Then ask her to add 2 and name the amount. [3] See the left figure below. Ask her to add another 2 and say the amount. [5] See the right figure below.

Continue to 1-ten 9. Ask: What kind of numbers were you saying (even or odd)? [odd]

Ask her to do it again using the regular math names.

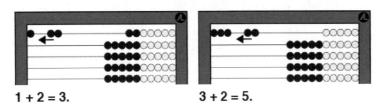

1 + 2 = 3.   3 + 2 = 5.

Adding twos on the stairs. Ask the child to say the odd numbers to 10. Now tell the child to construct the odd stairs. Next tell her to add 2 to the first row. See the left figure on the next page. Ask her to say the equation. [1 + 2 = 3]

EXPLANATIONS:

ACTIVITIES FOR TEACHING:

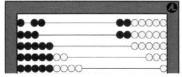

1 + 2 same as next row (3).

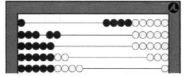

3 + 2 same as next row (5).

Ask her to add 2 to the next row and say the equation. [3 + 2 = 5] Repeat for 5 + 2 and 7 + 2.

Adding 2 with the even-odd patterns. Tell the child to turn her abacus sideways and enter 1 on the next to the last wire. Tell her: Add 2 and say the equation. [1 + 2 = 3] Enter 2 more and saying the equation. [3 + 2 = 5] See the figures below. Continue to 1-ten 9.

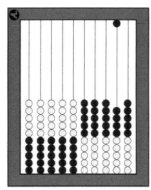 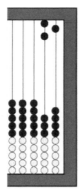 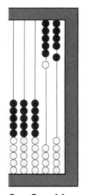

Entering 1.   **1 + 2 = 3.**   **9 + 2 = 11.**

Practice. Ask: Is 2 an even number or an odd number? [even number] What about 5? [odd number] What about 7? [odd number] What about 8? [even number]

Determining even or odd. Tell the child to enter 28 on her abacus. Ask: How can you tell if 28 is even or odd? Suggest they group by twos to find out. See the left figure below. Ask her to see if 37 is even or odd. See the right figure below.

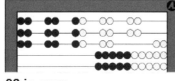 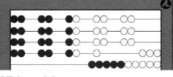

28 is even.   **37 is odd.**

Ask her to try 43 [odd] and numbers of her choosing.

In conclusion. Ask: What is 3 + 2? [5] What is 7 + 2? [9] What is 1 + 2? [3] What is 5 + 2? [7] What is 2 + 2? [4] Ask: If you start with 2 and keep adding twos, what kind of numbers will you get? [even numbers] If you start with 1 and keep adding twos, what kind of numbers will you get? [odd numbers]

EXPLANATIONS:

Lesson 17: The Doubles 1 to 5

OBJECTIVES:
1. To work with doubles
2. To write equations

MATERIALS:
1. Math balance
2. Dry erase board

ACTIVITIES FOR TEACHING:	EXPLANATIONS:
Warm up. Sing "The Months" from a previous lesson.	
Play the Comes After game with the months. Ask: What month comes after February? [March] What month comes after July? [August] What month comes after November? [December]	
Ask: What is 5 + 2? [7] What is 1 + 2? [3] What is 7 + 2? [9] What is 9 + 2? [11] What is 2 + 2? [4]	
Ask: If you start with 2 and keep adding twos, what kind of numbers will you get? [even numbers] If you start with 1 and keep adding twos, what kind of numbers will you get? [odd numbers]	
Doubles on the math balance. Place two weights on the left 1. Ask the child to balance it with one weight. Have the child write the equation on her dry erase board. [1 + 1 = 2] See the figure below. 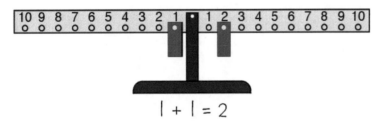 Doubling 1 on the math balance.	An expression such as 2 + 2 = 4 is properly call an *equation*—the word equation is derived from *make equal*. The term "number sentence," which was used for a while, makes no sense grammatically or mathematically and should be avoided. Engineers and scientists do not talk about number sentences.
Move the left weights from the left 1 to the left 2. Ask the child to balance it and have her write the equation. $$2 + 2 = 4$$	A sentence is a group of words making a complete thought or a sentence may refer to a punishment. Some children have thought that writing a number sentence meant spelling out the numbers.
Continue with doubling 3, 4, and 5. $$3 + 3 = 6$$ $$4 + 4 = 8$$ $$5 + 5 = 10$$	However, some older tests still use "number sentence." If the child will be taking such a test, tell her that the person who wrote the test might use the incorrect words "number sentence" instead of equation.

ACTIVITIES FOR TEACHING:	EXPLANATIONS:

After the child has written all five equations, ask her to read the equations. Then ask: What did you notice about the *sums*, the number after the equal sign? [even numbers]

Finding doubles on the math balance. Enter 1 weight on the left 2. Give the child two weights and tell the child to make it balance by putting both weights on the same peg. See the figure below.

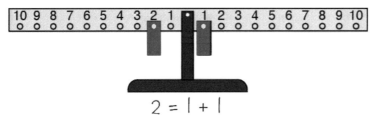

$$2 = 1 + 1$$

Finding the double for 2.

A deep understanding of equations requires that 2 = 1 + 1 also be recognized as a valid equation. Too many children mistakenly think the equal sign means "do something (a calculation)."

Say the equation: 2 equals 1 plus 1. Ask the child to write the equation. Continue with 4, 6, 8, and 10 as shown below.

$$4 = 2 + 2$$
$$6 = 3 + 3$$
$$8 = 4 + 4$$
$$10 = 5 + 5$$

Ask: Can you make it balance with two weights on the same number and one weight on 7? [no] Ask: Can you make it balance with two weights on the same number and one weight on 5? [no]

Ask: What other numbers will not work? [1, 3, 9] What is special about those numbers? [odd numbers]

In conclusion. Tell the child to say the doubles and their sums up to 5. [1 + 1 = 2, 2 + 2 = 4, . . . , 5 + 5 = 10]

© Activities for Learning, Inc. 2013

Lesson 18: Doubles 6 to 10

OBJECTIVES:
1. To work with doubles in the teens
2. To review naming and writing teens
3. To write equations

MATERIALS:
1. AL Abacus
2. Math balance
3. Place-value cards, 1–9 and 10
4. Dry erase board

ACTIVITIES FOR TEACHING:

Warm up. Sing "The Months" from a previous lesson.

Ask the child to say the even numbers starting at 2 to 20. [2, 4, 6, . . . , 20] Play the Comes After Game with even numbers. Repeat for the odd numbers.

Play the Comes After game using the days of the week. Ask: What day comes after Tuesday? [Wednesday] What day comes after Friday? [Saturday] What day comes after Wednesday? [Thursday]

Ask the child to enter 2 on her abacus and to name the quantity. [2] Ask her to add another 2 and name the amount. [4] See the figure below. Continue to 10. Ask: What was special about the numbers you said? [even numbers]

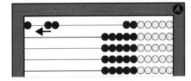 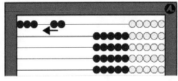

Adding 2s to count by twos.

Doubling 6 on the math balance. Put two weights on the left 1 and ask: In the last lesson, what did we need to make it balance? [2] Ask the child to balance it.

Move the two left weights to the left 2 and ask the child to balance it. [4] Continue by moving the two weights to the left 3, 4, and 5. [6, 8, 10]

Keeping the weight on the right 10, move the two weights to the left 6. Give the child a fourth weight and ask her to balance it. See below.

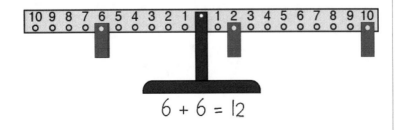

$6 + 6 = 12$

EXPLANATIONS:

ACTIVITIES FOR TEACHING:	EXPLANATIONS:

Tell the child to compose the sum with her place-value cards. See below. Ask her to say its name two ways. [ten 2 and twelve]

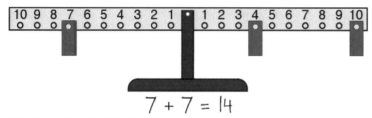

Composing 12 by placing 2 over the zero of the 10.

Tell the child to write the equation on her dry erase board.

$$6 + 6 = 12$$

Doubling 7 on the math balance. Continuing by removing the weight from the right 2 and moving the two weights on the left from the 6 to the 7. Ask the child to make it balance. Tell the child to compose the sum with her place-value cards and to name it. [ten-4, fourteen] Ask her to write the equation. See below.

$$7 + 7 = 14$$

Finding the double for 7.

Doubling 8–10 on the math balance. Continue in the same way for doubling 8, 9, and 10.

Then ask her to read her equations using the math way. Ask: What is special about the sums? [ten plus an even number] Ask her to read her equations again using the regular names.

Doubling 6–10 on the abacus. Tell the child to enter 6 on the first and second wires of her abacus. See the figure below. Ask: Can you see the ten? [the blue beads in both rows] How much is 6 + 6 using the math way? [ten-2] Continue to 10 + 10.

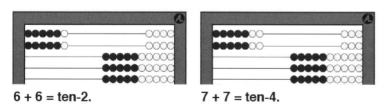

6 + 6 = ten-2.   7 + 7 = ten-4.

In conclusion. Ask the child to recite all the doubles from 1 + 1 to 10 + 10 using her abacus and the math names. Repeat with the regular names.

© Activities for Learning, Inc. 2013

LESSON 19: PRACTICING THE DOUBLES

OBJECTIVES:
1. To write the doubles
2. To play games involving the doubles

MATERIALS:
1. AL Abacus
2. Math journal
3. *Math Card Games* book, A15 and A17
4. Multiplication cards* (after sorting, use the 1s and 2s envelopes)

ACTIVITIES FOR TEACHING:

Warm up. Sing "The Months" from a previous lesson.

Ask the child to say the odd numbers starting at 1 to 19. [1, 3, 5, . . . , 19] Play the Comes After Game with odd numbers. Repeat for the even numbers.

Play the Comes After game using the days of the week. Ask: What day comes after Wednesday? [Thursday] What day comes after Saturday? [Sunday] What day comes after Monday? [Tuesday]

Ask the child to enter 2 on her abacus and to name the quantity. [2] Ask her to add another 2 and name the amount. [4] Continue to 10. Ask: What was special about the numbers you said? [even numbers]

Reciting the doubles 1 to 5. Ask the child to enter on the top wire of her abacus the quantities as you tell her and to name the sums. See the figure below.

$1 + 1 =$ __ [2]
$2 + 2 =$ __ [4]
$3 + 3 =$ __ [6]
$4 + 4 =$ __ [8]
$5 + 5 =$ __ [10]

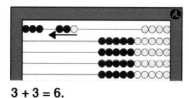

$3 + 3 = 6.$

Ask: What pattern do you hear with the sums? [even numbers]

Reciting the doubles 6 to 10. Ask the child to enter 6 on the top two wires of her abacus. See the figure below. Ask: How do you know how much it is? [The dark-colored beads make 10 and the light colored beads are recognized as 2.] Continue doubles to 10 + 10.

$6 + 6 =$ __ [12]
$7 + 7 =$ __ [14]
$8 + 8 =$ __ [16]
$9 + 9 =$ __ [18]
$10 + 10 =$ __ [20]

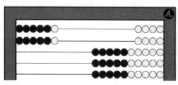

$6 + 6 = 12.$

EXPLANATIONS:

*Included with the multiplication cards are 10 envelopes, each printed with the multiples of a number from 1–10. Insert into each envelope 10 multiplication cards matching the numbers listed on the front of the envelope.

A new deck of multiplication cards is collated to make this task easy: the first 10 cards go into the 1s envelope; the next 10 cards go into the 2s envelope; and so forth.

ACTIVITIES FOR TEACHING:	EXPLANATIONS:
Recording the doubles in the math journal. Tell the child to find the doubles with her abacus and to write them in her math journal. See below.	

$1 + 1 = 2$
$2 + 2 = 4$
$3 + 3 = 6$
$4 + 4 = 8$
$5 + 5 = 10$
$6 + 6 = 12$
$7 + 7 = 14$
$8 + 8 = 16$
$9 + 9 = 18$
$10 + 10 = 20$

The math journal page showing the doubles and sums.

Ask her to read the equations, first using the math way of number naming and again using the regular names.

Doubles Memory game. This simply memory game found in the *Math Card Games* book, A15, has the players matching the doubles with their sums.

Advanced Doubles Memory game. This game is played like Doubles Memory, but uses multiplication cards. Use cards 1–10 from the 1s envelope for the doubles; use cards 2–20 from the 2s envelope for the sums.

Play is the same except only one card is picked up for a double. Tell the players that at the end of the game they need to return the cards to the correct envelopes.

Doubles Solitaire. This more difficult game, found in the *Math Card Games* book, A17, requires some strategy to win. Two people can play the solitaire together with the goal to "beat the cards."

In conclusion. Ask: What is 3 + 3? [6] What is 8 + 8? [16] What is 4 + 4? [8] What is 9 + 9? [18] What is 2 + 2? [4] What is 7 + 7? [14]

Explanations: The child need not play all the games. Choose the most appropriate ones.

© Activities for Learning, Inc. 2013

Lesson 20: The Commutative Property

OBJECTIVES:
1. To understand and apply the commutative property *(a + b = b + a)*

MATERIALS:
1. AL Abacus
2. Dry erase board
3. Worksheet 6, The Commutative Property

ACTIVITIES FOR TEACHING:

Warm-up. Ask the child to say the months of the year. Then play the Comes After game with the months. Ask: What month comes after April? [May] What month comes after August? [September] What month comes after January? [February]

Ask the child to enter 1 on her abacus and to name the quantity. [1] Ask her to add another 2 and name the amount. [3] See figure below. Continue to 9. Ask: What was special about the numbers you said? [odd numbers]

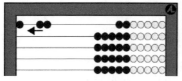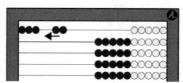

Adding 2s to count by twos.

Drawing part-whole circle sets. Show the child how to draw part-whole circle sets as shown below. First, draw the large circle. Second, draw the two lines. Third, draw the small circles by starting at the end of the lines.

  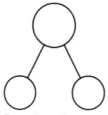

Drawing the large circle. Drawing the lines. Drawing the small circles.

Commutative property with part-whole circle sets. Ask the child to draw two part-whole circle sets. Ask her to write parts 4 and 6 in one set and parts 6 and 4 in the other as shown on the top of the next page. Ask the child to find the whole for both. [10]

EXPLANATIONS:

Part-whole circle sets are a visual tool that help children understand partitioning. The whole is written in the larger circle and the parts, in the smaller circles. Research shows children using them do better in solving story problems.

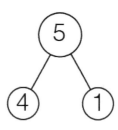

Some children discover the commutative property on their own, but others need experiences to realize and apply it.

Do not teach the term *commutative* at this point. The child must thoroughly understand the concept before the word is introduced.

ACTIVITIES FOR TEACHING:	EXPLANATIONS:

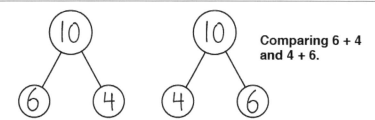

Comparing 6 + 4 and 4 + 6.

Commutative property with the abacus. Ask her to enter 5 + 1 on the first wire of her abacus and 1 + 5 on the second wire. Tell her to write the sums in the whole-circles and to write the equations. See the left figure below.

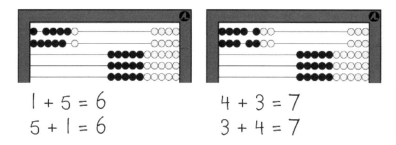

1 + 5 = 6
5 + 1 = 6

4 + 3 = 7
3 + 4 = 7

Repeat for 4 + 3 and 3 + 4. See the right figures above. Ask her to notice how the equations are the same and how they are different. [same parts, different order] Encourage her to try her own numbers and discuss her conclusions.

Worksheet 6. This worksheet provides more practice in applying the commutative property. Using the abacus helps the child "see" the concept.

4 + 5 = 9	7 + 2 = 9
5 + 4 = 9	2 + 7 = 9
6 + 3 = 9	3 + 5 = 8
3 + 6 = 9	5 + 3 = 8
4 + 3 = 7	7 + 1 = 8
3 + 4 = 7	1 + 7 = 8
8 + 1 = 9	3 + 7 = 10
1 + 8 = 9	7 + 3 = 10

In conclusion. Write on a dry erase board 40 + 30 = 70 and 30 + 40 = 70. Ask the child: What do you notice about the equations? [The answers are the same.]

The commutative property is sometimes referred to as the commutative law. Property, meaning attribute or quality, is the preferred term.

© Activities for Learning, Inc. 2013

Lesson 21: Applying the Commutative Property

OBJECTIVES:
1. To apply the commutative property *(a + b = b + a)*
2. Play Go to the Dump

MATERIALS:
1. AL Abacus
2. Tiles
3. Dry erase board
4. *Math Card Games* book, A3

ACTIVITIES FOR TEACHING:	EXPLANATIONS:

Warm-up. Ask the child to say the months of the year. Then play the Comes After game with the months. Ask: What month comes after May? [June] What month comes after December? [January]

Play the Comes After game using the days of the week. Ask: What day comes after Tuesday? [Wednesday] What day comes after Friday? [Saturday] What day comes after Wednesday? [Thursday]

Ask the child to recite all the doubles from 1 + 1 to 10 + 10 using her abacus and the math names. Repeat with the regular names.

Say: 50 + 40 = 90 and 40 + 50 = 90. Ask the child: What do you notice about the equations? [The answers are the same.]

The commutative property. Have the child pick up 5 green tiles with her left hand and 1 red tile with her right hand. Have the child put her left hand tiles in a line. Now put the tile in her right hand in the same line next to the green tiles. See the figure below.

Ask her to say the equation. [5 + 1 = 6] Now ask her to grab 1 red and 5 green and arrange the tiles with the red one to the left of the green tiles. Ask: What is the equation? [1 + 5 = 6] Ask: Do you get the same answer? [yes]

One way to compare 5 + 1 and 1 + 5 using tiles.

Have her repeat this activity with several numbers up to 10; 4 + 3 and 3 + 4 or 4 + 1 and 1 + 4. Tell the child to write the equations on her dry erase board.

ACTIVITIES FOR TEACHING:	EXPLANATIONS:

The commutative property on the abacus. Ask the child to make the stairs only to five on her abacus as shown below.

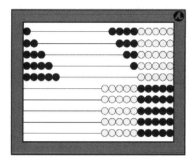

The stairs to five.

Tell her to look at her abacus to answer the following questions:

What do you need with 1 to make 10? [9]
Where is that on the abacus? [first row on the right]

What do you need with 4 to make 10? [6]
Where is that on the abacus? [fourth row on the right]

What do you need with 6 to make 10? [4]
Where is that on the abacus? [fourth row on the left]

What do you need with 8 to make 10? [2]
Where is that on the abacus? [second row on the left]

Go to the Dump game. Play the Go to the Dump game in the *Math Card Games* book, A3. Tell her to use the abacus stairs to 5, shown above, for her manipulative.

In conclusion. Give the child the following problem:

Nate rode his bike for 13 minutes in the morning and 18 minutes in the afternoon. (Write this down as shown below.) Abby rode her bike 18 minutes in the morning and 13 minutes in the afternoon. (Write this down.) Who rode for the longest time that day? [same] Ask: How do you know?

> Nate 13 and 18   Abby 18 and 13

© Activities for Learning, Inc. 2013

LESSON 22: SOLVING "ADD TO" PROBLEMS

OBJECTIVES:
1. To solve "Add To" problems

MATERIALS:
1. AL Abacus
2. Worksheet 7, Solving "Add To" Problems

ACTIVITIES FOR TEACHING:

Warm-up. Ask the child to say the even numbers starting at 2 to 20. [2, 4, 6, . . . , 20] Play the Comes After Game with even numbers. Repeat for the odd numbers.

Ask the child to enter 2 on her abacus and to name the quantity. [2] Ask her to add another 2 and name the amount. [4] Continue to 20. Ask: What was special about the numbers you said? [even numbers]

Ask the child to recite all the doubles from 1 + 1 to 10 + 10 using her abacus with the regular names.

Say: 60 + 30 = 90 and 30 + 60 = 90. Ask the child: What do you notice about the equations? [The answers are the same.]

Worksheet 7. Give the child the worksheet.

"Add To" problem 1. Ask the child to read the first story problem on her worksheet.

> Sam has 9 crayons. Then Sam gets 2 more crayons from a box. How many crayons does Sam have now?

Ask: Is 9 a whole or a part? [part] Write it in the part-circle. See the left figure below.

 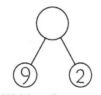

Writing 9 as a part.   **Writing 2 as a part.**   **Finding the whole.**

Next ask: Is 2 a part or a whole? [part] Write it in the other part-circle. See the second figure above. Next ask her to find the whole. [11] See the third figure above. Tell her to put a line under her answer. Ask her to write the equation on her worksheet.

$$9 + 2 = \underline{11}$$

EXPLANATIONS:

Problems in which a given quantity is increased are easiest for children to solve.

ACTIVITIES FOR TEACHING:	EXPLANATIONS:

Problem 2. Ask the child to read the second problem on her worksheet.

Jacob saw 2 butterflies on a flower. Some more butterflies landed on the flower. Now he sees 8 butterflies. How many butterflies landed on the flower?

Ask her: Is 2 a part or a whole? [part] Is 8 a part or a whole? [whole] Ask the child to write the numbers in her part-whole circle set. Ask her to find the other part and write it in the other part circle. See below.

Writing 2 as a part.　Writing 8 as a whole.　Finding the part.

Tell her to write the equation on her worksheet and to underline the answer.

$$2 + \underline{6} = 8$$

Tell her to reread the problem to be sure it makes sense.

Problem 3. Do the third problem as above.

Emily got 4 goldfish for her birthday. Now she has 8 goldfish. How many goldfish did she have before her birthday?

$$\underline{4} + 4 = 8$$

Many people will write the known 4 in the left part-circle, rather than the right part-circle. It doesn't matter which part-circle is used.

Problem 4. Ask the child to do the fourth problem independently.

Jack picked 8 apples. Jill picked the same amount. How many apples did they pick together?

$$8 + 8 = \underline{16}$$

In conclusion. Tell the child to make up a problem and ask you to solve it.

© Activities for Learning, Inc. 2013

Lesson 23: Quadrilaterals

OBJECTIVES:	MATERIALS:
1. To learn or review the term *parallel*	1. Dry erase board
2. To learn or review the term *quadrilateral*	2. One set of tangrams (7 pieces)
3. To construct quadrilaterals from tangram pieces	

ACTIVITIES FOR TEACHING:	EXPLANATIONS:

Warm-up. Review the days of the week. Ask: Are the number of days in a week even or odd? [odd] How do you know? [7 is odd]

Ask the child: How much is 4 + 1? [5] 9 + 1? [10] 3 + 1? [4] 7 + 1? [8] Then ask: How much is 4 + 2? [6] How did you know? [next even number] Continue with 6 + 2 [8] and 8 + 2? [10]

Ask the child to solve the following story problem using a part-whole circle set.

Max has 8 crayons. Then Max gets 4 more crayons from a box. How many crayons does Max have now? [12]

Parallel lines. To discuss parallel lines, draw sets of parallel lines as shown below on the left. Tell the child that these lines are *parallel*. Next draw non-parallel lines (shown on the right) and tell her they are not parallel.

Parallel lines.   Non-parallel lines.

Quadrilaterals. Draw the following figures and tell the child that they are quadrilaterals.

These figures are quadrilaterals.

Then draw the following figures and tell her that they are **not** quadrilaterals.

These figures are NOT quadrilaterals.

RightStart™ Mathematics Level B Second Edition © Activities for Learning, Inc. 2013

ACTIVITIES FOR TEACHING:	EXPLANATIONS:

Ask: How can you tell what is a quadrilateral? Guide her to discuss that it needs to have straight lines, exactly four lines, and it must be closed. Tell her that "quad" means four.

Point to each of the non-quadrilaterals in turn and ask why it is not a quadrilateral. [The first two do not have four sides, the third has a curved line, and the fourth is not closed.]

Tangram pieces. Tell the child to spread out her set of tangrams. Ask: Do you see any pieces with parallel lines? [2 pieces shown below]

   The two figures with parallel lines. They are quadrilaterals.

Ask her to find the two pieces that are quadrilaterals. [same two pieces] Discuss: Is the square a quadrilateral? [yes] Does it have straight lines? [yes] Does it have four lines? [yes] Is it closed? [yes] Is it a quadrilateral? [yes]

Composing quadrilaterals. Ask the child to combine two or three tangram pieces to form quadrilaterals. See some examples below.

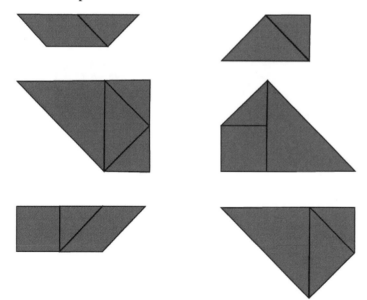

In conclusion. Ask: How many sides does a quadrilateral have? [4] Have the child show parallel lines with her arms.

© Activities for Learning, Inc. 2013

LESSON 24: BUILDING RECTANGLES

OBJECTIVES:
1. To form new rectangles from existing rectangles
2. To identify a rectangle as a quadrilateral
3. To identify a square as a special rectangle

MATERIALS:
1. AL Abacus
2. One set of five rectangles* (Appendix p. 3, there are four sets on the page)
3. **Child's scissors**
4. Dry erase board
5. **One sheet of construction paper, optional**

ACTIVITIES FOR TEACHING:	EXPLANATIONS:

Warm-up. Ask the child to solve the following story problem using a part-whole circle set.
 	
    Beth saw 4 bees on a picnic table. Some more bees landed on the picnic table. Now Beth sees 12 bees. How many bees landed on the picnic table? [8]
 	
Ask the child to say the months of the year. Then play the Comes After game with the months. Ask: What month comes after June? [July] What month comes after January? [February]
 	
Play a new version of the Comes After game. Say three numbers and ask what comes next: 7, 8, 9. [10] Ask: What number comes after 4, 5, 6? [7] What number comes after 2, 3, 4? [5]
 	
Ask the child to make the stairs only to five on her abacus. Tell her to look at her abacus to answer the following questions:
 	
    What do you need with 2 to make 10? [8]
    Where is that on the abacus? [second row on the right]
    What do you need with 3 to make 10? [7]
    Where is that on the abacus? [third row on the right]
    What do you need with 6 to make 10? [4]
    Where is that on the abacus? [fourth row on the left]
 	
Preparing the rectangles. Give the child a column of five rectangles as shown on the right. Tell her to write 1 on the smallest rectangle, 2 on the next smallest, 3 on the next smallest, 4 on the next, and 5 on the largest. Then tell her to cut them apart.
 	
Ask: Are these shapes quadrilaterals? [yes] Which are rectangles? [all of them] Which is a square? [number 3]
 	
    Column of rectangles with numbers.
	*Cut the rectangles on the appendix page into columns of five rectangles.

RightStart™ Mathematics Level B Second Edition

ACTIVITIES FOR TEACHING:	EXPLANATIONS:

New rectangles with three rectangles. Ask the child to take any three rectangles and create a new rectangle. Challenge her to find several ways. [There are nine different combinations of putting them in a row and four other arrangements as shown below.] Interchanging the same rectangles in a row or column is not a new arrangement. Tell her to record her results on the dry erase board using the numbers.

New rectangles using three of the five rectangles.

New rectangles with four rectangles. Now ask her to use four rectangles to construct new rectangles. [There are five different combinations of putting them in a row and three other arrangements as shown below on the left.]

 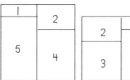 

New rectangles using four of the five rectangles.   **New rectangle with all five rectangles.**

Ask the child to add these solutions to the other group on the board.

New rectangle with five rectangles. Ask her to use all five rectangles to construct new rectangles. [There is one way of putting them in a row and one other arrangement.] See the right figure above. Add them to the board.

Pattern of the numbers. Ask the child: What pattern do you see with the numbers in your rectangle arrangements? [When there is more than a column, the sum of the numbers in each column are equal.]

Preserving the large rectangle (optional). Ask the child to construct a rectangle with all five rectangles and paste it onto construction paper.

In conclusion. Hold up a square. Ask: What are three names for this shape? [square, rectangle, and quadrilateral]

© Activities for Learning, Inc. 2013

Lesson 25: Triangles with Right Angles

OBJECTIVES:
1. To learn or review the term *perpendicular*
2. To learn the term *right angle*
3. To learn the term *right triangle*

MATERIALS:
1. Dry erase board
2. **Two pencils of unequal length**
3. One set of tangrams

ACTIVITIES FOR TEACHING:	EXPLANATIONS:
Warm-up. Ask: How many sides does a quadrilateral have? [4] Ask the child to show parallel lines with her arms. Now ask her to show non-parallel lines. Play the Comes After game by saying three number patterns and ask: What comes next: 3, 4, 5? [6] What number comes after 5, 6, 7? [8] What number comes after 9, 10, 11? [12] *Perpendicular lines.* To review perpendicular lines, draw sets of perpendicular lines as shown below on the left. Tell the child that these lines are *perpendicular.* Next draw non-perpendicular lines (shown on the right) and tell her that they are not perpendicular.   **Perpendicular lines.** **Non-perpendicular lines.** *Right angles.* To show forming a right angle, start with pencils in a parallel position. Then gradually move the top one until they are perpendicular. Tell her that is a *right angle.*  **Showing the formation of a right angle.** Show her how to make a right angle with her arm by bending at the elbow. See the figures below.   **Making a right angle with an arm.** Have her show right angles by starting with hands together and opening them to a right angle. See the pictures on the next page.	 The pencils need to be of unequal length to prevent the child from thinking angles are related to the lengths of the sides. The term *perpendicular* refers to the relationship between lines, while *right angle* refers to the space between the lines.

ACTIVITIES FOR TEACHING:	EXPLANATIONS:

Showing making a right angle with hands.

Triangles. Hold up a large triangle from the tangrams. Ask: Is this a quadrilateral? [no] Why not? [It doesn't have four sides.] Ask: What is it called? [a triangle] What is special about this triangle? [It has a right angle.] Tell her it is called a *right triangle*.

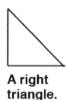

A right triangle.

Right triangles. Tell the child to spread out her seven tangram pieces. Ask her: How many of the pieces are right triangles? [5] How many right angles are there in all the pieces? [9, 5 in the triangles and 4 in the square]

Two right angles. Tell the child to place her two large right triangles next to each other. Ask her: What happens to the right angles? [They turned into a straight line.] See the figure below. What is the new shape? [another right triangle]

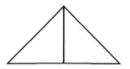

Two right angles together give a straight line.

Constructing right triangles. Ask her to make the following constructions with her tangram pieces:

1. a right triangle from the two smallest triangles,
2. a right triangle from the two smallest triangles and the medium triangle,
3. a right triangle from the two smallest triangles and the square,
4. a right triangle from the two smallest triangles and the parallelogram (the piece with two sets of parallel lines).

   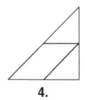

1. 2. 3. 4.

In conclusion. Ask: Which capital letters of the alphabet have right angles? [E, F, H, L, T] Write them. Ask: Which letter has only one right angle? [L] Which letter has two right angles? [T] How many right angles does E have? [4] How many does H have? [4]

There might be some variation in answers depending on how the child is taught to write their letters.

© Activities for Learning, Inc. 2013

Lesson 26: Adding Ten to a Number

OBJECTIVES:
1. To learn the term *digit*
2. To add 10 to any number up to 90

MATERIALS:
1. AL Abacus
2. *Math Card Games* book, N43
3. Place-value cards
4. Worksheet 8, Adding Ten to a Number

ACTIVITIES FOR TEACHING:

Warm-up. Ask the child to solve the following story problem using a part-whole circle set.

> Tom got 3 balloons for his birthday. Now he has 6 balloons. How many balloons did he have before his birthday? [3]

Ask: How many sides does a quadrilateral have? [4] Tell the child to name a quadrilateral in the room.

Ask the child to show parallel and perpendicular lines with her arms. Then ask her to show a right angle.

Ask the child: How much is 4 + 1? [5] 9 + 1? [10] 3 + 1? [4] 7 + 1? [8] How much is 4 + 2? [6] How did you know? [next even number] Then continue with 6 + 2, [8] and 8 + 2. [10]

The term digit. Explain to the child that when we write words, we use letters. When we write numbers, we use *digits*. Say: We have 26 letters in our alphabet. How many digits do we have to write our numbers? [10] Tell her to name them; write them as the child says them. [1, 2, 3, 4, 5, 6, 7, 8, 9, 0] If she omits zero, ask: What about zero?

Write the following numbers and ask how many digits in each: 7, [1] 11, [2] 100, [3] 76, [2] 2413. [4]

Adding 10 to a number on the abacus. Tell the child to enter 2-ten 7 on her abacus. Then tell her to enter 10 on the next wire. See the figures below.

EXPLANATIONS:

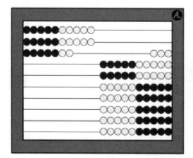
2-ten 7.

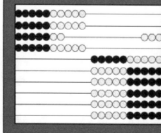
2-ten 7 plus 10.

ACTIVITIES FOR TEACHING:

Ask the child: How much is entered now? [3-ten 7] Tell her to say the equation. [2-ten 7 + 10 = 3-ten 7] Repeat for 6-ten 6 plus 10 [7-ten 6] and for 4-ten 9 plus 10. [5-ten 9] See figures below.

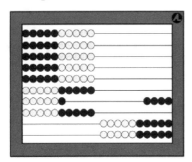 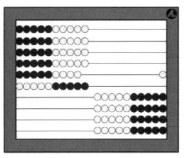

6-ten 6 plus 10.   4-ten 9 plus 10.

Can You Find Plus Ten game. This game is another variation of the Can You Find game from the *Math Card Games* book, N43. Here the child is to find 10 more than the number you say.

Below are suggested numbers you say; the numbers in brackets are the place-value cards the child pick up, overlap, and set aside. All the cards will be collected by the end of the game.

Can you find 8 + 10?   [10 & 8]
Can you find 6-ten 5 + 10?   [70 & 5]
Can you find 2-ten 7 + 10?   [30 & 7]
Can you find 71 + 10?   [80 & 1]
Can you find 59 + 10?   [60 & 9]
Can you find 36 + 10?   [40 & 6]
Can you find 13 + 10?   [20 & 3]
Can you find 84 + 10?   [90 & 4]
Can you find 42 + 10?   [50 & 2]

Worksheet 8. Ask the child to do the worksheet while using her abacus. The problems and solutions are below.

49 + 10 = **59**
23 + 10 = **33**
51 + 10 = **61**
18 + 10 = **28**
65 + 10 = **75**
 4 + 10 = **14**
76 + 10 = **86**
82 + 10 = **92**
37 + 10 = **47**

In conclusion. Ask: How much is 10 + 10? [20] How much is 20 + 10? [30] How much is 30 + 10? [40] How much is 40 + 10? [50] Continue to 90 + 10. [100]

EXPLANATIONS:

Some children will benefit by using an abacus.

© Activities for Learning, Inc. 2013

Lesson 27: Adding Ones and Adding Tens

OBJECTIVES:
1. To realize the similarity between partitioning ones and tens
2. To realize the similarity between adding ones and adding tens

MATERIALS:
1. AL Abacus
2. Worksheet 9, Adding Ones and Adding Tens

ACTIVITIES FOR TEACHING:

Warm-up. Write the following numbers and ask how many digits in each: 5, [1] 34, [2] 432, [3] 87, [2] 4652. [4]

Ask: How much is 20 + 10? [30] How much is 40 + 10? [50] How much is 10 + 10? [20] How much is 30 + 10? [40]

Tell the child to enter 3-ten 7 on her abacus. Tell her to enter 10 on the next wire. Ask: How much is entered on the abacus now? [4-ten 7 or 47] Tell her to enter 23 and then add 10 on the next wire. Ask: How much is entered now? [33]

Partitioning 10. Ask her to enter 10 on her abacus. Then ask her to move 1 bead to the right and say the equation. [10 = 9 + 1] Ask her to move another bead and say the equation. [10 = 8 + 2] Continue to 10 = 0 + 10.

Partitioning 10-ten. On the abacus, enter 10-ten. To partition 1 part, offset it slightly from the edge as shown below. Ask the child to say it: 10-ten = 9-ten + 1-ten. Move over another 10 and say: 10-ten = 8-ten + 2-ten.

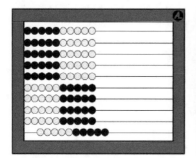 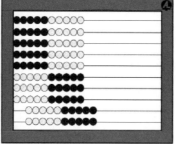

Partitioning 10-ten into 9-ten and 1 to ten.   Partitioning 10-ten into 8-ten and 2-ten.

Continue to 10-ten = 0-ten + 10-ten.

Adding tens. Write the following equation:

$$30 + 20 = \underline{}. \quad [50]$$

Ask the child to first enter the 3-ten, then to enter the 2-ten (see the figure on the next page), and finally to

EXPLANATIONS:

Even though a child may know that 70 and 8 is 78, they often are unsure about 70 + 8. Apparently, it takes a while for the meaning of "+" to be really understood.

ACTIVITIES FOR TEACHING:

EXPLANATIONS:

write the sum. Ask the child to name the parts [30, 20] and the whole. [50]

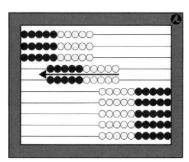

Adding 3-ten and 2-ten.

Repeat for the following equations: 50 + 30 = ___. [80] and 80 + 10 = ___. [90]

Comparing adding ones and tens. Ask the child to add:

$$6 + 3 = \underline{}. [9]$$

Next add:

$$60 + 30 = \underline{}. [90]$$

See the figures below.

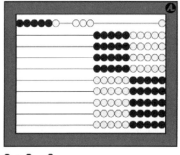 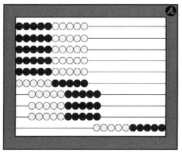

6 + 3 = 9   60 + 30 = 90

Tell her to think about both equations and ask: Are they alike in some way? Repeat for 1 + 5 [6] and 10 + 50. [60]

Worksheet 9. Have the child do the worksheet with her abacus. The solutions are shown below:

5 + 2 = 7	4 + 2 = 6
50 + 20 = 70	40 + 20 = 60
4 + 4 = 8	8 + 1 = 9
40 + 40 = 80	80 + 10 = 90
7 + 2 = 9	3 + 4 = 7
70 + 20 = 90	30 + 40 = 70
2 + 6 = 8	4 + 5 = 9
20 + 60 = 80	40 + 50 = 90

In conclusion. Ask: What pattern did you see on the worksheet? [Adding tens is like adding ones.] What is 5 + 3? [8] What is 50 + 30? [80]

© Activities for Learning, Inc. 2013

Lesson 28: Introducing Hundreds

OBJECTIVES:
1. To learn that a hundred is 10 tens
2. To practice finding two quantities that total 1 hundred

MATERIALS:
1. AL Abacus
2. Abacus tiles
3. Place-value cards
4. Math journal

ACTIVITIES FOR TEACHING:

Warm-up. Ask: How much is 50 + 10? [60] How much is 80 + 10? [90] How much is 70 + 10? [80] How much is 60 + 10? [70]

Tell the child to enter 6-ten 7 on her abacus. Tell her to enter 10 on the next wire. Ask: How much is entered on the abacus now? [7-ten 7 or 77] Say: Clear your abacus and now enter 53. Tell her to enter 10 on the next wire. Ask: How much do you have entered now? [63]

10-ones as one ten. Tell the child to enter 10 on her abacus. See left figure below. Ask her: How many ones do you see? [10] How many tens? [one]

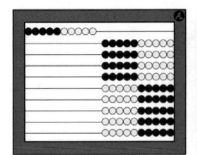 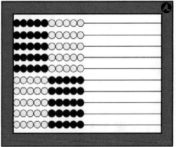

Ten ones, also 1-ten.   Ten tens, also 1 hundred.

10-tens as one hundred. Tell the child to enter all the beads on her abacus. See right figure above. Ask: How many tens are entered? [ten] How many hundreds? [1 hundred] Ask: How many tens are in 10-ten? [ten] Then ask: How many tens are in one hundred? [10]

Ask her to think about how she could show two hundred. Lay out 2 abacus tiles as shown below on the left.

2 hundred.   4 hundred.

Tell the child to add another 2 abacus tiles, laying them out as shown in the right figure above.

EXPLANATIONS:

RightStart™ Mathematics Level B Second Edition   © Activities for Learning, Inc. 2013

ACTIVITIES FOR TEACHING:	EXPLANATIONS:

Ask: How much is it? [4 hundred] Tell the child to continue laying out the abacus tiles and naming the amounts. Continue to 10 hundred.

7 hundred.

Name the hundreds. Start with 5 abacus tiles and ask the child: How many beads do you see? [5 hundred] Then add 3 more abacus tiles and again ask for the quantity. [8 hundred] Continue adding or removing 1 or 2 abacus tiles at a time and asking the child to name the quantities; include 0 and 10 hundred.

Making 100s game. This solitaire game requires the player to find four sets of four place-value cards, two tens and two ones, that total 100. Use the following 16 place-value cards: 10 to 80, 1 to 4, and 6 to 9.

Each player proceeds as follows:
    Composes a number with two digits.
    Enters that quantity on the abacus.
    Finds the amount on the abacus needed to make 100.
    Composes that amount with place-value cards.

Have the child repeat three times. Then have her write the four equations in the form of 48 + 52 = 100 in her math journal. See the figures below.

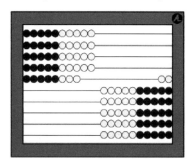

Entering 48 and seeing 52 needed to make 100.

One possible arrangement to make 100s with the cards.

There are 147,456 different arrangements for this game.

In conclusion. Before the child collects the place-value cards, ask: What is the total of all the numbers on your cards? [4 hundred]

If necessary, ask her how much each group totals, [100] and how many groups she has. [4]

© Activities for Learning, Inc. 2013

Lesson 29: Numbers 100 to 120

OBJECTIVES:
1. To represent and compose numbers 100 to 120
2. To write and read numbers 100 to 120

MATERIALS:
1. AL Abacus
2. Place-value cards
3. Abacus tiles
4. Math journal

ACTIVITIES FOR TEACHING:	EXPLANATIONS:
Warm-up. Ask the child to solve the following story problem using a part-whole circle set.	
Zach picked 9 apples. Ann picked the same amount. How many apples did they pick together? [18]	
Ask: What is 6 + 3? [9] What is 60 + 30? [90] How much is 2 + 1? [3] How much is 20 + 10? [30] How much is 5 + 2? [7] How much is 50+ 20? [70]	
Tell the child to enter 5-ten 8 on her abacus. Tell her to enter 10 on the next wire. Ask: How much is entered on the abacus now? [6-ten 8 or 68] Say: Clear your abacus and now enter 84. Tell her to enter 10 on the next wire. Ask: How much do you have entered now? [94]	
Show the 300 place-value card and ask the child to build the number with abacus tiles. Repeat for 600 and 900.	
Adding ones from 100 to 120. Tell the child to lay one abacus tile to the left. Now tell the child to add 1 on her abacus. See below.	When child learn to count by rote, they learn the pattern that the number following a 9 is a new word. For example, the number following 29 is 30 (not twenty-10) and the number following 99 is 100 (not ninety-10). Therefore, they find the number following 109 confusing because it is one hundred 10.
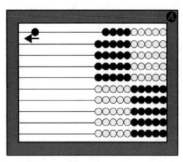 **Adding 1 to 1 hundred to get 1 hundred 1.**	Understanding the hundreds structure eliminates the problem. It is acceptable to say "one hundred *and* one."
Tell the child: Now we have one hundred one. Ask the child to add another 1. Ask: Now how much do we have? [102] Continue to 120 using the math way having the child alternate adding 1 and saying the amount.	Counting in the hundreds is said 1-hundred 1, 1-hundred 2, till you reach the tens then it is said 1-hundred ten, 1-hundred ten-1, 1-hundred ten-2, and so forth.

| ACTIVITIES FOR TEACHING: | EXPLANATIONS: |

The place-value cards to 120. Tell child to lay out the following place-value cards: 100, 10, 20, and 1 to 9. Ask the child to use an abacus tile and put 1 on the abacus as before.

Now ask her to put the corresponding place-value cards below the abacus and abacus tile. See below.

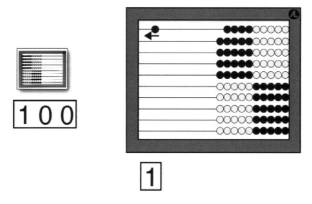

Now show her how to stack the cards. Be sure the right edges line up. See below.

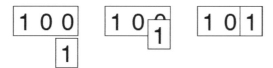

Recording 101 to 120. Ask her to write the number 101 in her math journal, each digit in a separate rectangle. Ask the child to continue adding one bead, showing it with place-value cards, and recording it in her math journal in columns. See below.

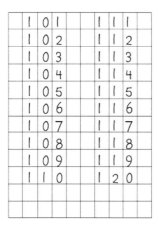

The math journal page with numbers 101 to 120.

When she reaches 120, ask her to read the numbers using the math way. Repeat with regular number names.

In conclusion. Ask her to count from 100 to 120, using both ways of number naming. Ask: How many digits do you need to write 9? [1] 109? [3] 19? [2] 119? [3]

© Activities for Learning, Inc. 2013

Lesson 30: More Hundreds

OBJECTIVES:
1. To read and write hundreds
2. To combine hundreds, tens, and ones

MATERIALS:
1. Dry erase board
2. Abacus tiles
3. Place-value cards
4. AL Abacus
5. *Math Card Games* book, N43

ACTIVITIES FOR TEACHING:

Warm-up. Ask the child to count from 100 to 120, using both ways of number naming. Ask: How many digits do you need to write 7? [1] 108? [3] 17? [2] 116? [3]

Ask: How much is 60 + 10? [70] How much is 80 + 10? [90] How much is 10 + 10? [20] How much is 70 + 10? [80]

Play the Comes After game: say three numbers and ask what comes next: 34, 35, 36. [37] Ask: What number comes after 55, 56, 57? [58] What number comes after 59, 60, 61? [62]

Draw a square. Ask: What are three names for this shape? [square, rectangle, and quadrilateral]

Recording hundreds. Lay out 10 abacus tiles. Hold up one abacus tile and ask: How much is this? [1 hundred] Have the child write 100 on the dry erase board.

Then hold up two abacus tiles and ask: How much is this? [2 hundred] Write 200 and say: This is how we write 200. Point to the 2 while saying two; point to the first 0 while saying "hun"; and point to the second 0 while saying "dred." See below.

Practicing reading hundreds. Ask the child to lay out the place-value cards with hundreds, tens, and ones. Then ask her to find the hundreds, naming them in random order: 900, 700, 200, and so on.

Lay out 10 abacus tiles. Take one tile and start a new column next to the first column. Point to each column and tell the child to find the place-value card for each quantity. [900, 100] See the figures on the next page.

EXPLANATIONS:

ACTIVITIES FOR TEACHING:	EXPLANATIONS:

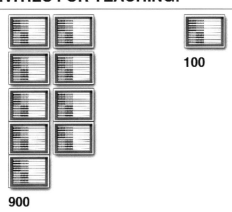

900   100

Move another abacus tile from the 9 and add it to the one. Again ask her to find the place-value cards. [800, 200] Repeat twice more. [700, 300] [600, 400]

Combining hundreds, tens, and ones. Make a column of abacus tiles showing 700 and enter 48 on the abacus. See the figure below. Ask: How many beads are entered? [748] Tell her to find the place-value cards for these numbers. Demonstrate how to stack the cards.

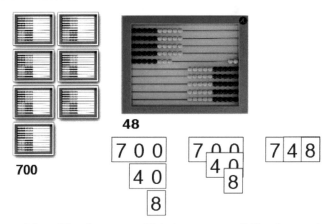

700

Can You Find game. This is a more difficult version of Can You Find game in the *Math Card Games* book, N43. Ask the child to lay out the hundreds, tens, and ones place-value cards.

Below are suggested numbers to say. Tell the child to pick up, stack, and set aside the corresponding cards. All the cards will be picked up at the conclusion of the game.

1. Can you find 400?
2. Can you find 43?
3. Can you find 104?
4. Can you find 57?
5. Can you find 629?
6. Can you find 760?
7. Can you find 215?
8. Can you find 998?
9. Can you find 371?
10. Can you find 502?
11. Can you find 86?
12. Can you find 830?

Some children will need to hear each number spoken more than once.

In conclusion. Ask the child: How many digits do you need after the 4 to write 400? [2] How many digits do you need after the 4 to write 40? [1] How many digits do you need after the 4 to write 4? [0]

Noting the number of digits following the leftmost digit(s) in a number is a more accurate determination of place value than the total number of digits. For example, 2700 can be read correctly as "27 hundred" by observing the two digits following the 27.

© Activities for Learning, Inc. 2013

Enrichment Lesson 31: Working with 100s and 1000s

OBJECTIVES:
1. To build the quantities 1, 10, 100, and 1000 with paper squares
2. To construct quantities with the paper squares

MATERIALS:
1. AL Abacus
2. Abacus tiles
3. Flat Hundreds Squares, at least 37 (Appendix p. 4)
4. **2 crayons, 1 dark-colored and 1 light-colored**

ACTIVITIES FOR TEACHING:

Warm-up. Ask: What is 7 + 3? [10] What is 70 + 30? [100] How much is 4 + 2? [6] How much is 40 + 20? [60] How much is 6 + 4? [10] How much is 60 + 40? [100]

Tell the child to enter 6-ten 7 on her abacus. Tell her to enter 10 on the next wire. Ask: How much is entered on the abacus now? [7-ten 7 or 77] Say: Clear your abacus and now enter 53. Tell her to enter 10 on the next wire. Ask: How much do you have entered now? [63]

Have the child build 1, 10, 100, and 1000 with her abacus and abacus tiles.

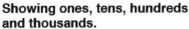

Showing ones, tens, hundreds and thousands.

Point to the 1 and ask: How many 1s would we need to make it look like the 10? [10] Point to the abacus showing 10 and ask: How many 10s do we need to make 100? [10] Repeat for the 100 and ask how many 100s we need to make 1000. [10] You might conclude by asking her why she keeps saying 10. [our special, or magic, number]

EXPLANATIONS:

This the first of several enrichment lessons designed to bring the world of math into everyday life. If necessary because of time restraints, the lesson may be omitted without loss of continuity.

This particular lesson does take a lot of time but child will build a deeper understanding from the process. Perhaps do these activities over a number of days.

ACTIVITIES FOR TEACHING:	EXPLANATIONS:

Building 1s & 10s. Give the child the blank Flat Hundred Squares. Explain to her that she will need to make nine squares showing 1s and nine squares showing 10s.

Ask her to color the top left square so it looks like a 1 on an abacus. Ask her to color the 10s in two colors. See the figures below.

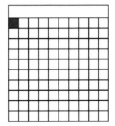
The 1-square:
9 are needed.

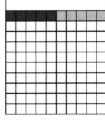
The 10-square:
9 are needed.

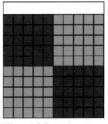
The 100-square:
19 are needed.

The child will use these representations of 1, 10, 100, and 1000 to construct various quantities up to 9999.

Building 100s & 1000s. Ask how she could make 100s. [by coloring ten rows of 10s] At least 19 hundreds are needed; 9 to make individual hundreds and 10 to staple together make a thousand. Additional groups of ten 100s will make more thousands. When the 100s are colored as shown above, ask how she could make a 1000. [by stacking ten 100s] Staple or clip (in the clear area at the top) stacks of ten hundreds to make the thousands.

Fetching quantities. Ask the child to fetch four 1s. The child picks up four sheets showing a 1. Tell her to return the sheets. Ask her to fetch 6 hundred.

Continue with other quantities, such as 7-ten, 1 thousand, 5 hundred, and so forth.

Challenge the child to remember and fetch two quantities. For example, ask her to fetch 7 hundred 5-ten. Ask the child to repeat the quantities before retrieving them. Ask if she wants to try to remember 3 quantities. If so, ask for 1 thousand, 3 hundred, 5 ones.

In conclusion. Ask: How many 1s in 10? [10] How many 10s in 100? [10] How many 100s in 1000? [10]

© Activities for Learning, Inc. 2013

Lesson 32: Two-Fives Strategy

OBJECTIVES:
1. To introduce the two-fives strategy

MATERIALS:
1. AL Abacus
2. Worksheet 10, Two-Fives Strategy
3. *Math Card Games* book, A3

ACTIVITIES FOR TEACHING:

Warm-up. Ask: How many sides does a quadrilateral have? [4] Have the child show parallel and perpendicular lines with her arms.

Ask her to count from 100 to 120, using both ways of number naming.

Ask: How many digits do you need to write 2? [1] 101? [3] 11? [2] 111? [3]

Ask: How many 1s in 10? [10] How many 10s in 100? [10] How many 100s in 1000? [10]

Ask: How much is 34 + 10? [44] How much is 46 + 10? [56] How much is 17 + 10? [27] How much is 31 + 10? [41]

Play the Comes After game say three numbers and ask what comes next: 54, 55, 56. [57] Ask: What number comes after 25, 26, 27? [28] What number comes after 79, 80, 81? [82]

Two-fives strategy preparation. On the abacus enter 1 on the first wire and 3 on the second wire. Ask the child: How much is 1 + 3? [4] See the left figure below.

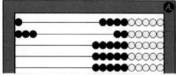 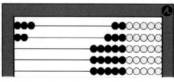

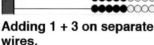

Adding 1 + 3 on separate wires.

Adding 3 + 2 on separate wires.

Repeat for 3 and 2. [5] See the right figure above.

Repeat for 2 and 4. [6]

Repeat for 4 and 3. [7]

Repeat for 4 and 4. [8]

Repeat for 1 and 2. [3]

EXPLANATIONS:

ACTIVITIES FOR TEACHING:	EXPLANATIONS:

Two-fives strategy. Enter 6 on the top wire and 8 on the second wire. Tell the child: Look for a way to find the sum of 6 + 8. Guide her to seeing the two groups of 5s with the dark-colored beads, outlined in the figure below. Ask: How many dark-colored beads are there? [10] How many light-colored beads? [4] So how much is 6 + 8? [1-ten 4 or 14]

The two-fives strategy is useful when both addends are between 5 and 9.

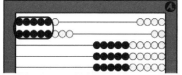 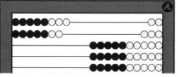

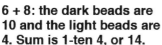

6 + 8: the dark beads are 10 and the light beads are 4. Sum is 1-ten 4, or 14.

8 + 7: the dark beads are 10 and the light beads are 5. Sum is 1-ten 5, or 15.

Ask the child to try 8 + 7 on her abacus. See the right figure above. Ask her to explain the method. [Two 5s make 10 while 3 and 2 make 5, so 1-ten 5 or 15.] Ask her to find 7 + 9. [1-ten 6 or 16] Repeat for 5 and 9. [1-ten 4 or 14]

Worksheet 10. Ask the child to do only the first column on the worksheet. She is to use her abacus. The solutions are as follows:

6 + 8 = **14**
9 + 7 = **16**
6 + 9 = **15**
6 + 5 = **11**
9 + 6 = **15**
7 + 5 = **12**
9 + 8 = **17**
8 + 9 = **17**
6 + 6 = **12**
8 + 7 = **15**
7 + 7 = **14**

Go to the Dump with Fifteens game. Play Go to the Dump with Fifteens, an advanced version of the game Go to the Dump from the *Math Cards Games* book, A3. Use the Basic Deck of cards but only the numbers from 5 to 10. The pairs are two cards whose numbers total 15. The remaining rules of the game are the same.

The card decks with numbers from 5 to 10 will be needed for the Addition War game in the next lesson.

The facts that total 15 will be needed in the Corners™ game, which will be played in a future lesson.

In conclusion. Ask the child to name what she needs to make 15: 10 and what? [5] 6 and what? [9] 8 and what? [7] 5 and what? [10] 9 plus what? [6] 7 plus what? [8]

© Activities for Learning, Inc. 2013

LESSON 33: MORE TWO-FIVES STRATEGY

OBJECTIVES:
1. To practice the two-fives strategy

MATERIALS:
1. AL Abacus
2. Worksheet 10, Two-Fives Strategy
3. *Math Card Games* book, A44

ACTIVITIES FOR TEACHING:	**EXPLANATIONS:**
Warm-up. Ask the child to name what she needs to make 15: 10 and what? [5] 6 and what? [9] 8 and what? [7] 5 and what? [10] 9 plus what? [6] 7 plus what? [8]	The child may use the abacus, if needed.
Ask her to count from 100 to 120, using both ways of number naming.	
Ask: How much is 36 + 10? [46] How much is 47 + 10? [57] How much is 19 + 10? [29] How much is 71 + 10? [81]	
Play the Comes After game say three numbers and ask what comes next: 44, 45, 46. [47] Ask: What number comes after 15, 16, 17? [18] What number comes after 89, 90, 91? [92]	
Two-fives strategy with fingers. Another way to use the two-fives strategy involves fingers. The amounts over 5 from each addend are shown on each hand.	
For example, to add 8 + 7, 3 fingers (the amount that 8 is over 5) are raised on the left hand and 2 fingers (the amount that 7 is over 5) are raised on the right hand. The sum is 10 plus 2 and 3, which equals 1-ten 5 or 15. See the figures below.	
Adding 8 + 7 by showing with fingers only the amounts over 5. **8 + 7 = 10 + 3 + 2 = 15.** 8 = 5 + <u>3</u> 7 = 5 + <u>2</u>	
	Note that the child is not counting on her fingers, but can subitize the sum.
Ask the child to use it for 7 + 6. 7 + 6 = 10 + 2 + 1 = 13.	

ACTIVITIES FOR TEACHING:	EXPLANATIONS:

Comparing the two-five strategies. Tell the child to enter 7 and 6 on her abacus. Ask: How is the abacus like her fingers? [The light-colored beads are the same as the fingers.]

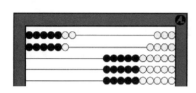

$7 = 5 + \underline{2}$ $6 = 5 + \underline{1}$

Repeat for 6 and 8.

Worksheet 10. Ask the child to do the second column on the worksheet. She is to use her abacus. The solutions are as follows:

9 + 5 = **14**
6 + 7 = **13**
8 + 5 = **13**
7 + 9 = **16**
5 + 6 = **11**
5 + 9 = **14**
7 + 6 = **13**
7 + 8 = **15**
8 + 6 = **14**
5 + 7 = **12**
8 + 8 = **16**
5 + 8 = **13**

Addition War game. Play the game Addition War from *Math Cards Games* book, A44. Use only the cards with numbers from 5 to 10. Encourage the child to use her abacus or her fingers, but do not insist. Tell the child she is to say the sums aloud before comparing them.

In conclusion. Ask the child: What is 8 + 5? [13] What is 9 + 6? [15] What is 7 + 5? [12] What is 7 + 8? [15] What is 6 + 8? [14]

LESSON 34: ADDING FIVE TO A NUMBER

OBJECTIVES:
1. To add fives and tens up to 200
2. To count by fives to 200

MATERIALS:
1. AL Abacus
2. Abacus Tiles
3. Tiles
4. **A brown paper bag*** for tiles

ACTIVITIES FOR TEACHING: | **EXPLANATIONS:**

Warm-up. Ask the child: What is 9 + 6? [15] What is 6 + 8? [14] What is 7 + 5? [12] What is 8 + 5? [13] What is 7 + 8? [15]

*This bag will be used for the child to remove tiles without seeing them.

Ask the child to name what she needs to make 15: 10 and what? [5] 6 and what? [9] 8 and what? [7] 5 and what? [10] 9 plus what? [6] 7 plus what? [8]

The child can use the abacus, if needed.

Ask: How much is 24 + 10? [34] How much is 56 + 10? [66] How much is 37 + 10? [47] How much is 71 + 10? [81]

Adding fives on the abacus. Tell the child to enter 20 on her abacus. Next tell her to add 5 more and say how much it is. [25] See the left figure below.

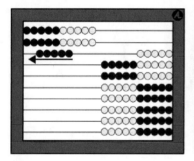 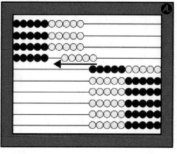

20 + 5 = 25   35 + 5 = 40

Ask her to enter 35 plus 5 and say how much it is. [40] See the right figure above.

Repeat for 65 + 5, [70] 80 + 5, [85] and 95 + 5. [100]

Counting by fives (math way). Ask the child to start with zero and add fives until she reaches 200.

Tell her to use the math way for naming numbers. After moving each set of 5 beads, have the child say the amount aloud.

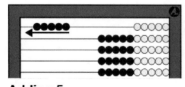 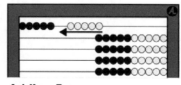

Adding 5.   Adding 5 more.

RightStart™ Mathematics Level B Second Edition © Activities for Learning, Inc. 2013

ACTIVITIES FOR TEACHING:

Continue to 100. At 100, exchange the 100 on the abacus for a abacus tile, then clear the abacus. Continue adding fives. See the figures below.

 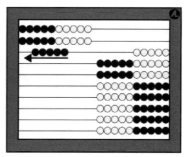

Child adding 5, and saying one hundred 2-ten 5.

Continue until she has reached 200.

Counting by fives (regular names). Repeat the above activity using the regular names.

Race to 100. The goal of this game is to reach 100 exactly using the abacus. Use the bag for the tiles. Remove the green tiles (or she gets another turn if she draws a green tile). A yellow tile is worth 5, a blue tile is worth 10, and a red tile is 0.

To play, the child takes a tile from the bag and adds that quantity on her abacus. The goal is to reach 100.

In conclusion. Ask the child: What is 35 + 5? [40] What is 50 + 5? [55] What is 35 + 10? [45] What is 85 + 5? [90] What is 20 + 15? [first add the 10 and then the 5, 35] What is 60 + 15? [75]

EXPLANATIONS:

Lesson 35: Partitioning 5, 10, and 15

OBJECTIVES:
1. To practice the sums totaling 5, 10, and 15
2. To add 15 to a number

MATERIALS:
1. Dry erase board
2. Math journal
3. AL Abacus
4. *Math Card Games* book, A3

ACTIVITIES FOR TEACHING:	EXPLANATIONS:
Warm-up. Ask the child: What is 25 + 5? [30] What is 60 + 5? [65] What is 15 + 10? [25] What is 75 + 5? [80] What is 40 + 15? [first add the 10 and then the 5, 55] What is 70 + 15? [85] Ask the child to name what she needs to make 15: 10 and what? [5] 7 and what? [8] 9 and what? [6] 5 and what? [10] 8 plus what? [7] 6 plus what? [9] Ask: How much is 26 + 10? [36] How much is 53 + 10? [63] How much is 38 + 10? [48] How much is 72 + 10? [82] How much is 94 + 10? [104] *Partitioning 5.* Explain to the child that in the next lesson she will be learning to play a game that uses the facts that total 5, 10, and 15. So today she will be partitioning those numbers and writing them in her math journal. Draw two part-whole circle sets and write 5 in the whole-circles. Ask: What is a way to make 5? [1 + 4 or 2 + 3] See the figures below. 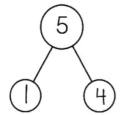 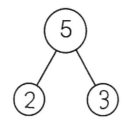 5 partitioned into 1 + 4. 5 partitioned into 2 + 3. Ask the child to write the two equations in her math journal. See the figure on the next page. Ask: Do we need to write 4 and 1, or is it the same as 1 + 4? [same] *Partitioning 10.* In the same way, partition 10. Ask the child to write those equations in her math journal. See the figure on the next page.	

ACTIVITIES FOR TEACHING:	EXPLANATIONS:

		5	=	1	+	4		
		5	=	2	+	3		
	1	0	=	1	+	9		
	1	0	=	2	+	8		
	1	0	=	3	+	7		
	1	0	=	4	+	6		
	1	0	=	5	+	5		
	1	5	=	5	+	1	0	
	1	5	=	6	+	9		
	1	5	=	7	+	8		

Math journal page with partitioning 5, 10, and 15.

Partitioning 15. Draw three part-whole circle sets and write 15 in the whole-circles and 5 in the first left part-circle. Ask the child to find the other ways to partition, but no numbers greater than 10. Then ask her to write the equations in her math journal as shown above.

Adding 15. Ask the child to enter 20 on her abacus. Then ask her to add 15. Tell her to first add the 10, then the 5. See the left figure below.

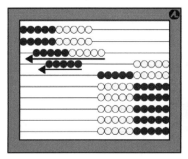 

Adding 15 by adding 10 and then 5.   **Using two hands to add 10.**

Even though 5 + 10 is not a "fact," it will be needed for the Corners™ activities.

Some have asked why 5 + 10 is not a fact. Addition facts are adding numbers up to 9 plus 9. Adding 10 to a number is a function of place value. So looking at 5 + 10 = 15, using the transparent number naming: five plus ten equals ten five (or one-ten five). Turning it around to 10 + 5 = 15, or ten plus five equals ten five, its just combining the numbers!

Repeat for 40 + 15. [55] and 70 + 15. [85]

Now ask her to enter 25 and to add 15. To add the 10 together, show her how to use both hands as shown above on the right. Then she adds the 5. [40]

Ask her to enter 20. Next add 15. [35] Next add 10 to that answer. [45] Next add 10 to that answer. [55] Next add 5 to that answer. [60]

Go to the Dump game. Ask the child to play Go to the Dump, found in the *Math Card Games* book, A3.

In conclusion. Ask: What do you need with 7 to make 10? [3] What do you need with 7 to make 15? [8] What do you need with 4 to make 10? [6] What do you need with 4 to make 5? [1] What do you need with 9 to make 15? [6]

© Activities for Learning, Inc. 2013

Lesson 36: Corners™ Exercise without Scoring

OBJECTIVES:
1. To practice the sums totaling 5, 10, and 15
2. To learn how to join Corners™ cards

MATERIALS:
1. Corners™ cards*
2. *Math Card Games* book, A8
3. Math journal

ACTIVITIES FOR TEACHING:

Warm-up. Ask: What do you need with 8 to make 10? [2] What do you need with 8 to make 15? [7] What do you need with 6 to make 10? [4] What do you need with 3 to make 5? [2] What do you need with 9 to make 15? [6]

Ask the child: What is 50 + 5? [55] What is 70 + 5? [75] What is 25 + 10? [35] What is 55 + 5? [60] What is 30 + 15? [45]

Ask the child to name what she needs to make 15: 10 and what? [5] 7 and what? [8] 9 and what? [6] 5 and what? [10] 8 plus what? [7] 6 plus what? [9]

Ask: How much is 27 + 10? [37] How much is 58 + 10? [68] How much is 48 + 10? [58] How much is 62 + 10? [72] How much is 98 + 10? [108]

Joining Corners™ cards. Place the following two Corners™ cards in view of the child. Explain that the colors must always match when we put them together.

    Two of the 50 Corners™ cards.

Further explain that the two numbers touching must equal 5, 10, 15, or 20. Ask the child: Look at the red numbers; do they equal 5, 10, 15, or 20? [yes] Say: So we can put them together. See the left figure below.

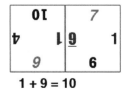 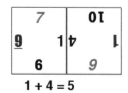

Ask: Can we put the green numbers together? [no] Why not? [6 + 7 does not equal 5, 10, 15, or 20.] Can we put the blue numbers together? [yes] What do they equal? [5] See the right figure above.

EXPLANATIONS:

*These 50 small white cards each have four colored numbers between 1 and 10 along the sides. No two cards are alike.

Find these six Corner™ cards to begin the lesson.

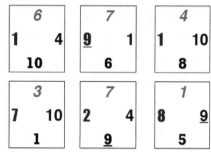

Different fonts are used in the figures to compensate for lack of color.

Every other card will be upside down.

To distinguish sixes from nines, nines are underlined, or to put it in different words, nine has a line, six does not.

RightStart™ Mathematics Level B Second Edition © Activities for Learning, Inc. 2013

ACTIVITIES FOR TEACHING:

Corners™ Exercise game. The game, Corners™ Exercise, is found in the *Math Card Games* book, A8. Take the four Corners™ cards shown below and ask the child to help you put all four of them together matching colors and the sums equaling 5, 10, 15, or 20.

Four solutions for the same cards are shown below:

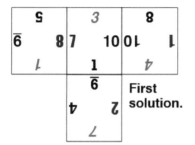
First solution.

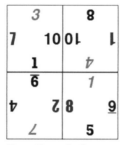
Second solution.

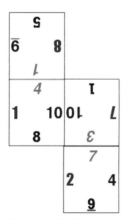
Third solution.

Fourth solution.

Give the child the full deck of Corners™ cards. Ask her to take four cards and join them. Remind her to refer to her math journal list of sums, as needed. Tell her that sometimes it is not possible to join all four cards.

After she has joined her four cards, she takes four more cards. Continue until only two cards remain.

In conclusion. Ask: What are the ways to make 15? [10 + 5, 9 + 6, and 8 + 7] What is the way to make 20? [two 10s] What are the ways to make 5? [1 + 4 and 2 + 3]

EXPLANATIONS:

Scoring for Corners™ Exercise will be done in the next lesson.

These four will cards will be used in the next lesson.

Remember every other card will be upside down. Children quickly adapt to reading them upside down.

LESSON 37: CORNERS™ EXERCISE WITH SCORING

OBJECTIVES:
1. To practice the sums totaling 5, 10, and 15
2. To add 5, 10, and 15 to a number

MATERIALS:
1. Corners™ cards*
2. AL Abacus
3. *Math Card Games* book, A8
4. Math journal

ACTIVITIES FOR TEACHING:

Warm-up. Ask: What are the ways to make 15? [10 + 5, 9 + 6, and 8 + 7] What is the way to make 20? [two 10s] What are the ways to make 5? [1 + 4 and 2 + 3]

Ask: What do you need with 8 to make 10? [2] What do you need with 8 to make 15? [7] What do you need with 6 to make 10? [4] What do you need with 3 to make 5? [2] What do you need with 9 to make 15? [6]

Ask the child: What is 50 + 5? [55] What is 70 + 5? [75] What is 25 + 10? [35] What is 55 + 5? [60] What is 30 + 15? [45]

Ask the child to name what she needs to make 15: 10 and what? [5] 7 and what? [8] 9 and what? [6] 5 and what? [10] 8 plus what? [7] 6 plus what? [9]

Scoring with Corners™ cards. Join the four Corners™ cards as shown below. Tell the child that to find the score for the four cards, she needs to add the numbers that are touching.

EXPLANATIONS:

*Find these four Corners™ cards.

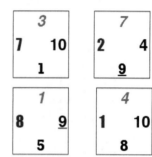

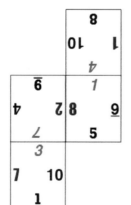

Score: 3 + 7 and 2 + 8 and 4 + 1 = 25.

Ask her: What numbers do you need to add? [3 + 7, 2 + 8, 4 + 1] Challenge her to add in her head. Discuss how she does it. One way is to add the two 10s, which is 20, and then add the 5, to get 25.

ACTIVITIES FOR TEACHING:	EXPLANATIONS:

Scoring with the abacus. Rearrange the four cards as shown below.

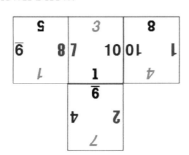

Score: 8 + 7 and 10 + 10 and 1 + 9 = 45.

On the abacus one solution is shown below where 20 is entered first, then 15 added, and then 10:

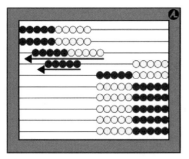 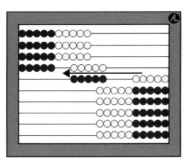

Entering 20 and adding 15.   Adding 10.

Ask the child if she could add the numbers in a different order. Another solution is shown below where 10 is entered first, then 20 added, and then 15:

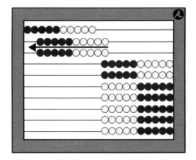 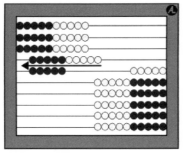

Entering 10 and adding 20.   Adding 15.

Here the child is applying the associative property.

Ask: Is one way of adding easier than another way? [yes] Does the answer stay the same? [yes]

Corners™ Exercise game. Ask the child to play the Corners Exercise found in the *Math Card Games* book, A8. Today she finds her scores, writing them in her math journal.

In conclusion. Tell the child you have a hard question for her: What is the highest score you could get joining four cards? [70, two 15s and two 20s]

You might need to ask: How many 20s could you have? [only two, because no card has two 10s]

© Activities for Learning, Inc. 2013

Lesson 38: Basic Corners™ Game

OBJECTIVES:
1. To practice the sums totaling 5, 10, and 15
2. To add 5, 10, and 15 to a number in the context of the Corners™ game

MATERIALS:
1. *Math Card Games* book, A9
2. Corners™ cards
3. Math journal for scoring
4. AL Abacus

ACTIVITIES FOR TEACHING:

Warm-up. Ask: In the Corners™ game, what are the ways to make 15? [10 + 5, 9 + 6, and 8 + 7] What is the way to make 20? [two 10s] What are the ways to make 5? [1 + 4 and 2 + 3]

Ask: What do you need with 8 to make 10? [2] What do you need with 8 to make 15? [7] What do you need with 6 to make 10? [4] What do you need with 3 to make 5? [2] What do you need with 9 to make 15? [6]

Ask the child: What is 50 + 5? [55] What is 80 + 5? [85] What is 25 + 10? [35] What is 55 + 5? [60] What is 30 + 15? [45]

Ask the child to name what she needs to make 15: 10 and what? [5] 7 and what? [8] 9 and what? [6] 5 and what? [10] 8 plus what? [7] 6 plus what? [9]

Corners™ game. Explain that the Corners™ game from the *Math Card Games* book, A9, is generally played in groups of three or four, but two will work also. Place the Corners™ cards face down on a pile near the players. Each player takes four cards and puts them face up in a row in view of all players.

The card with the lowest green number starts the game. In the event that there is more than one card having the lowest number, then of those cards, the one with the lowest blue number starts. After a player plays a card, she takes another card, so she always has four cards.

The player to the left of the first player joins one of his cards to the first card. The colors must match and the numbers touching must either be the same or have a sum of 5, 10, 15, or 20. However, only the sums of 5, 10, 15, or 20 are added to the score. Players take turns playing one card and must play if possible.

Emphasize that in this game, a player can play *only* to the last card played, which is different from the Corners™ exercise.

EXPLANATIONS:

This basic variation of the Corners™ game explained here ignores the "corners" and ends when the first player reaches 100.

Playing only to the last card is important to prevent the game from becoming excessively slow after a few turns.

ACTIVITIES FOR TEACHING:	EXPLANATIONS:

A basic Corners™ game. Below is the beginning of a Corners™ game with two players.

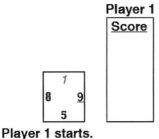
Player 1 starts.

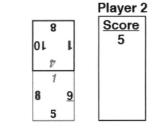
Player 2 gets 5 points.

The card with the darker outline is the last card added.

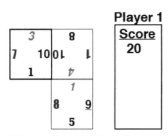
Player 1 gets 20 points.

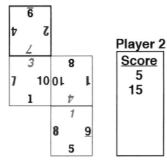
Player 2 gets 10 points.

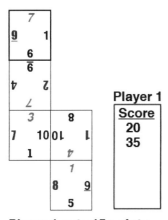
Player 1 gets 15 points.

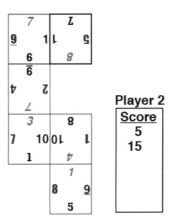
Player 2 gets 0 points.

Matching numbers, such as one and one here, is a valid play providing the colors also match. The resulting score is zero.

There is no reason to cross out previous scores.

Scoring. Players keep an accumulative score in the math journal. That is, write down only the result of the latest addition, no intermediate steps. For example, player 2 on his second turn, adds 10 to his previous 5 and writes 15. Also, player 1 on her third turn adds 15 to her previous 20 and writes 35.

The child may need an abacus for scoring. The first player to reach 100 is the winner.

In conclusion. Ask: In the Corners™ game, what three numbers can you join with 9? [1, 6, and 9] How many points would a 1 give you? [10] How many points would a 6 give you? [15] How many points would a 9 give you? [0]

© Activities for Learning, Inc. 2013

LESSON 39: SOLVING "COMBINE" PROBLEMS

OBJECTIVES:
1. To solve "Combine" problems

MATERIALS:
1. Worksheet 11, Solving "Combine" Problems
2. Corners™ cards

ACTIVITIES FOR TEACHING:

Warm-up. Ask: What do you need with 7 to make 10? [3] What do you need with 7 to make 15? [8] What do you need with 5 to make 10? [5] What do you need with 4 to make 5? [1] What do you need with 9 to make 15? [6]

Ask the child: What is 30 + 5? [35] What is 80 + 5? [85] What is 15 + 10? [25] What is 75 + 5? [80] What is 50 + 15? [65]

Ask the child to name what she needs to make 15: 10 and what? [5] 7 and what? [8] 9 and what? [6] 5 and what? [10] 8 plus what? [7] 6 plus what? [9]

Ask: How much is 17 + 10? [27] How much is 48 + 10? [58] How much is 78 + 10? [88] How much is 42 + 10? [52] How much is 93 + 10? [103]

Worksheet 11. Give the worksheet to the child.

"Combine" problem 1. Ask the child to read the first story problem:

> Levi has 6 red apples and 9 green apples to sell. How many apples does Levi have to sell?

Then ask her to fill in her part-whole circle set. See the figures below.

  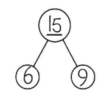

Writing 6 as a part.   **Writing 9 as a part.**   **Finding the whole.**

If necessary, explain that 6 and 9 are parts and 15 is the whole.

EXPLANATIONS:

These problems are harder for children to solve because no physical change occurs.

It is critically important for children to think through a problem and not attempt to memorize any pattern or key words by rote.

The child should correct any errors she makes on her worksheet. She will learn more by finding her own errors rather than having someone else doing it for her.

ACTIVITIES FOR TEACHING:	EXPLANATIONS:

Ask the child to write the equation on her worksheet.

$$6 + 9 = \underline{15}$$

Problem 2. Ask the child to read the second problem on her worksheet and fill in the part-whole circle set and write the equation.

There are 15 children playing tag. In the group, 7 children are girls. How many of the children are boys?

Ask the child to explain her work. See below.

Writing 15 as whole.   Writing 7 as a part.   Finding the part.

$$7 + \underline{8} = 15$$

or

$$15 = 7 + \underline{8}$$

Tell her to reread the problem to be sure it makes sense.

Problems 3 and 4. Do them in the same way as above.

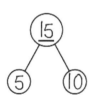

Lydia is waiting for her birthday. There are 5 days in May and 10 days in June until her birthday. How many days must Lydia wait?

$$5 + 10 = \underline{15}$$

There are 12 months in a year. Two months start with the letter A. How many months do not start with A?

$$2 + \underline{10} = 12$$

Corners™ game. Play the Corners™ game from the previous lesson.

In conclusion. Ask: What is 30 + 15? [45] What is 35 + 10? [45] What is 35 + 15? [50]

This problem requires the child to conceptually combine boys and girls into a group, which is harder than physical combining or time change problems.

© Activities for Learning, Inc. 2013

Lesson 40: Sums Equal to 11

OBJECTIVES:
1. To partition 11 based on facts equaling 10
2. To practice adding sums equal to 11

MATERIALS:
1. Math balance
2. Dry erase board
3. *Math Card Games* book, A24

ACTIVITIES FOR TEACHING:	EXPLANATIONS:
Warm-up. Using a part-whole circle set, ask the child to solve the following problem: Chad has 7 red apples and 8 green apples to sell. How many apples does Chad have to sell? [15 apples] Ask them to say the even numbers to 20. [2, 4, 6, . . . , 20] Ask the child: What is 7 + 3? [10] What is 6 + 4? [10] What is 5 + 5? [10] What is 8 + 2? [10] 9 + 1? [10] Ask: 10 is 1 and what? [9] Ten is 2 and what? [8] Ten is 3 and what? [7] Ten is 4 and what? [6] Ten is 5 and what? [5] ***Partitioning 11 with the math balance.*** Enter a weight on the left 10 of the math balance and a weight on the right 2. Ask: What is needed to make it balance? [weight on right 8] What is the equation? [10 = 2 + 8] 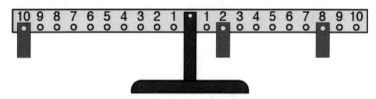 Partitioning 10 into 2 and 8. Now place a another weight at the left 1 and ask: Where does the weight on 8 need to move to make it balance? [to 9] See below. Ask her to say the equation. [11 = 2 + 9] 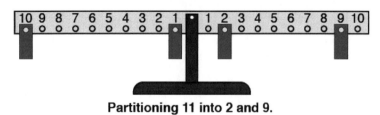 Partitioning 11 into 2 and 9.	

ACTIVITIES FOR TEACHING:	EXPLANATIONS:

Have the child write the equation on her dry erase board.

Next move the weight from the right 2 to the right 3. Ask the child to balance it and say the equation. [11 = 3 + 8] Ask her to write it. Continue to 11 = 5 + 6.

Partitioning 11 with the abacus. Enter 11 and slide the 1 in the second row to the right, as shown in the left figure below. Tell the child to say the partitioning: 11 = 10 + 1. Move the last bead on the top wire to the right a short ways and ask the child to say the partitioning: 11 = 9 + 2. See the right figure. Continue to 11 = 2 + 9.

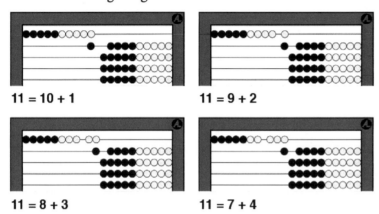

11 = 10 + 1   11 = 9 + 2

11 = 8 + 3   11 = 7 + 4

Show her another way. Enter 11 and separate 2 to see 11 = 9, (8 and 1) + 2. See the left figure below. Move over another bead for 11 = 8 + 3. See the right figure below. Continue to 11 = 2 + 9.

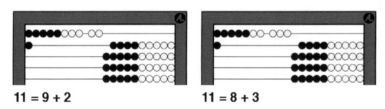

11 = 9 + 2   11 = 8 + 3

Ask: How does partitioning 11 compare to partitioning 10? [With 11, one of the addends is one more than partitioning 10.]

Go to the Dump with Elevens. Play Go to the Dump with Elevens, found in the *Math Card Games* book, A24. Encourage the child to use her abacus as needed.

In conclusion. Ask the child: 11 = 5 + what? [6] 11 = 7 + what? [4] 11 = 9 + what? [2] 11 = 6 + what? [5] 11 = 4 + what? [7]

Before playing this game, the child must have mastered the facts equaling 10, which form the basis for this variation. A child not knowing the 10 facts could confuse the two sets of facts.

For a child needing a little more help, she could play Finding the Pairs Equaling Eleven, in the *Math Card Games* book, A21.

© Activities for Learning, Inc. 2013

Lesson 41: Review

OBJECTIVES:
1. To review concepts learned in previous lessons

MATERIALS:
1. *Yellow is the Sun* book
2. Worksheet 12, Review
3. AL Abacus

ACTIVITIES FOR TEACHING:	EXPLANATIONS:

Warm-up. Read the book *Yellow is the Sun* to the child.
 	
What comes next. Give the child Worksheet 12. Ask her the following questions:
  1. What comes next in the pattern 6, 7, 8? [9]
  2. What comes next in the pattern 28, 29, 30? [31]
  3. What comes next in the pattern 98, 99, 100? [101]
  4. What comes next in the pattern 107, 108, 109? [110]
 	
Adding on. Ask her the following questions:
  5. Start with 70 and add 1. [71]
  6. Tell her to add 1 more. [72]
  7. Ask her to continue the rest of the numbers until all the blanks on the worksheet are filled in. [73, 74, 75, 76, 77, 78, 79, 80]
 	
Even stairs. Tell her to build the even stairs on her abacus. See the left figure below and have her fill in the blanks to the following questions.
  8. Look at the left side of the abacus. Write the even numbers starting with 2. [2, 4, 6, 8, 10]
 	
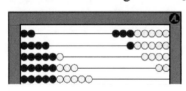 The even stairs.
 	
Odd stairs. Tell her to build the odd stairs on her abacus. See the right figure below and have her fill in the blanks to the following questions.
  9. Look at the left side of the abacus. Write the odd numbers starting with 1. [1, 3, 5, 7, 9]
 	
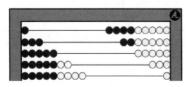 The odd stairs.
	This lesson is a review of concepts learned so far. It is designed to prepare the child for the assessment in the following lesson.

ACTIVITIES FOR TEACHING:	EXPLANATIONS:

Addition. Tell the child the following questions are addition problems and she needs to write the answers on her worksheet.

10. 2 + 4 = **6**
11. 2 + 7 = **9**
12. 4 + 4 = **8**
13. 6 + 6 = **12**
14. 4 + 3 = **7**
15. 3 + 4 = **7**
16. 42 + 10 = **52**
17. 8 + 1 = **9**
18. 80 + 10 = **90**
19. 6 + 8 = **14**
20. 9 + 7 = **16**
21. 35 + 5 = **40**
22. 70 + 15 = **85**

Part-whole circle sets. Use the part-whole circle set to solve the following problems.

23. Emma has 4 books on the desk. Then Emma gets 5 more books from a box. How many books does Emma have on the desk now? [9 books]

24. There are 3 boys and 6 girls at the swimming pool. How many kids are at the swimming pool? [9 kids]

25. Six hundred trees are to be planted in a park. Three hundred trees have already been planted. How many more trees must still be planted? [three hundred trees]

Shapes.

26. Ask the child to circle all the rectangles.

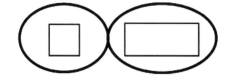

© Activities for Learning, Inc. 2013

LESSON 42: ASSESSMENT 1

OBJECTIVES:
1. To assess concepts learned in previous lessons

MATERIALS:
1. *Yellow is the Sun* book
2. AL Abacus
3. Worksheet 13, Assessment 1

ACTIVITIES FOR TEACHING:

Warm-up. Read the book *Yellow is the Sun* to the child. Sing the "The Months" with the child.

What comes next. Give the child Worksheet 13. Ask her the following questions:
1. What comes next in the pattern 3, 4, 5? [6]
2. What comes next in the pattern 48, 49, 50? [51]
3. What comes next in the pattern 107, 108, 109? [110]

Adding on. Ask her the following questions:
4. Start with 50 and add 1. [51]
5. Tell her to add 1 more. [52]
6. Ask her to continue the rest of the numbers until all the blanks on the worksheet are filled in. [53, 54, 55, 56, 57, 58, 59, 60]

Even stairs. Tell her to build the even stairs on her abacus. See the left figure below and have her fill in the blanks to the following questions.
7. Look at the left side of the abacus. Write the even numbers starting with 6. [6, 8, 10, 12, 14]

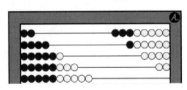

The even stairs.

Odd stairs. Tell her to build the odd stairs on her abacus. See the right figure below and have her fill in the blanks to the following questions.
8. Look at the left side of the abacus. Write the odd numbers starting with 3. [3, 5, 7, 9, 11]

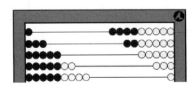

The odd stairs.

EXPLANATIONS:

ACTIVITIES FOR TEACHING:	EXPLANATIONS:

Addition. Tell the child the following questions are addition problems and she needs to write the answers on her worksheet.

9. 2 + 8 = **10**
10. 2 + 5 = **7**
11. 5 + 5 = **10**
12. 8 + 8 = **16**
13. 5 + 3 = **8**
14. 3 + 5 = **8**
15. 74 + 10 = **84**
16. 6 + 1 = **7**
17. 60 + 10 = **70**
18. 6 + 9 = **15**
19. 8 + 5 = **13**
20. 65 + 5 = **70**
21. 80 + 15 = **95**

Part-whole circle sets. Use the part-whole circle set to solve the following problems.

22. Danny has 6 pillows on the bed. Then Danny gets 5 more pillows from the closet. How many pillows does Danny have on the bed now? [11 pillows]
23. There are 4 boys and 5 girls at the park. How many kids are at the park? [9 kids]
24. Five hundred trees are to be planted in a park. Four hundred trees have already been planted. How many more trees must still be planted? [one hundred trees]

Shapes. Ask the child to name the three shapes.

25. Triangle
26. Rectangle
27. Square or rectangle

© Activities for Learning, Inc. 2013

Lesson 43: Making Rectangles with Tangrams

OBJECTIVES:
1. To review the term *parallelogram*
2. To learn the term *congruent*
3. To draw geometric figures

MATERIALS:
1. Two sets of tangrams
2. Dry erase board

ACTIVITIES FOR TEACHING:	EXPLANATIONS:
Warm-up. Ask: How many sides does a quadrilateral have? [4] Have the child to show parallel lines with her arms. Have her to show perpendicular lines. Ask the child: 11 = 5 + what? [6] 11 = 7 + what? [4] 11 = 9 + what? [2] 11 = 6 + what? [5] 11 = 4 + what? [7] Ask the child to solve the following problem. There are 20 dogs playing in the grass. In the group, 7 dogs are black. The others are white. How many of the dogs are white? [13 white dogs] Ask: How much is 13 + 10? [23] How much is 44 + 10? [54] How much is 76 + 10? [86] How much is 41 + 10? [51] How much is 96 + 10? [106] Ask: What is 40 + 15? [55] What is 65 + 10? [75] What is 55 + 15? [70] ***Naming the tangram pieces.*** Ask: How many of the tangram pieces are triangles? [5] Tell her to make a right angle with an arm or hand. Then ask: How many right angles do you see on the seven tangrams? [9, 5 triangles and 4 on the square] How many shapes do not have a right angle? [1] Tell her: Find the pieces that have parallel lines. See the figure below. Ask: What is special about the opposite sides? [parallel] Tell her they are called *parallelograms*. Ask her to point to the parallelogram that has right angles. [the square] Tangram pieces that are parallelograms. Explain that people usually call the parallelogram piece with right angles a square.	

RightStart™ Mathematics Level B Second Edition © Activities for Learning, Inc. 2013

ACTIVITIES FOR TEACHING:	EXPLANATIONS:

Making squares. Ask the child to make a square with the two large triangles. Then ask her to make a square with the two smallest triangles. See the figures below.

Square from large triangles.   **Square from small triangles.**   **Square tangram shape.**

Ask: Which of the squares you made is exactly the same size as the tangram square? [the square with small triangles] Tell her to place the square on top of the new square to check. Tell the child when shapes exactly fit on top of each other, they are *congruent*.

Next tell the child to use the large triangles from the second tangram set. Put all four together to make a larger square. See the figure at the right.

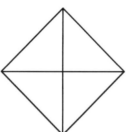

Larger square made with four large triangles.

Constructing rectangles. Tell the child to make a rectangle using the two smallest triangles and the square. See the left figure below.

Three ways to make non-square rectangles from the two smallest triangles and another shape.

Tell the child to copy that figure onto her dry erase board.

Next tell her to make a rectangle that is not a square with the two smallest triangles and the medium triangle. See the second figure above. Ask the child to copy this figure below her first figure on her dry erase board.

Lastly, tell the child to make a rectangle with the two smallest triangles and the parallelogram. See the third figure above. Ask the child to copy this last figure below the other two figures.

In conclusion. Ask: Do you think the three rectangles you made are congruent? [yes]

Copying figures helps the child focus on important details.

© Activities for Learning, Inc. 2013

Lesson 44: Continuing Patterns

OBJECTIVES:
1. To continue a simple pattern
2. To work repeating patterns

MATERIALS:
1. Tiles
2. Two set of tangrams

ACTIVITIES FOR TEACHING:	EXPLANATIONS:
Warm-up. Ask the child to say the even numbers to 10. Repeat for odd numbers. Then play the Comes Before game using only even or odd numbers. For example, say 7, [5] 10, [8] 5, [3] and so forth. Ask: 6 is 5 plus what? [1] 8 is 5 plus what? [3] 7 is 5 plus what? [2] 9 is 5 plus what? [4] ***Simple patterning.*** Using tiles, demonstrate making a pattern by alternating two colors. Tell her: This simple pattern is called an AB pattern. Ask the child to take two handfuls of tiles and make the same AB pattern, using as many of her tiles as possible. 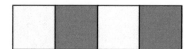 **The AB pattern.** Next show her the following ABB pattern. Ask her to copy it and to continue it until she runs out of tiles.  **The ABB pattern.** Ask the child to make an ABC pattern. If she shows hesitancy, ask her to guess what it means.  **The ABC pattern.** ***A increasing pattern with tiles.*** Tell the child to make a row with 1 green tile, 2 red tiles, 3 blue tiles. Then to continue with the same colors: 4 green tiles, 5 red tiles, 6 blue tiles. See the figure at the top of the next page.	There is no "BA" or "BAA" pattern; the names must start with "A" and proceed in alphabetical order.

ACTIVITIES FOR TEACHING:	EXPLANATIONS:

Two patterns: ABC and an increasing pattern.

Ask: If you think only about the color, what kind of simple pattern is it? [ABC] Ask: Do you see another kind of pattern? [Each time there is one more tile.] Tell her: The tiles are an increasing, or growing pattern. We have two patterns!

Ask: What three parts in the patterns come next? [7 green, 8 red, and 9 blue tiles]

Patterning with tangram triangles. Tell the child to take three triangles from one tangram set, each a different size and to lay them out as follows:

An increasing pattern.

Ask: What kind of pattern do you have? [increasing, or growing pattern]

Now ask the child to repeat the pattern with the second set of triangles. See below.

The repeating triangle pattern.

Ask: If you think only about the color, what kind of pattern is it? [AB] Tell her: So, this is a pattern within a pattern.

In conclusion. Ask: What are the two types of patterns talked about today? [simple and increasing] What comes next in this pattern: small, medium, large, small, medium? [large]

© Activities for Learning, Inc. 2013

Lesson 45: Continuing Patterns with Geoboards

OBJECTIVES:
1. To make patterns on the geoboard
2. To combine geoboard patterns to make new patterns

MATERIALS:
1. Geoboards

ACTIVITIES FOR TEACHING:

Warm-up. Ask: What are two types of patterns? [simple and increasing] What comes next in this pattern: small, medium, large, small, medium? [large]

Ask the child to say the even numbers to 20. Repeat for odd numbers. Then play the Comes Before game using only even or odd numbers. For example, say 9, [7] 18, [16] 15, [13] and so forth.

Square pattern on geoboard. Tell the child that today she will make patterns on the geoboard. Make the square pattern as shown below on the left. Ask the child to copy the pattern and to continue it to the top of the geoboard. Create the same pattern on the second geoboard.

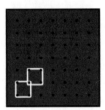 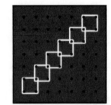

Square pattern.   **Square pattern continued.**

Now tell the child that she will make a pattern with the square patterns. Suggest she lay them in a row. See the figure below.

A pattern made with square patterns.

Ask: Can you think of another design? See below.

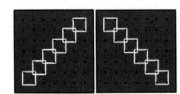

Other patterns made with square patterns.

EXPLANATIONS:

ACTIVITIES FOR TEACHING:

Ask: Can you think of another design? See below.

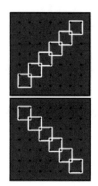 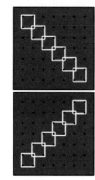

Still more patterns made with square patterns.

Increasing rectangle pattern on the geoboard.

Make the increasing rectangle pattern as shown below on the left. Ask the child to continue the pattern. Create the same pattern on the second geoboard.

Increasing rectangles.   **Increasing rectangles continued.**

Now ask her to combine her geoboards to make interesting patterns. See below for some suggestions.

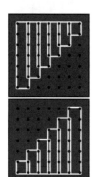 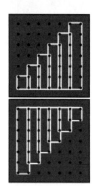

More patterns made with the increasing rectangles geoboards.

In conclusion. Ask the child to find patterns in her house or outside.

EXPLANATIONS:

Lesson 46: Designs with Diagonals

OBJECTIVES:
1. To introduce the terms *vertex*, *vertices*, and *diagonal*
2. To learn to draw straight lines with a ruler or other straightedge
3. To plan and color designs in hexagons

MATERIALS:
1. 4-in-1 ruler
2. **Blank sheet of paper**
3. Worksheet 14, Designs with Diagonals
4. **Crayons**

ACTIVITIES FOR TEACHING:	EXPLANATIONS:

Warm-up. Ask the child what new patterns she sees in the house or outside.

Ask: What are the two types of patterns? [simple and increasing] What comes next in this pattern: red, white, blue, red, white? [blue]

Play the Comes Before game using only even or odd numbers. For example, say 7, [5] 16, [14] 17, [15] and so forth.

Vertex and vertices. Draw a rectangle and point to a corner and tell the child that it is called a *vertex*. Tell her that when we are talking about more than one vertex, we say *vertices* (VER-tah-seez). Ask: How many vertices does a rectangle have? [4] How many vertices does a square have? [4]

Diagonals in a rectangle. Draw a diagonal as shown and explain that it is a straight line drawn from one vertex to another vertex. Say that it is called a *diagonal*. Ask the child to draw another diagonal. Ask: Could you draw any more diagonals in the rectangle? [no]

People often incorrectly believe that diagonals lines cannot be horizontal or vertical.

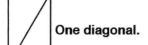
One diagonal.

Two diagonals.

Drawing a line with a ruler. Draw two dots on a piece of paper and explain that you want to draw a line between them. Emphasize placing the ruler slightly below the dots to allow for the pencil thickness. Connect the dots. See below.

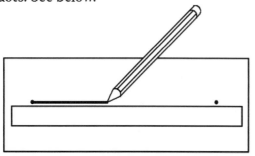
Drawing a line between dots.

RightStart™ Mathematics Level B Second Edition © Activities for Learning, Inc. 2013

ACTIVITIES FOR TEACHING:	EXPLANATIONS:

Worksheet 14. Give the child the worksheet. Ask the her to look at the first figure, the pentagon. Tell her to draw the diagonals by connecting the dots. Tell her to turn the paper so the dots are easier to draw. See the figures below.

Pentagon with 1 diagonal. **Pentagon with 5 diagonals.**

After she finishes, ask: How many diagonals does the pentagon have? [5] How many diagonals do you see at each vertex? [2] What do the diagonals make? [a star]

Tell her that there is a famous building in Washington D.C. built in that shape, which is called The Pentagon.

Show her how to draw a star freehand. See below.

Drawing a star freehand.

Before attempting to draw the star on paper, some children may find it helpful to use a finger and trace the star in the pentagon.

Diagonals in a hexagon. Tell her the next figure on the worksheet is a *hexagon*. Ask: How many sides does the hexagon have? [6] How many vertices does a hexagon have? [6] Tell her each vertex has three diagonals.

Ask: How many sets of parallel lines does a hexagon have? [3] How many sets of parallel lines in a pentagon? [0]

A hexagon with 1 diagonal. **A hexagon with 9 diagonals.**

Designs in a hexagon. Tell the child to make designs in the last two hexagons by coloring. A few examples are shown below.

Designs using hexagons and diagonals.

In conclusion. Ask: What do you call a line drawn between two vertices? [a diagonal] How many vertices does a square have? [4] How many vertices does a triangle have? [3]

© Activities for Learning, Inc. 2013

Lesson 47: The Greater Than Symbol

OBJECTIVES:
1. To learn to write the > symbol
2. To practice using the > symbol

MATERIALS:
1. 6 blue tiles and 4 yellow tiles
2. Place-value cards
3. Math journal
4. Worksheet 15, The Greater Than Symbol

ACTIVITIES FOR TEACHING:	EXPLANATIONS:
Warm-up. Ask: What do you call a line drawn between two vertices? [a diagonal] How many vertices does a square have? [4] How many vertices does a triangle have? [3]	

Ask: What are the two types of patterns? [simple and increasing] What comes next in this pattern: book, pencil, paper, book, pencil? [paper]

Ask: 7 is 5 plus what? [2] 9 is 5 plus what? [4] 7 is 4 plus what? [3] 9 is 4 plus what? [5]

Greater or less. Place the 6 blue tiles in a group and the 4 yellow tiles in another group as shown below. Then ask the child: Which group has the greater number of tiles? [blue] Which group has the lesser number of tiles? [yellow] If necessary, remind her that greater means more.

■ ■ ■   □ □   6 is greater than 4.
■ ■ ■   □ □   4 is less than 6.

Tell her: In mathematics we say "6 is greater than 4" and "4 is less than 6."

Greater than symbol. Tell the child that there is a math symbol for "is greater than." Write 6 and 4 with a space between them. See below.

Show her how to make the symbol by placing two dots by the larger number, one at the top and one at the bottom, and one dot in the middle by the smaller number as shown on the next page. Then connect the dots, starting at the larger number.

6   4   Decide which number is greater.

6 **:** 4   Draw two dots near the greater number.

RightStart™ Mathematics Level B Second Edition   © Activities for Learning, Inc. 2013

ACTIVITIES FOR TEACHING:	EXPLANATIONS:

6 : · 4   Draw one dot near the lesser number.

6 > 4   Connect the dots.

Making 100s game. Play the Making 100s game (Lesson 28). A sample is shown below.

|6|8| |3|2| |2|4| |7|6| Numbers generated
|5|9| |4|1| |1|3| |8|7| from Making 100s.

These numbers will be used in the next activity.

Numbers in order. Tell the child to put her numbers in order from greatest to least. Ask her to find the largest number to start the row. [87 in this example] Next, ask her to find the next largest number and put it in the row. Continue with the numbers as shown below.

|8|7| |7|6| |6|8| |5|9| |4|1| |3|2| |2|4| |1|3|
The place-value cards in order from greatest to least.

Ask the child to look at the row and read the numbers. For this example, 87 > 76, 76 > 68, 68 > 59, and so forth.

Now tell the child to write these "statements" in her math journal. See the sample at the right.

8	7	>	7	6
7	6	>	6	8
6	8	>	5	9
5	9	>	4	1
4	1	>	3	2
3	2	>	2	4
2	4	>	1	3

Math journal page with >.

Worksheet 15. Give the child the worksheet. The problems and solutions are shown below:

6 ⊖ 4
9 ⊖ 7
17 ⊜ 17
31 ⊖ 13
8 + 3 ⊖ 4 + 6
21 + 10 ⊜ 31
60 + 5 ⊖ 50 + 6
7 + 8 ⊜ 8 + 7
1 + 90 ⊖ 19
200 ⊖ 50 + 50
110 ⊖ 100 + 1

In conclusion. Ask the child: What number is greater than 10, but less than 12? [11] What numbers are greater than 12, but less than 15? [13 and 14]

© Activities for Learning, Inc. 2013

Lesson 48: Adding 9 to a Number

OBJECTIVES:
1. To learn the complete the ten strategy for adding facts with 9s
2. To practice adding 9s

MATERIALS:
1. AL Abacus
2. Dry erase board
3. Worksheet 16, Adding 9 to a Number

ACTIVITIES FOR TEACHING:	EXPLANATIONS:
Warm-up. Ask the child: What number is greater than 10, but less than 12? [11] What numbers are greater than 12, but less than 15? [13 and 14]	
Ask: 8 is 4 plus what? [4] 9 is 6 plus what? [3] 7 is 3 plus what? [4] 9 is 7 plus what? [2]	
Say: Count by 5s up to 150. [5, 10, 15, . . . , 150]	
Say: Count by tens starting with 3 to 103. [3, 13, 23, . . . , 103]	
Review 10 + a number. Ask the child: What is 10 + 4? [14] Ask how she knew the answer and ask her to enter it on the abacus. Continue by asking: What is 10 + 8? [18] and the remaining 10 facts. Write some of them on the dry erase board and ask the child to give the sums.	
9 plus a number. Tell the child that she is going to learn a new way to add 9 to a number. Ask her to enter 9 on the first wire and 6 on the second wire. See the figure below. 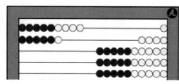 **Adding 9 + 6.**	
Ask: How could you change the 9 into a 10? Suggest she *takes* 1 from the 6 and *gives* 1 to the 9, to get 10 and 5, which is 15. See the figures below. 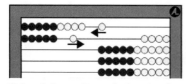 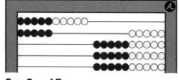 **Take 1 from 6 and give to 9.** **9 + 6 = 15.**	The "take and give" procedure was used in Level A. Using two hands, moving in opposite directions, provides a physical sense of making the change.
Ask her to say the equation. [9 + 6 = 15]	
Repeat for 9 + 4, [13] 9 + 2, [11] and 9 + 8. [17]	
Next enter 9 + 5 and challenge the child to move the beads in her head if she can. Practice with 9 + 3, [12] 9 + 7, [16] and 9 + 9. [18]	Moving beads mentally is a step to help children in developing a mental abacus.

ACTIVITIES FOR TEACHING:	EXPLANATIONS:

9 + a number with the even/odd pattern. Tell the child to turn her abacus sideways. Then ask her to enter 9, then leave a space and enter 6. See the left figure below. To see the sum, move up 1 bead from the 6 to form a 10. See the right figure below.

 9 + 6.

 Take 1 from 6 to form 10 and 5.

Repeat for 9 + 8, [17] 9 + 4, [13] and so on.

Adding with 9s in higher decades. Write 39 + 6 = and ask the child to find the sum on her abacus. [Take 1 from 6 to change the 39 into 40, so sum is 45.]

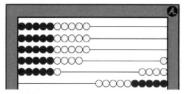

Adding 39 + 6.

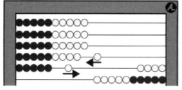

Take 1 from 6 and give to 9.

Repeat for 89 + 7, [96] 79 + 5, [84] 19 + 8, [27] and 49 + 3. [52]

Next write 25 + 9. Tell the child to use take and give in the same way to take 1 from 5 and give it to the 9, giving 34 as the sum. See the figures below.

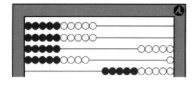

Adding 25 + 9.

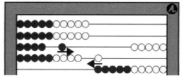

Take 1 from 5 and give to 9.

Repeat for 78 + 9 [87] and 56 + 9. [65]

Worksheet 16. Give the child the worksheet. Tell her to use her abacus. Problems and solutions are shown below.

9 + 3 = **12** 9 + 9 = **18**   79 + 5 = **84** 19 + 8 = **27**
9 + 7 = **16** 9 + 4 = **13**   59 + 4 = **63** 29 + 6 = **35**
3 + 9 = **12** 9 + 2 = **11**   89 + 2 = **91** 15 + 9 = **24**
9 + 8 = **17** 5 + 9 = **14**   69 + 9 = **78** 49 + 1 = **50**
6 + 9 = **15** 9 + 5 = **14**   33 + 9 = **42** 57 + 9 = **66**
4 + 9 = **13** 7 + 9 = **16**
                8 + 9 = **17**

In conclusion. Ask the child to use her abacus to solve the following problem:

Tracy has 28 chickens. She gets 9 more chickens. How many chickens does Tracy have now? [37]

© Activities for Learning, Inc. 2013

Lesson 49: Adding 8 to a Number

OBJECTIVES:
1. To learn the complete the 10 strategy for adding facts with 8s
2. To practice adding 8s

MATERIALS:
1. AL Abacus
2. Dry erase board
3. Worksheet 17, Adding 8 to a Number

ACTIVITIES FOR TEACHING:

EXPLANATIONS:

Warm-up. Ask the child: What number is greater than 20, but less than 22? [21] What numbers are greater than 22, but less than 25? [23 and 24]

Ask: What is 10 + 9? [19] What is 10 + 8? [18] What is 10 + 7? [17] What is 10 + 10? [20]

Ask the child to count by 5s up to 100. [5, 10, 15, . . . , 100]

Tell her: Count by tens starting with 6 to 56. [6, 16, 26, . . . , 56]

8 + a number. Ask the child to think of how she learned to find 9 + 7 in the previous lesson. Then ask if she could use the same method to find 8 + 7. [15]

Ask: How could you change the 8 into a 10? [Take 2 from the 7 and give them to the 8.]

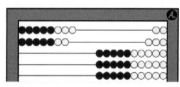

Adding 8 + 7.

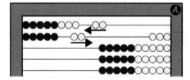 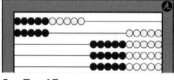

Take 2 from 7 to give to 8.   8 + 7 = 15.

Ask her to use this method for finding 8 + 4 [12] and 8 + 6. [14] Then enter the following and ask the child to find the answers by mentally moving the beads: 8 + 8, [16] 8 + 3, [11] 8 + 5, [13] and 8 + 9. [17]

8 + a number with the even/odd pattern. Tell the child to turn her abacus sideways. Then ask her to enter 8 and 6 with a space between them. See the left figure on the next page. To see the sum, move up 2 beads from the 6 to form a 10. See the right figure on the next page.

ACTIVITIES FOR TEACHING:	EXPLANATIONS:

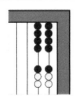 8 + 6.   Take 2 from 6 to form 10 and 4.

Repeat for 9 + 8, [17] 8 + 4, [12] and so on.

Adding with 8s in higher decades. Write 28 + 4 = ____ and ask the child to find the sum. [Take 2 from 4 to change the 28 into 30, giving 32.] See figures below.

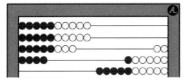 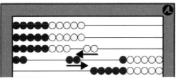

Adding 28 + 4.   **Take 2 from 4 and give to 8.**

Repeat for 85 + 8 = ____, [93] 68 + 5 = ____, [73] and 28 + 9 = ____. [37]

Next write 15 + 8. Tell the child to use take and give in the same way to take 2 from 5 and give it to the 8, giving 23 as the sum. See the figures below.

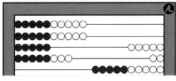 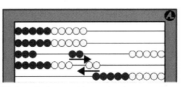

Adding 15 + 8.   **Take 2 from 5 and give to 8.**

Repeat for 64 + 8 [72] and 46 + 8. [54]

Worksheet 17. Give the child the worksheet. Tell her to use her abacus. Problems and solutions are shown below.

```
              3 + 8 = 11
8 + 6 = 14    4 + 8 = 12    18 + 8 = 26    78 + 8 = 86
8 + 8 = 16    9 + 8 = 17    68 + 7 = 75    18 + 2 = 20
8 + 9 = 17    8 + 5 = 13    58 + 6 = 64    28 + 5 = 33
5 + 8 = 13    7 + 8 = 15    38 + 4 = 42    88 + 9 = 97
2 + 8 = 10    6 + 8 = 14    28 + 3 = 31    48 + 5 = 53
8 + 4 = 12    8 + 3 = 11
```

In conclusion. Ask the child to use her abacus to solve the following problem:

Tony has 85 nails. He finds 7 more nails. How many nails does Tony have now? [92]

© Activities for Learning, Inc. 2013

Lesson 50: Two-Fives Strategy Practice

OBJECTIVES:
1. To practice adding with the two-fives strategy in higher decades
2. To practice some of the facts by playing Short Chain Solitaire game

MATERIALS:
1. Dry erase board
2. AL Abacus
3. *Math Card Games* book, A47
4. Worksheet 18, Two-Fives Strategy Practice

ACTIVITIES FOR TEACHING:

EXPLANATIONS:

Warm-up. Play the Figure Riddle game; describe a figure and ask the child to name it. For example, ask: What figure has 3 vertices? [triangle] What figures always have right angles? [rectangle, square] What figure has all the sides congruent? [equilateral triangle, square]

Ask the child: What is 45 + 5? [50] What is 60 + 10? [70] What is 40 + 15? [55] What is 25 + 15? [40] What is 48 + 2? [50]

Two-fives strategy in higher decades. Write 27 + 6 = __ and ask the child to enter 27 on her abacus. Then ask her to enter 6 on the next wire. See the figure below.

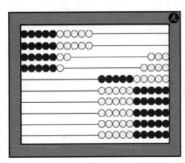

7 and 6 make 10 + 3.
So 27 + 6 = 33.

Ask: How many tens do you see? [Three: the first two wires have tens and the two fives make another ten.] How much is 27 + 6? [33]

Practice with oral facts such as 17 + 5 [22] and 68 + 5. [73] Also write the following for the child to solve: 16 + 6 = __ [22] and 27 + 8 = __. [35]

Short Chain Solitaire game. Play Short Chain Solitaire, found in the *Math Card Games* book, A47. Have the child play it several times.

ACTIVITIES FOR TEACHING:

Worksheet 18. Give the child the worksheet. Tell her to mark each answer on the hundred chart by either coloring in the corresponding square or crossing it out. The pattern and answers are shown below.

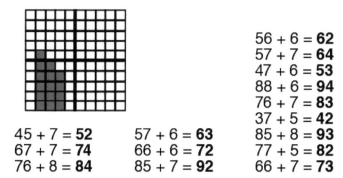

45 + 7 = **52**
67 + 7 = **74**
76 + 8 = **84**

57 + 6 = **63**
66 + 6 = **72**
85 + 7 = **92**

56 + 6 = **62**
57 + 7 = **64**
47 + 6 = **53**
88 + 6 = **94**
76 + 7 = **83**
37 + 5 = **42**
85 + 8 = **93**
77 + 5 = **82**
66 + 7 = **73**

In conclusion. Ask the child to use her abacus to solve these problems. Ask her to say the answers orally. What is 27 + 5? [32] What is 78 + 5? [83] What is 56 + 6? [62]

EXPLANATIONS:

Lesson 51: Adding 8s and 9s Practice

OBJECTIVES:
1. To practice adding with 8s and 9s

MATERIALS:
1. Dry erase board
2. AL Abacus
3. *Math Card Games* book, A57
4. Worksheet 19, Adding 8s and 9s Practice

ACTIVITIES FOR TEACHING:

EXPLANATIONS:

Warm-up. Ask the child to use her abacus to solve these problems. Ask her to say the answers orally. What is 37 + 5? [42] What is 58 + 5? [63] What is 76 + 6? [82]

Play the Figure Riddle game; describe a figure and ask the child to name it. For example, ask: What figure has 3 vertices? [triangle] What figures always have right angles? [rectangle, square] What figure has all the sides congruent? [equilateral triangle, square]

Ask the child: What is 35 + 5? [40] What is 70 + 10? [80] What is 60 + 15? [75] What is 95 + 15? [110] What is 98 + 2? [100]

Reviewing adding 9s in higher decades. Write 23 + 9 = ___ and ask the child to enter 23 on her abacus. Then ask her to enter 9 on the next wire. See the left figure below.

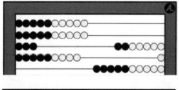 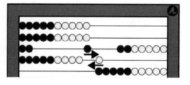

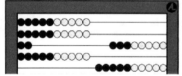

Making a ten to find:
23 + 9 = 32.

Tell her to make a ten by taking 1 from 3 and giving it to 9. See the remaining figures above. Then ask: How many tens do you see? [Three: the first two wires and the third wire have tens.] Ask: How much is 23 + 9? [32]

Repeat for 17 + 9 [26] and 68 + 9. [77]

Reviewing adding 8s in higher decades. Write 23 + 8 = ___ and ask the child to enter both 23 and 8 on her abacus. See the left figure at the top of the next page.

ACTIVITIES FOR TEACHING:	EXPLANATIONS:

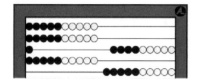

Making a ten to find: 23 + 8 = 31.

Ask: How can you make another ten? [by taking 2 from the 3 and giving it to the 8] See the remaining figures above. Ask: How much is 23 + 8? [31]

Repeat for 44 + 8 [52] and 65 + 8. [73]

Mental Addition game. Play the Mental Addition game, found in the *Math Card Games* book, A57.

Worksheet 19. Give the child the worksheet. Tell her to mark each answer on the hundred chart by either coloring in the corresponding square or crossing out it out. The pattern and answers are shown below.

For the multiplication card, use the cards from the envelopes for the 6s, 7s, 8s, and 9s.

Adding 8s and 9s has been done separately before; here they are done together on the worksheet.

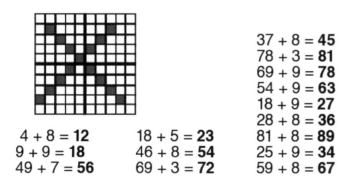

4 + 8 = **12**   18 + 5 = **23**   37 + 8 = **45**
9 + 9 = **18**   46 + 8 = **54**   78 + 3 = **81**
49 + 7 = **56**   69 + 3 = **72**   69 + 9 = **78**
                                    54 + 9 = **63**
                                    18 + 9 = **27**
                                    28 + 8 = **36**
                                    81 + 8 = **89**
                                    25 + 9 = **34**
                                    59 + 8 = **67**

In conclusion. Ask the child to solve the following problem.

While walking along the river, Tracy and Tony found 65 rocks. Tony found 8 more rocks. How many rocks do they have altogether? [73] Then, Tracy finds 9 more rocks. How many rocks do they have altogether? [82]

LESSON 52: THOUSANDS

OBJECTIVES:
1. To learn that one thousand is 10 hundreds
2. To read thousands

MATERIALS:
1. AL Abacus
2. Place-value cards
3. Abacus tiles
4. Base-10 picture cards

ACTIVITIES FOR TEACHING:

Warm-up. Expand the Comes After game to larger numbers. For example, ask what comes after 200, 400, 600? [800]

Enter 10 on the abacus and ask the child: How much is this? [ten 1s or 1-ten] If she gives only one answer ask her if there is another name for it. Let her explain why there are two answers.

Enter 100 and ask: How much is this? [ten 10s or 100] Use the same technique to get to both answers.

Ask the same questions with the place-value cards. Show 10 and ask: How do we read this? [ten 1s or 1-ten] Again seek both answers and let her explain. Repeat for 100. [ten 10s or 100]

Show her 60 and 600 from the place-value cards and ask how she could tell which is 6-ten and which is 6 hundred. [6-ten has one digit after the 6 while 6 hundred has 2 two digits.]

Thousands. Lay out 10 abacus tiles and ask: What do we call this? [10 hundred] If necessary, remind her that 10 hundred has another name, 1 thousand. Ask: How many beads are here? [1 thousand] Ask: Is that a lot of beads?

Ask: How many abacus tiles would you need to show 2 thousand? [twenty] Ask: How many abacus tiles would you need to show 4 thousand? [forty]

Ten abacus tiles showing 1 thousand beads.

EXPLANATIONS:

ACTIVITIES FOR TEACHING:	EXPLANATIONS:

Place-value cards. Show the child the 1000 card; point to the 10 and say that we can read it as "ten hun-dred." See the left figure below.

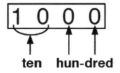 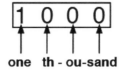

The place-value card seen as "ten hun-dred."   **The place-value card seen as "one th-ou-sand."**

While pronouncing "thousand" with three syllables is phonetically incorrect, it is the best that can be done.

Tell her the usual way to read it is one thousand: Point to each digit in turn while saying "one-th-ou-sand." See the right figure above. Ask: In 1000, how many digits come after the 1? [3]

Noting the number of digits following the leftmost digit(s) in a number is a more accurate determination of place value than the total number of digits. For example, 2700 can be read correctly as "27 hundred" by observing the two digits following the 27.

Base-10 picture cards. Ask the child: What would 2000 beads would look like? [20 abacus tiles] Explain it takes too long to build, so we will use pictures. Show her a thousand from the base-10 picture cards. See the figure below.

Base-10 picture card for 1000.

Place-value cards. Tell the child to spread out her place-value cards with the thousands.

Lay out three thousands pictures as shown below on the left. Ask the child: How much is this? [3000] Tell her to find the 3000-card from the place-value cards. Repeat for 6000, 9000, and 7000.

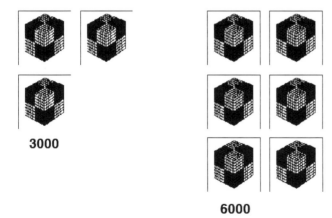

3000   **6000**

Grouping in twos is important for quick recognition. Also, it parallels how quantities will be entered on side 2 of the abacus.

In conclusion. Ask the child: How much is 2000 plus 4000? [6000] How much is 2000 plus 6000? [8000] How much is 3000 plus 5000? [8000]

© Activities for Learning, Inc. 2013

Lesson 53: Base-10 Picture Cards

OBJECTIVES:
1. To review that one thousand is 10 hundreds
2. To read thousands

MATERIALS:
1. AL Abacus
2. Place-value cards
3. Abacus tiles
4. Base-10 cards
5. 4-in-1 ruler

ACTIVITIES FOR TEACHING:

Warm-up. Ask: How many 1s in 10? [10] How many 10s in 100? [10] How many 100s in 1000? [10]

Ask the child: How much is 3000 plus 4000? [7000] How much is 3000 plus 6000? [9000] How much is 2000 plus 5000? [7000]

Show her 50 and 500 from the place-value cards and ask how she could tell which is 5-ten and which is 5 hundred. [5-ten one digit after the 5 while 5 hundred has two digits.]

The base-10 picture cards. With abacus tiles nearby, ask the child to enter 1 on the abacus. Tell her to find the base-10 card showing 1. Next ask her to enter 10 on the abacus and find the base-10 card showing 10. Now ask her to enter 100 on the abacus and find the 100 base-10 card showing 100. Ask the child to make one thousand with the abacus tiles and find the 1000 base-10 card. See the figures below.

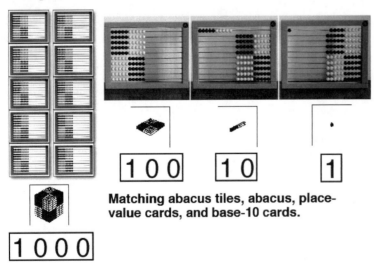

Matching abacus tiles, abacus, place-value cards, and base-10 cards.

Point to the abacus tiles and ask: How much is this? [1000] Point to the base-10 card showing 100 and ask: How much is this? [100] Continue with the next base-10 cards. [10 and 1]

EXPLANATIONS:

ACTIVITIES FOR TEACHING:	EXPLANATIONS:

Ask the child to set the corresponding place-value cards in front of the base-10 card. See the figure on the previous page.

Point to the base-10 card with 1 and ask: How many 1s do we need to make it like the 10? [10] Point to the base-10 card with 10 and ask: How many 10s do we need to make it like the 100? [10] Point to the base-10 card with 100. Ask: How many 100s we need to make it like the 1000? [10] You might conclude by asking: Why do you keep saying 10? [our special number]

Matching place-value cards to base-10 cards. Lay out 2 thousands and 4 hundreds with the base-10 cards, as shown below. Tell the child to find the place-value cards to place below.

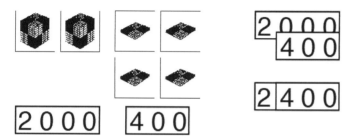

Then tell her to stack the cards and read them. [2 thousand 4 hundred] See the right figure above.

Repeat for 1 thousand fifty-four. See below.

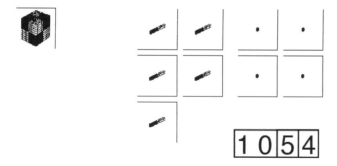

Feet in a mile. Demonstrate the length of a foot with a ruler or your hands. Tell the child there are 5280 feet in a mile. Tell her to compose the number with her place-value cards. Repeat for the number of days a child has lived on the day she turns five: 1826 days.

In conclusion. Ask: Which is more, 4 thousand or 8 hundred? [4 thousand] Which is greater, 10 hundred or 1 thousand? [same] Which is less, 1 hundred or 17? [17]

Lesson 54: Trading with Base-10 Cards

OBJECTIVES:
1. To experience trading with the base-10 cards

MATERIALS:
1. Place-value cards
2. Base-10 cards

ACTIVITIES FOR TEACHING:	EXPLANATIONS:
Warm-up. Ask: Which is more, 3 thousand or 7 hundred? [3 thousand] Which is greater, 10 hundred or 1 thousand? [same] Which is less, 2 hundred or 13? [13]	
Ask the child: How much is 2000 plus 4000? [6000] How much is 3000 plus 3000? [6000] How much is 4000 plus 5000? [9000]	
Show her 50 and 500 from the place-value cards and ask how she could tell which is 5-ten and which is 5 hundred. [5-ten one digit after the 5 while 5 hundred has 2 two digits.]	
Lay out 10 ones from the base-10 cards grouped in 2s and ask: 10 ones is the same as . . . .? [1 ten] Show her the picture of the 10 card. Repeat for 10 tens being the same as 1 hundred. Repeat for 10 hundreds being the same as 1 thousand.	
Trading with base-10 cards. Place 4 thousands, 20 hundreds, 15 tens, and 22 ones from the base-10 cards in a jumbled mess in view of the child. Keep the remaining cards neatly stacked by denomination a short distance away at a place called the "bank."	
Tell the child that she is to find out how much the "mess" is. Discuss how she could figure out how much there is. [Trade when there is more than 10 of any denomination.]	
Ask the child to arrange the cards neatly in rows of two as shown on the next page. Tell her to trade one of the denominations. She need not start with the 1s. Tell the child to start at the bottom of the column to gather tens.	
The child then takes the ten cards and make the appropriate trade. For example, if gathering hundreds, she trades 10 hundreds for 1 thousand. The child then places the thousand with the other thousands. Have her check to see if there is another group of 10.	The order of trading is not important. Calculating mentally or on a calculator is easier to do when starting at the left; only on paper is it easier to start at the right.
	Counting from the bottom is more orderly and will be done later on side 2 of the abacus.

ACTIVITIES FOR TEACHING:

EXPLANATIONS:

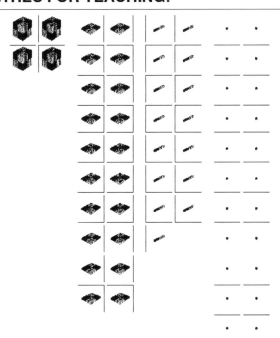

4 thousands, 20 hundreds, 15 tens, and 22 ones.

Ask the child to do the trading for the remaining denominations. After the trading is complete, ask the child to find the corresponding place-value card for each denomination. Ask her to construct the whole number by stacking the parts and to read the result. [6172; 6 thousand 1 hundred seventy-two]

The same quantity after trading.

Repeat. Repeat the activity using 2 thousands 19 hundreds 19 tens and 12 ones, [4102] or let the child decide on her own numbers, but keep at least two cards of each denomination in the bank.

In conclusion. Show a picture of 10 and ask: Suppose I had 60 of these pictures. How much would I have? [600] Ask the child to explain it. [Each ten is 100, so 60 would be 600.] Show the 600 place-value card and ask: Is it the same? [yes] Why? [it shows 60-ten or 6 hundred]

Lesson 55: Adding with Base-10 Cards

OBJECTIVES:
1. To add four-digit numbers with the base-10 cards

MATERIALS:
1. Base-10 cards
2. Place-value cards
3. *Math Card Games* book, A44 or A45
4. **The following numbers on separate slips of paper, 1549, 2735, and 3817**

ACTIVITIES FOR TEACHING:	EXPLANATIONS:
Warm-up. Show a 10 from the base-10 picture cards and say: Suppose I had 80 of these cards. How much would I have? [800] Ask the child to explain it. [Each ten is 100, so 80 would be 800.] Show the 800 place-value card and ask: Is it the same? [yes] Why? [it shows 80-ten or 8 hundred]	
Ask: Which is more, 2 thousand or 6 hundred? [2 thousand] Which is greater, 1 thousand or 10 hundred? [same] Which is less, 1 hundred or 11? [11]	This lesson is not intended to teach the paper and pencil algorithm for adding numbers, but only to extend the concept of trading to a more abstract form.
Ask the child: How much is 1000 plus 5000? [6000] How much is 6000 plus 2000? [8000] How much is 2000 plus 5000? [7000]	
Show her 70 and 700 from the place-value cards and ask how she could tell which is 70 and which is 7 hundred. [70 has one digit after the 7 while 7 hundred has two digits.]	
Addition War game. Play the Addition War game, found in the *Math Card Games* book, A44. If a game for three is needed, use game A45.	
Preparation for adding with base-10 cards. Tell the child the following story.	
There were three shepherds, named Abe, Amy, and Adrian. Abe had 1549 sheep, Amy had 2735 sheep, and Adrian had 3817 sheep (point to the numbers on the three slips of paper as you say them). The shepherds called a meeting and decided they wanted to know how many sheep they had altogether.	To keep track of the shepherds, note that the number of syllables in the name is the same as the number of thousands.
Give the child one of the shepherd's numbers. Tell her to construct her numbers with her place-value cards and then collect the corresponding base-10 cards. Repeat for the other shepherd's numbers using separate base-10 cards.	

RightStart™ Mathematics Level B Second Edition

ACTIVITIES FOR TEACHING:

EXPLANATIONS:

Adding. Ask the child to add her base-10 pictures together, combining denominations. Lay the three sets of place-value cards in a column. See below.

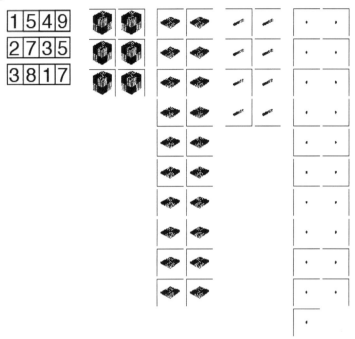

The base-10 cards for all three quantities added together.

The gathering and trading proceed the same as the previous lesson.

At the conclusion of the trading, the child composes the sum with her place-value cards.

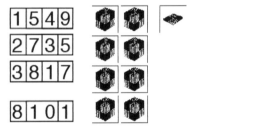

The sum after trading.

Summarize. Ask: Which numbers are the parts? [shepherd's numbers] Which is the whole? [8101] How many sheep did the three shepherds have in all? [8101]

Tell the child to write the numbers in a column in her math journal. Show her how to draw a line below the third number to separate the parts from the whole.

In conclusion. Ask: When do you need to trade? [When the number of the same cards gets to 10]

© Activities for Learning, Inc. 2013

Lesson 56: More Adding with Base-10 Cards

OBJECTIVES:
1. To add two 4-digit numbers with base-10 cards
2. To practice trading

MATERIALS:
1. Base-10 cards
2. Worksheet 20, More Adding with Base-10 Cards
3. Place-value cards

ACTIVITIES FOR TEACHING:	EXPLANATIONS:
Warm-up. Show a 10 from the base-10 picture cards. Say: Suppose I had 40 of these pictures. How much would I have? [400] Ask the child to explain it. [Each ten is 100, so 40 would be 400.]	
Ask: Which is more, 3 thousand or 3 hundred? [3 thousand] Which is less, 9 hundred or 9? [9] Which is greater, 1 thousand or 10 hundred? [same]	
Ask the child: How much is 2000 plus 4000? [6000] How much is 4000 plus 3000? [7000] How much is 1000 plus 5000? [6000]	
Worksheet 20. Tell the child to do the six addition problems in order: first, A and then B and so forth.	
Do the first one with her as follows: Ask her to prepare the first number with place-value cards and base-10 cards. Then she does the same for the second number.	
When both numbers are ready, have her combine the cards. Next she does the trading. Then she constructs the sum with her sets of place-value cards and writes the answer on her worksheet.	
The next page shows both numbers of the first problem composed with the place-value cards and the base-10 cards. Below the dotted line is the combining and trading.	

RightStart™ Mathematics Level B Second Edition   © Activities for Learning, Inc. 2013

ACTIVITIES FOR TEACHING:

EXPLANATIONS:

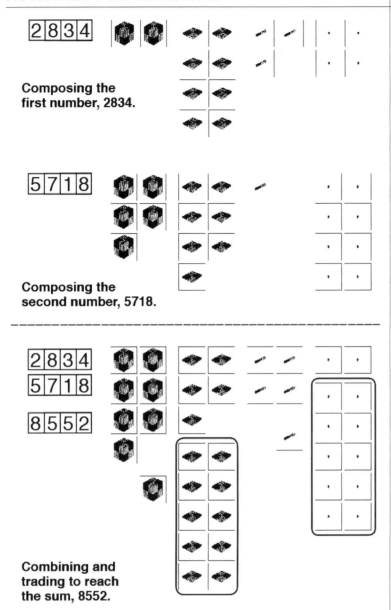

Composing the first number, 2834.

Composing the second number, 5718.

Combining and trading to reach the sum, 8552.

The child does the five remaining sums on the worksheet the same way.

The problems and solutions for the worksheet are listed below:

A. 2834	B. 2473
+ 5718	+ 3647
8552	6120

C. 4791	D. 2649
+ 1288	+ 1877
6079	4526

E. 1509	F. 1678
+ 3246	+ 3529
4755	5207

In conclusion. Ask: How many ones in 10? [10] How many tens in 100? [10] How many hundreds in one thousand? [10]

© Activities for Learning, Inc. 2013

Enrichment Lesson 57: Cotter Tens Fractal—Prep

OBJECTIVES:

1. To construct the ten-triangles for the Cotter Tens Fractal
2. To appreciate the ten-for-one pattern of our number system through building the Cotter Tens Fractal

MATERIALS:

1. AL Abacus
2. Cotter Tens Fractal drawing (Appendix p. 5)
3. 100 small triangles* (10 copies of Appendix p. 6)
4. 100 medium triangles** (25 copies of Appendix p. 7)
5. **Scissors and glue**

ACTIVITIES FOR TEACHING:

Warm-up. Ask: Which is more, 1 thousand or 5 hundred? [1 thousand] Which is greater, 10 tens or 1 hundred? [same] Which is less, 2 hundred or 2? [2]

Ask the child: How much is 1000 plus 100? [1100] How much is 6000 plus 600? [6600] How much is 2000 plus 200? [2200]

Ask the child: What number is greater than 100, but less than 102? [101] What numbers are greater than 112, but less than 115? [113 and 114]

Ask the child: What number is greater than 1000, but less than 1002? [1001] What numbers are greater than 1002, but less than 1005? [1003 and 1004]

Cotter Tens Fractal. Show the child the Cotter Tens Fractal shown below or on Appendix p. 5.

The Cotter Tens Fractal.

Explain: This special project will take several days to make. When it is completed, it will be taller than you are. Point out to her that a little triangle is 1; a group of ten triangles is 1-ten, ten tens is a hundred, and ten hundreds is a thousand. See above.

EXPLANATIONS:

*Copy these onto colored paper.

For a single child, you could download a copy of the medium triangles each with 10 small triangles in color. Link can be found here: http://rightstartmath.com/resources/cotter-tens-fractal.

**The four triangles on the page need to be cut apart, either by the child or beforehand.

The Cotter Tens Fractal helps the child experience our place-value system concretely. This fractal actually expands indefinitely in the same way as does our number system.

Building the Cotter Tens Fractal is best done with a group of children.

The small-triangles measure 1.3 by 1.125 inches high; the ten-triangles, 5.2 by 4.5 inches high; the hundred-triangle, 20.8 by 18 inches high; and the thousand, or final, triangle will be 83.2 by 72 inches (212 by 183 cm) high. The completed work can be attached to a wall along with the explanation on Appendix p. 5.

A one, a ten-triangle, and a hundred-triangle are shown below:

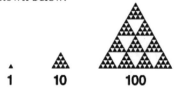

1 10 100

RightStart™ Mathematics Level B Second Edition © Activities for Learning, Inc. 2013

ACTIVITIES FOR TEACHING:	EXPLANATIONS:

Tens arrangement. Tell the child: Make the stairs to 4; see the left figure below. Ask: How many beads are entered? [10]

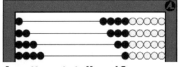 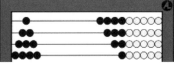

A pattern totaling 10.   The same pattern centered.

Next show her how to move the beads on the first 3 wires so they are centered over the 4 beads. See the right figure above. Tell her: This is the pattern we need to make for the tens-triangles.

Triangles. Give the child the strips of small triangles to cut out. Remind her that they must be cut very carefully.

Each sheet has 105 triangles, or 5 extra triangles.

Making the ten-triangles. Show her how to make the pattern with 10 of the triangles. Start by placing four triangles in a row along the bottom edge of the medium triangle. Then place three triangles above those, two above those, and the last one on top. See the figures below.

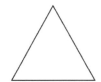 

The tens outline.   The first two glued.   The first row glued.

Two rows glued.   Three rows glued.   A ten-triangle.

Gluing starts the same way, from the bottom row. Apply weights overnight to keep them flat.

Cutting and gluing the ten-triangles.

In conclusion. Ask: How many little colored triangles are in each medium triangle? [10] How many medium triangles do you need to make a hundred? [10]

© Activities for Learning, Inc. 2013

ENRICHMENT LESSON 58: COTTER TENS FRACTAL

OBJECTIVES:
1. To complete the Cotter Tens Fractal
2. To help the child experience and visualize the repeating tens structure of our number system
3. To integrate mathematics and art

MATERIALS:
1. 100 ten-triangles made in the previous lesson
2. 10 sheets of paper for the hundred-triangles*, 20.8" by 18"
3. Background paper,** 83.2" wide and 72" high
4. **Glue**

ACTIVITIES FOR TEACHING:

Warm-up. Ask the child: Which is more, 2 thousand or 6 hundred? [2 thousand] Which is greater, 10 tens or 1 hundred? [same] Which is less, 3 hundred or 3? [3]

Ask the child: How much is 1000 plus 400? [1400] How much is 7000 plus 700? [7700] How much is 5000 plus 500? [5500]

Ask the child: What number is greater than 300, but less than 302? [301] What numbers are greater than 312, but less than 315? [313 and 314]

Ask: What does ten ones make? [a ten] What does ten tens make? [a hundred] What does ten hundreds make? [a thousand]

Making the hundred-triangles. Take 10 ten-triangles and lay them out in the same pattern. Ask the child: How many ten-triangles do you see? [10] How many small triangles do you see? [10-ten, or 1 hundred] To help her understand, count the ten-triangles as 1-ten, 2-ten, 3-ten, and so forth. At 10-ten ask: What is another name for 10-ten? [1 hundred]

Tell the child that now she can make the hundred-triangles. Tell her how to lay out the ten-triangles on the paper for the hundred-triangles the same way as she did in the previous lesson: four on the bottom row, three in the next row, then two, then the last one. Then tell her to glue them in place.

EXPLANATIONS:

*Some people omit making the hundred-triangles, preferring to proceed directly to the thousand-triangle.

**Two sheets 36" wide and 83.2" long work well.

If your family is part of a larger group, each family could make one or two of the hundreds. Then at a gathering, the families combine their hundreds into the Cotter Tens Fractal.

ACTIVITIES FOR TEACHING:

Making the thousand-triangle. When the 10 hundred-triangles are completed, ask the child to guess what is next. [building the thousand-triangle]

Lay out the 10 hundred-triangles, using the same pattern as before to build the thousand-triangle, which is the Cotter Tens Fractal. When the glue is dry, fasten it to a wall.

In conclusion. Ask: How many little triangles are in the Cotter Tens Fractal? [1000]

EXPLANATIONS:

© Activities for Learning, Inc. 2013

Lesson 59: Adding Even Numbers Practice

OBJECTIVES:
1. To practice composing large numbers with the place-value cards
2. To introduce the vertical form of addition
3. To discover that two even numbers results in an even number

MATERIALS:
1. The Cotter Tens Fractal (App. p. 5)
2. *Math Card Games* book, N43 and A48
3. Place-value cards
4. AL Abacus

ACTIVITIES FOR TEACHING:	EXPLANATIONS:

Warm-up. Standing in front of the Cotter Tens fractal (use Appendix p. 5, if one is not available), point to a ten-triangle and ask the child how many small triangles are in the triangle. [10] Then point to a hundred-triangle and ask how many of the ten-triangles are in that triangle. [10] Finally point to the whole large triangle and ask how many 100 triangles are here? [10]
 	
 Ask the child: How many 10s are in 1 thousand? [100]
 	
 Ask: Which is more, 2 thousand or 3 hundred? [2 thousand] Which is greater, 10 tens or 1 hundred? [same] Which is less, 4 hundred or 40? [40]
 	
 Ask the child: How much is 3000 plus 300? [3300] How much is 4000 plus 400? [4400] How much is 7000 plus 700? [7700]
 	
 Can You Find game. Play the Can You Find game, found in the *Math Card Games* book, N43. Ask the child to use all the place-value cards. As you name a quantity, the child look for the corresponding cards, stack them, and set them aside near the bottom of their workspace.
 	
 The following numbers will include all the cards:
 	
     5-ten
     2 hundred
     6 thousand 3 hundred
     9 thousand 3-ten
     5 hundred 7
     7 thousand 5
     1 hundred 90
     5 thousand 8 hundred 4
     7 hundred 81
     3 thousand 23
     4 thousand 76
     2 thousand 4 hundred 68
     8 thousand 6 hundred 42
     1 thousand 9 hundred 19	

ACTIVITIES FOR TEACHING:	EXPLANATIONS:

Adding evens in the even/odd pattern. Write the following in the vertical format as follows:

$$\begin{array}{r}4\\+\,8\\\hline\end{array}$$

Explain to the child that today we will write numbers to be added under each other.

Ask her to turn her abacus sideways and use the even/odd pattern to add 4 and 8. See the left figure below.

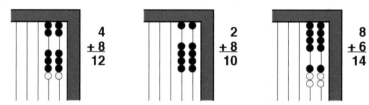

Adding even numbers.

Repeat for 2 + 8 [10] and 8 + 6. [14] See the right figures above. Ask her: What kind of numbers are you adding? [even numbers] Can you think of some more even numbers to add that are less than 11? Ask her to write them and to add them as above.

Then ask: What kind of numbers are the addends, the numbers being added? [even numbers] What kind of numbers are the sums? [even numbers]

Even Chains Solitaire. Have the child play the Even Chains Solitaire, found in the *Math Card Games* book, A48. This game uses all the facts in which both addends are even numbers.

In conclusion. Ask: What kind of number do you always get when you add two even numbers? [even number]

There are enough cards in the basic number card deck to prepare card decks for both the Short Chain Solitaire and the Even Chain Solitaire games.

Lesson 60: Adding up to 10 and up to 15

OBJECTIVES:
1. To partition a number into three parts
2. To practice adding several numbers together

MATERIALS:
1. Dry erase board
2. *Math Card Games* book, A55

ACTIVITIES FOR TEACHING:	EXPLANATIONS:
Warm-up. Ask: What kind of number do you always get when you add two even numbers? [even number]	
Ask the child to give the ways to make 11: 2 and what? [9] 5 and what? [6] 9 and what? [2] 7 and what? [4]	
Ways to make 10 with 3 numbers. Draw a part-whole circle set with three parts and write 10 in the whole circle as shown below.	
Tell the child the following problem:	
Tegan has 10 pet treats and 3 pets. How could Tegan split the treats among the 3 pets?	
You might ask the child to think of some reasons for giving the pets different numbers of treats. [size, rewards]	
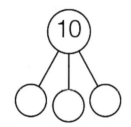 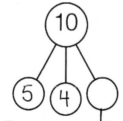 The part-whole circle set with three parts. One way to partition 10 into 3 parts.	There are 45 possible ways.
Ask the child for the numbers to put in the parts circles and ask how she did it. Tell the child to write the equation. $$10 = 5 + 4 + 1$$ $$5 + 4 + 1 = 10$$	
Ask the child to write down more ways to partition 10 into three parts.	

ACTIVITIES FOR TEACHING:	EXPLANATIONS:
Adding three numbers. Write 9, 3, and 1 as parts in a part-whole circle set as shown below on the left. Ask the child: How can you find the sum? If she suggests 9 + 3 and then add the 1, ask: Are there other ways? Do you always get the same answer? [yes] Which is the easiest way? [9 + 1 + 3]	

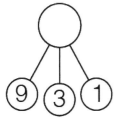
Adding 3 parts.

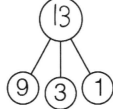
Easiest way: 9 + 1 + 3

Preparation for On the Number game. Draw a part-whole circle set with four parts and numbers as shown below on the left. Ask the child to find the remaining part. [1] Ask how she did it? One way is to add the three numbers in any order to get 9; then 1 is needed with 9 to make 10. Another way is 3 + 2 makes 5; 4 needs 1 to make another 5. The solution is shown in the right figure below.

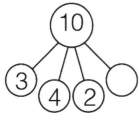
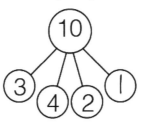
Finding the missing part.

Repeat with 15 as the whole. See the figures below.

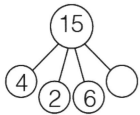
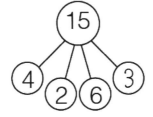
Finding the missing part.

On the Number game. Play the game On the Number found in the *Math Card Games* book, A55. Use the target number 10 for the first game and 15 for the next games.

In conclusion. Ask: How can you add three numbers? [First add any two numbers, then add the last number.]

© Activities for Learning, Inc. 2013

Lesson 61: Adding Several Numbers

OBJECTIVES:
1. To practice adding several numbers
2. To find 2, 3, or 4 numbers that total 15

MATERIALS:
1. Dry erase board
2. Worksheet 21, Adding Several Numbers
3. Basic number cards
4. *Math Card Games* book, A53

ACTIVITIES FOR TEACHING:

Warm-up. Ask: How can you add three numbers? [First add any two numbers, then add the last number.]

Ask the child to solve the following problem using a part-whole circle set:

John has 11 apples and 3 friends to share the apples with. How could John split the apples among the 3 friends?

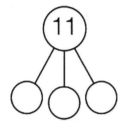 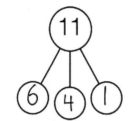

The part-whole circle set with three parts.   **One way to partition 11 into 3 parts.**

Ask the child: 9 and what equals 15? [6] 7 and what equals 15? [8] 5 and what equals 15? [10] 8 and what equals 15? [7] 6 and what equals 15? [9]

Ask: What kind of number do you always get when you add two even numbers? [even number]

Ask the child to give the ways to make 11: 3 and what? [8] 4 and what? [7] 10 and what? [1] 9 and what? [2]

EXPLANATIONS:

ACTIVITIES FOR TEACHING:

Worksheet 21. Give the child the worksheet. Remind her she can add the numbers in any order. The problems and solutions are below:

$3 + 2 + 1 = \mathbf{6}$
$5 + 2 + 2 = \mathbf{9}$
$4 + 3 + 2 = \mathbf{9}$
$1 + 2 + 7 = \mathbf{10}$
$2 + 3 + 6 = \mathbf{11}$

$3 + 5 + 5 = \mathbf{13}$
$2 + 7 + 8 = \mathbf{17}$
$10 + 2 + 3 = \mathbf{15}$
$6 + 5 + 6 = \mathbf{17}$
$2 + 9 + 9 = \mathbf{20}$

Preparation for Rows and Columns game. Lay out the following basic number cards:

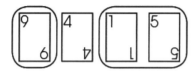

and ask the child which numbers she could use to make 15. [9, 1, 5] Ask how she found the numbers. She may see the 9 and 1 making 10 and with the 5 making 15.

Repeat for

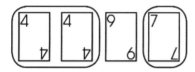

This sum [4, 4, 7] can be seen with the 4 and 4 giving 8, which added to 7 is 15.

Repeat for

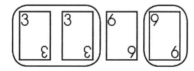

This time there are two solutions. [3, 3, 9 or 6, 9] Since the object of this new game will be to collect the most cards, the first solution is preferred.

Rows and Columns game. Play the Rows and Columns game from the *Math Card Games* book, A53.

In conclusion. Ask: What is $1 + 2 + 3 + 4 + 5$? [15]

EXPLANATIONS:

There are many different ways to find the numbers. Encourage the child to discuss which ways are easiest, or fastest.

Lesson 62: Solving Problems with Three Addends

OBJECTIVES:
1. To practice adding several numbers
2. To find 2, 3, or 4 numbers that total 15

MATERIALS:
1. Worksheet 22, Solving Problems with Three Addends
2. *Math Card Games* book, A53

ACTIVITIES FOR TEACHING:	EXPLANATIONS:
Warm-up. Ask: What is 1 + 2 + 3 + 4 + 5? [15]	
Ask the child: 6 and what equals 15? [9] 8 and what equals 15? [7] 10 and what equals 15? [5] 7 and what equals 15? [8] 9 and what equals 15? [6]	
Ask the child to give the ways to make 11: 2 and what? [9] 5 and what? [6] 9 and what? [2] 7 and what? [4]	
Worksheet 22. Give the child the worksheet.	
Problem 1. Tell her to read Problem 1 twice:	
James picked 3 red flowers, 6 blue flowers, and 7 yellow flowers. How many flowers did James pick? [16]	
Tell the child to solve it any way she likes. Then ask her to share her solution. Discuss writing the equation as follows:	
$$3 + 6 + 7 = \underline{}$$	
Also discuss how she found the solution. Emphasize seeing 3 + 7 as 10 and 6 more is 16.	The line under the problem on the child's worksheet is the place to write the equation.
$$3 + 6 + 7 = \underline{16}$$	
Problem 2. Tell her to read Problem 2 twice:	
On a trail, Kaitlyn saw 4 children riding bicycles, 10 children walking, and 1 child getting a drink. How many children did Kaitlyn see?	
Ask the child to solve the problem and write the equation.	
$$4 + 10 + 1 = \underline{}$$ $$4 + 10 + 1 = \underline{15}$$	

RightStart™ Mathematics Level B Second Edition

ACTIVITIES FOR TEACHING:	EXPLANATIONS:

As before, ask how she solved the equation. [4 and 1 is 5; 10 and 5 is 15]

Problem 3. Do Problem 3 in the same way.

Alex has 3 chapter books, 2 nursery rhyme books, and 8 picture books. How many books does Alex have?

$$3 + 2 + 8 = \underline{}$$
$$3 + 2 + 8 = \underline{13}$$

Problem 4. Problem 4 has added complications. It does not say explicitly how many shoes Michael and Matthew have. Also, there is an extra number, three, unrelated to the shoes.

Michael and Matthew each have 6 shoes. Matilda has 8 shoes. How many shoes do the three children have in all?

If necessary, ask: How many shoes does Michael have? [6] How many shoes does Matthew have? [6] How many shoes does Matilda have? [8] What do we need to find out? [the total number of shoes]

The equation is:

$$6 + 6 + 8 = \underline{}$$
$$6 + 6 + 8 = \underline{20}$$

In this problem, the child cannot merely add the numbers she sees; she must understand the problem before attempting to solve it.

Rows and Columns game. Play the Rows and Columns game in the *Math Card Games* book, A53.

In conclusion. Ask the child to make up a story problem like the ones on the worksheet.

Children gain much by playing the same game more than once. She is more proficient the second time and can spend more time on the mathematics of the game and less time on the rules of the game.

© Activities for Learning, Inc. 2013

Lesson 63: Introducing Side 2 of the Abacus

OBJECTIVES:
1. To compose numbers on side 2 of the abacus

MATERIALS:
1. "Yellow is the Sun" CD or "Thirty Days Has September" (Appendix p. 8)
2. AL Abacus
3. Place-value cards
4. Base-10 cards
5. *Math Card Games* book, N41

ACTIVITIES FOR TEACHING:

Warm-up. Using a year calendar, show the child that some months of the year have 30 days and some have 31. Show how February, has only 28 days, and discuss that every fourth year it has 29. Tell her she is going to learn a song that will help her remember how many days each month has.

Teach the child the new song "Thirty Days has September" using the "Yellow is the Sun" CD or Appendix page 8.

Thirty Days Has September
Thirty days has September,
April, June, and November.
The rest have 31 to carry,
But only 28 for February,
Except in leap year, that's the time
When February has 29.

Ask the child: How many ones are in 1-ten? [ten] How many tens are in 1 hundred? [ten] How many hundreds are in 1 thousand? [ten]

Review ordinal numbers. Ask the child to move 10 beads toward the middle of the abacus. Point to the first bead and ask: What position is this bead? [first] Point to each bead in turn and ask the same question. [second, . . . , tenth]

Composing 4-digit numbers. Ask the child to lay out in a row the place-value cards, 4000, 300, 50, and 2. Ask her to lay out the base-10 cards with the same amount.

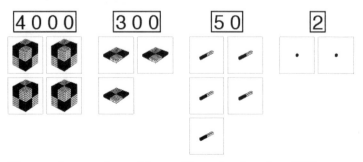

Place-value cards and base-10 cards showing 4352.

EXPLANATIONS:

ACTIVITIES FOR TEACHING:

Turn the abacus to side 2, with 1000, 100, 10, 1 on top. Tell the child that today she is going to use the abacus in a new way. Tell her that we are going to enter the same number on the abacus. Point out the thousand columns on the abacus and ask: How many thousands does the number have? [4] Raise 4 beads in the thousands columns, 2 in each column.

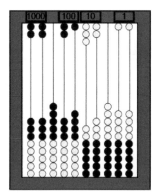

Side 2 displaying 4352.

Then ask: How many 100s in the hundreds place? [3] Raise 3 beads in the 100s columns. Continue with the 10s columns, [5] and the 1s columns. [2] Ask the child to compare the quantities with the lay out of the base-10 cards.

Stress that on this side of the abacus we do not enter actual tens, but only the number of tens. This is also true with the hundreds and thousands.

Practice. Give the child various quantities to enter, such as 4-ten, 900, 7, 1000, 50, and 800.

Modified Let's Compare game. The original Let's Compare game is found in the *Math Card Games* book, N41. For the modified version, the two players lay out all the place-value cards.

One player enters an amount on side 2 of the abacus. Then the other player makes that quantity with the place-value cards. Discuss if the numbers are the same.

Players take turns entering a number on the abacus.

In conclusion. Ask: On side 2 of the abacus, how many wires are there for the thousands? [2] How many wires for the hundreds? [2] How many wires for the tens? [2] How many wires for the ones? [2] How many wires are not used? [2]

EXPLANATIONS:

Side 2 of the abacus emphasizes trading and prepares the child for adding 4-digit numbers on paper.

Quantities are entered from left to right for several reasons. We read from left to right, do mental arithmetic from left to right, and enter quantities on a calculator from left to right. It also is the way we say numbers (except the teens).

It is important to keep the two wires as even as possible to make trading easier. See the figures below, both showing 12 ones entered. The right figure is clearly easier for trading.

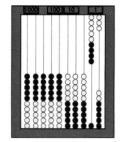 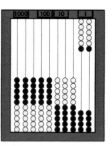

Incorrectly entering 12.   Correctly entering 12.

On side 1, 50 beads are entered to represent 50. On side 2, only 5 beads are entered to represent 50 because each bead represents 10.

© Activities for Learning, Inc. 2013

Lesson 64: Bead Trading

OBJECTIVES:
1. To learn to trade on side 2 of the abacus

MATERIALS:
1. Place-value cards
2. AL Abacus
3. *Math Card Games* book, A7.1

ACTIVITIES FOR TEACHING:	EXPLANATIONS:
Warm-up. Sing "Thirty Days has September" from the previous lesson.	

Using a year calendar, show the child that some months of the year have 30 days and some have 31. Show how February, has only 28 days, and discuss that every fourth year it has 29. Repeat the song if the child is interested.

Ask: On side 2 of the abacus, how many wires are there for the thousands? [2] How many wires for the hundreds? [2] How many wires for the tens? [2] How many wires for the ones? [2] How many wires are not used? [2]

Ask: How many ones are in 1-ten? [ten] How many tens are in 1 hundred? [ten] How many hundreds are in 1 thousand? [ten]

Adding the Place-Value Cards game. Ask the child to lay out all her place-value cards. Explain that you will say a number, which she is to compose with her place-value cards, then enter that number on side 2 of her abacus. The cards are then set aside. Next say another number, which she adds to the numbers already entered on the abacus.

All the ones, tens, and hundreds place-value cards, along with the 1000 and 2000 cards, will be used by the end of the activity. Start with the first numbers:

    5-ten
    2 hundred
    1 thousand 3 hundred
    35
    5 hundred 7

Shown on the left on the top of the next page is the abacus after the first five numbers are added. Tell the child: We need to do a trade because we have too many ones.

RightStart™ Mathematics Level B Second Edition   © Activities for Learning, Inc. 2013

ACTIVITIES FOR TEACHING:	EXPLANATIONS:

Demonstrate trading with the words, "ready, set, trade." The right hand gets *ready* to move 10 beads down, the left thumb gets *set* to move 1 ten-bead up, and the hands move simultaneously in opposite directions to *trade*. See the right figure below.

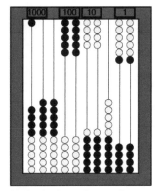

Side 2 after 5 numbers.   **Trading 10 ones for 1 ten.**

The extra bead can be moved to either of the two columns.

Ask the child: Do you see another place we need to trade? [the hundreds] The figure on the right shows that trade.

Trading 10 hundreds for 1 thousand.

Continue with remaining numbers, trading as necessary:

    1 hundred 90
    8 hundred 4
    7 hundred 81
    6 hundred 42
    2 thousand 23
    76
    4 hundred 68
    9 hundred 19

The final sum is 7995.

Bead Trading game. The Bead Trading game is found in the *Math Card Games* book, A7.1.

An error to watch for: some children after trading 10 tens for 1 hundred will continue entering ones in the tens column rather than the ones column.

Tell her to write down her number at the end of class so she may continue the activity at a later time.

In conclusion. Ask: When you play the Bead Trading game, does it take a long time to get to 10? [no] Does it take a long time to get to 100? [a little while] Does it take a long time to get to 1000? [yes]

Lesson 65: Adding 2-Digit Numbers and Tens

OBJECTIVES:
1. To learn to add a multiple of 10 to 2-digit numbers

MATERIALS:
1. AL Abacus
2. Worksheet 23, Adding 2-Digit Numbers and Tens

ACTIVITIES FOR TEACHING:

Warm-up. Sing "Thirty Days has September" from a previous lesson.

Ask: When you play the Bead Trading game, does it take a long time to get to 10? [no] Does it take a long time to get to 100? [a little while] Does it take a long time to get to 1000? [yes]

Ask the child to give the ways to make 10: 1 and what? [9] 4 and what? [6] 7 and what? [3] 2 and what? [8]

Ask the child: How many ones are in 1-ten? [ten] How many tens are in 1 hundred? [ten] How many hundreds are in 1 thousand? [ten]

Say: Count by 10s to 200. [10, 20, 30, . . . , 200]

Then say: Count by 5s to 200. [5, 10, 15, . . . , 200]

Ask the child to give the sums for 30 + 60, [90] 90 + 80, [170] 40 + 70, [110] 80 + 70, [150] and 30 + 90. [120] Tell her she may use the side 2 of the abacus if necessary.

Adding multiples of tens. Write:

        48 + 30 = ___. [78]

Ask the child to solve the equation on side 2. First enter 48 and then add 30, giving 78. See the figures below.

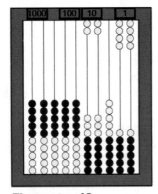 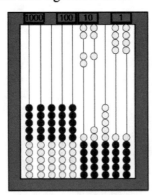

First enter 48.   **Next add 30, giving 78.**

Then ask her to find 14 + 20, [34] 57 + 40, [97] and 29 + 30. [59]

EXPLANATIONS:

RightStart™ Mathematics Level B Second Edition © Activities for Learning, Inc. 2013

ACTIVITIES FOR TEACHING:	EXPLANATIONS:

Next ask the child to enter 67 (left figure below) and move her thumb as if to add 20, but not actually touch the beads. Ask: What is 67 + 20? [87]

Research suggests that moving the fingers to simulate adding seems to be a helpful step in developing the ability to add mentally.

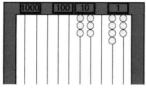
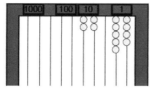

Finding 67 + 20 by mentally adding 20. [87]

Finding 49 + 30 by mentally adding 30. [79]

Ask her to find 49 + 30 by entering 49 and pretending to add 30. [79] See the right figure above.

Ask her to find 25 + 40 by entering 25 and pretending to add 40. [65]

Worksheet 23. Give the child the worksheet. Ask her to do it either by entering the first addend and pretending to add the second addend or to do it without the abacus. The problems and solutions are as follows:

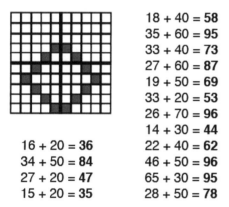

18 + 40 = **58**
35 + 60 = **95**
33 + 40 = **73**
27 + 60 = **87**
19 + 50 = **69**
33 + 20 = **53**
26 + 70 = **96**
14 + 30 = **44**
16 + 20 = **36**   22 + 40 = **62**
34 + 50 = **84**   46 + 50 = **96**
27 + 20 = **47**   65 + 30 = **95**
15 + 20 = **35**   28 + 50 = **78**

In conclusion. Ask the child to solve the following problem:

The Brown family planted 36 strawberry plants and 20 bean plants. How many plants did they plant altogether? [56]

Lesson 66: Corners™ Game

OBJECTIVES:
1. To practice scoring and trading in the hundreds

MATERIALS:
1. *Math Card Games* book, A9
2. Corners™ cards
3. AL Abacus
4. Math journal for scoring

ACTIVITIES FOR TEACHING:	EXPLANATIONS:
Warm-up. Sing "Thirty Days has September" from a previous lesson. Ask the child to solve the following problem: Andy planted 23 corn plants and 50 pumpkin plants. How many plants did he plant altogether? [73 plants] Ask: What do you need with 8 to make 10? [2] What do you need with 8 to make 15? [7] What do you need with 6 to make 10? [4] What do you need with 3 to make 5? [2] What do you need with 9 to make 15? [6] Ask the child: What is 50 + 5? [55] What is 80 + 5? [85] What is 25 + 10? [35] What is 55 + 5? [60] Ask the child: How many ones are in 1-ten? [ten] How many tens are in 1 hundred? [ten] How many hundreds are in 1 thousand? [ten] **Corners™ game.** Play the Corners™ game found in the *Math Card Games* book, A9. This game was played previously without the Corners™ option. Also the game ended when the first player reached 100 points. Playing to the corners adds more interest and excitement to the game. Now players can play to a corner, a place where the card joins two or more edges of a "corner." Both sides of the card must follow the usual rules for play: matching colors and totaling 5, 10, 15, 20 or matching the same number. Play then continues from that card. The game continues until all cards are played or no one can play.	

ACTIVITIES FOR TEACHING:

EXPLANATIONS:

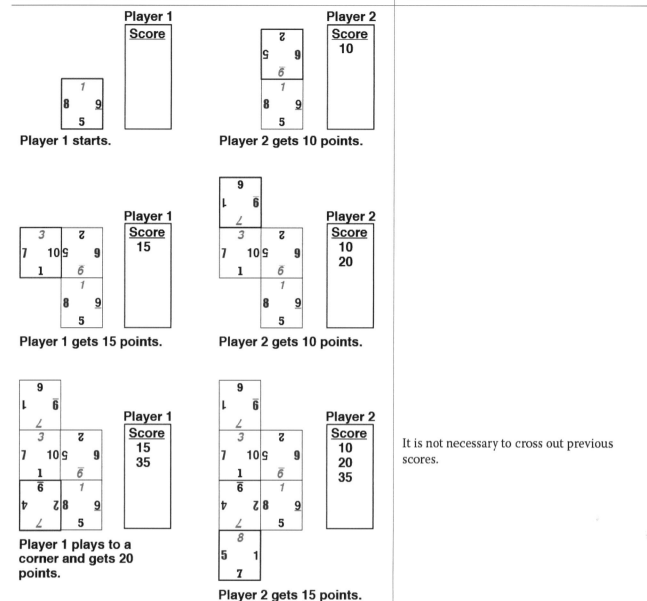

It is not necessary to cross out previous scores.

Scoring. Tell her to do her scoring on side 2 of her abacus. Remind her that to add 15, she needs to add the 10 first and then the 5. She writes only the result of the latest addition in her math journal with no intermediate steps.

The child will experience frequent trading 10 ones for 1 ten and less frequent trading 10 tens for 1 hundred.

In conclusion. Ask: What is 90 + 10? [100] What is 95 + 5? [100] What is 95 + 10? [105] What is 90 + 15? [105]

© Activities for Learning, Inc. 2013

Lesson 67: Mentally Adding 2-Digit Numbers

OBJECTIVES:
1. To mentally add two-digit numbers whose sums are less than 100

MATERIALS:
1. AL Abacus
2. *Math Card Games* book, A57
3. Worksheet 24, Mentally Adding 2-Digit Numbers

ACTIVITIES FOR TEACHING:	EXPLANATIONS:
Warm-up. Sing "Thirty Days has September" from a previous lesson. Ask: What is 80 + 10? [90] What is 85 + 5? [90] What is 95 + 15? [110] What is 90 + 15? [105] Ask the child to give the sums for 32 + 60, [92] 92 + 6, [98] and 58 + 20, [78] 78 + 8, [86] and 46 + 40, [86] 86 + 8. [94] ***Adding two-digit numbers.*** Give the child the following problem: There are 24 boys and 20 girls playing at the park. Then 3 more girls arrive. How many children are playing now at the park? [47] Read the problem several times. After the child arrive at the answer, ask her to write the equation: $$24 + 20 + 3 = 47$$ Ask the child how she did the adding. The numbers in the problem were given in the most efficient order for adding two-digit numbers orally. Discuss whether she thinks it is a good way to add the numbers. ***Practice for oral adding.*** Write and say: $$35 + 24 = \underline{}$$ Ask the child if she could add these numbers by starting with 35, then adding the tens, 20, and then 4. Model it for the child by saying: 35 + 20 = 55 and 55 + 4 = 59. Also ask her to do it on the abacus as shown on the next page. Ask the child to practice with 47 + 32. [77, 79] Encourage the child to say the intermediate sum. Repeat for 26 + 44. [66, 70]	 Studies show that in the course of everyday life, most people needing to add 2 two-digit numbers do so in their head. They do not reach for paper and pencil, nor do they use a calculator. This lesson gives the child a systematic method, or algorithm, for accomplishing mental addition. Future lessons will focus on shortcuts. Research shows that, generally, writing equations does not help young children solve problems. When the addends are not written down, starting with the first addend and adding the tens and then the ones of the second addend presents less of a memory load. For example, $$35 + 24 = 35 + 20 + 4.$$ Here the 5 is less likely to be forgotten if it is part of the 35. However, when addends are written down, adding the tens followed by the ones is also acceptable. So, 35 + 24 = (30 + 20) + (5 + 4).

ACTIVITIES FOR TEACHING: | EXPLANATIONS:

 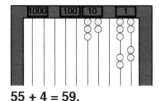

35 + 20 = 55.   **55 + 4 = 59.**

Ask her to do the following:

46 + 26 = ___. [66, 72]

The problem is shown below. The left figure shows adding 20 and the right figure shows adding the 6 ones. Trading can be done by pretending to trade or by noticing an extra 10 from the 6 + 6. Let the child decide which method to use for herself.

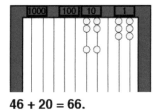 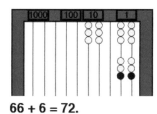

46 + 20 = 66.   **66 + 6 = 72.**

Repeat with the following:

64 + 28 = ___ [84, 92] and

46 + 39 = ___. [76, 85]

Mental Addition game. Play the Mental Addition game found in the *Math Card Games* book, A57.

Worksheet 24. Give the child the worksheet. Ask her to do it either by entering the first addend and pretending to add the second addend or to do it without the abacus. The problems and solutions are as follows:

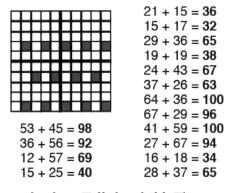

21 + 15 = **36**
15 + 17 = **32**
29 + 36 = **65**
19 + 19 = **38**
24 + 43 = **67**
37 + 26 = **63**
64 + 36 = **100**
67 + 29 = **96**

53 + 45 = **98**   41 + 59 = **100**
36 + 56 = **92**   27 + 67 = **94**
12 + 57 = **69**   16 + 18 = **34**
15 + 25 = **40**   28 + 37 = **65**

In conclusion. Tell the child: There are 24 hours in a day. Ask: Can you find out in your head, how many hours are in Saturday and Sunday? [48 hours]

LESSON 68: LONG CHAIN SOLITAIRE

OBJECTIVES:
1. To practice adding all the facts
2. To list hard to remember sums

MATERIALS:
1. Math journal
2. *Math Card Games* book, A49
3. AL Abacus

ACTIVITIES FOR TEACHING:

Warm-up. Ask: In the Corners™ game, what are the ways to make 15? [10 + 5, 9 + 6, and 8 + 7] What is the way to make 20? [two 10s] What are the ways to make 5? [1 + 4 and 2 + 3]

Ask: What is 90 + 10? [100] What is 95 + 5? [100] What is 95 + 10? [105] What is 90 + 15? [105]

Ask the child to mentally add 35 + 35, [65, 70] 52 + 31, [82, 83] 47 + 27, [67, 74] and 66 + 34. [96, 100]

Ask the child to write the equations and sums in her math journal: What is 60 + 5? [65] What is 90 + 5? [95] What is 15 + 10? [25] What is 65 + 5? [70] What is 40 + 15? [55]

Ask: On side 2 of the abacus, how many wires are there for the thousands? [2] How many wires for the hundreds? [2] How many wires for the tens? [2] How many wires for the ones? [2] How many wires are not used? [2]

Ask the child: How many ones are in 1-ten? [ten] How many tens are in 1 hundred? [ten] How many hundreds are in 1 thousand? [ten]

Hardest sums. Tell the child that today she will play Long Chain Solitaire, which is like Short Chain Solitaire, but longer. Explain that while she is playing, she should write in her math journal the two or three sums she thinks are the hardest to remember.

Long Chain Solitaire game. Play the Long Chain Solitaire game in the *Math Card Games* book, A49. The child should use the abacus for any facts she is unsure of.

The first figure on the next page shows the completed columns of the four chains. The lower figure shows the columns continuing into the next column, with the last column continuing into the first column.

EXPLANATIONS:

ACTIVITIES FOR TEACHING:	EXPLANATIONS:

A completed game of Long Chain Solitaire.

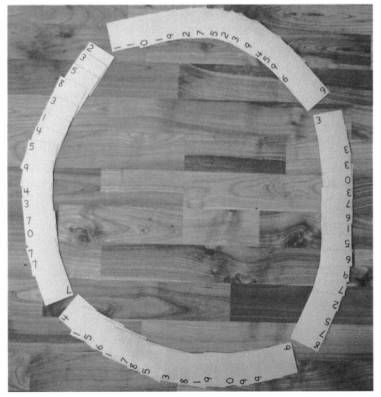

Here the four columns are connected to form a complete circle.

In conclusion. Ask: Why do think this game is called Long Chain? [The chains are long and they fit together to make a long chain.]

© Activities for Learning, Inc. 2013

Lesson 69: Addition Bingo Game

OBJECTIVES:
1. To practice adding all the facts
2. To find ways to remember hard sums

MATERIALS:
1. Math journal
2. *Math Card Games* book, A50
3. AL Abacus

ACTIVITIES FOR TEACHING:

Warm-up. Ask: What is 70 + 10? [80] What is 85 + 5? [90] What is 95 + 15? [110] What is 80 + 15? [95]

Ask the child to mentally add 45 + 45, [85, 90] 62 + 31 [92, 93] 37 + 27, [57, 64] and 56 + 34. [86, 90]

Ask the child: How many ones are in 1-ten? [ten] How many tens are in 1 hundred? [ten] How many hundreds are in 1 thousand? [ten]

Ask: 9 and what equals 15? [6] 7 and what equals 15? [8] 5 and what equals 15? [10] 8 and what equals 15? [7] 6 and what equals 15? [9]

Hardest facts. Tell her to look at her list of hardest facts from the previous lesson. Ask her to name or write one of her hardest facts. Then ask her to think how she could remember it or figure it out.

Repeat for other facts.

EXPLANATIONS:

ACTIVITIES FOR TEACHING:

Addition Bingo game. Play the Addition Bingo game in the *Math Card Games* book, A50. Encourage the child to use her abacus when needed. Play the game several times, using the same array for each game.

In conclusion. Ask her to name her three hardest facts and how she can figure them out.

EXPLANATIONS:

LESSON 70: DAYS IN A YEAR PROBLEM

OBJECTIVES:
1. To find the number of days in a year
2. To practice reading and trading quantities on side 2

MATERIALS:
1. Math journal
2. AL Abacus

ACTIVITIES FOR TEACHING:

Warm-up. Sing "Thirty Days has September" from a previous lesson.

Play the Comes After game. Ask: What month comes after March? [April] What month comes after November? [December] What month comes after June? [July]

Say: Count by tens to 200. [10, 20, 30, ..., 200]

Review the teen names by asking: What does 11 look like on the abacus? [10 and 1] What does 12 look like? [10 and 2] What does 13 look like? [10 and 3]

Ask the child how many days are in a week. [7]

Number of days in the months. Ask: How many days are in a month? [28–31] Tell the child he will make a table in his math journal giving the number of days in each month. Explain that we often abbreviate the names of the months by writing only the first three letters of the month. Ask him to write the abbreviations in a column as shown below. Ask him to write the number of days in each month in his table. Use 28 days for February.

Jan	31
Feb	28
Mar	31
Apr	30
May	31
Jun	30
Jul	31
Aug	31
Sep	30
Oct	31
Nov	30
Dec	31

Math journal: months and number of days.

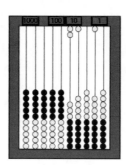

Jan has 31 days.

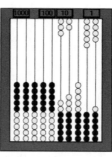

Jan and Feb have 59 days together.

Days in a year. Now ask: How many days do you think are in a year? Invite the child to make a guess. Ask how could we find out. Lead the child to think of adding on side 2 of the abacus.

Ask the child to enter January's days. Then ask him to add February's days. See the figures above.

EXPLANATIONS:

The first half of the RightStart™ Mathematics lessons referred to the child as a female and the second half refers to the child as a male.

ACTIVITIES FOR TEACHING:	EXPLANATIONS:

Ask him to read the sum by saying: How many days do January and February have together? [59] Can we trade? [no] Continue by adding March's days. Ask the child to read the sum before trading [90] and after trading. [90] See the figures below.

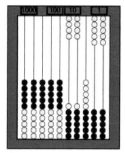 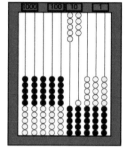

Adding Mar days gives 90.   **Still 90 after trading.**

Ask the child to enter April's days. Then ask him to read the total [120] before and after trading. Ask: Is the sum getting larger or smaller? [larger]

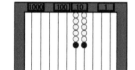 

Adding Apr days gives 120.   **Still 120 after trading.**

Continue in the same way with the remaining months. At the conclusion, discuss his guess. Also discuss why we have 365 days in a year: The earth takes 365 days and part of another day to travel around the sun.

Leap year. Tell the child that we have leap year only every four years. Ask: What change do you need to make in the listing of the number of days in the months for a leap year? [February has 29 days.] Then ask: How many days are in a leap year? [366]

Dishes in the cupboard. Ask the child to make a list of the different dishes in the cupboard, and count the number of each type. He may draw pictures of plates, cups, bowls, and so forth, and then write tally marks beside the pictures to indicate the number of each type. Then he writes the number beside each set of tally marks.

After he has seen the numbers, ask him to guess the sum of them. Let the child work alone to add the list. Assist only as necessary.

When he has completed the work, ask him if his answer makes sense—if he thinks he is right. Ask how many there would be if he broke a dish or bought a new one.

In conclusion. Ask: How many days are in a regular year? [365] How many days are in a leap year? [366]

© Activities for Learning, Inc. 2013

Lesson 71: Adding 1, 10, and 100

OBJECTIVES:
1. To add 1, 10, and 100 to various numbers

MATERIALS:
1. *Math Card Games* book, N42
2. AL Abacus
3. Base-10 cards
4. Place-value cards
5. Worksheet 25, Adding 1, 10, and 100

ACTIVITIES FOR TEACHING:

Warm-up. Ask: How many days are in a year? [365] How many days are in a leap year? [366]

Ask the child to count by tens to 300. [10, 20, 30, . . . , 300]

Ask the child to count by fives to 100. [5, 10, 15, . . . , 100]

Tell the child that you will say three numbers; he is to think about the pattern. Ask the child what number comes next: 4, 6, 8; [10] 35, 40, 45; [50] 6, 5, 4. [3]

Station Game. Play the following variation of the Station Game in the *Math Card Games* book, N42. Set up the station as follows:

  a) place-value cards;

  b) abacus, side 2;

  c) base-10 cards, and

  d) abacus, side 1 and abacus tiles. See the figure below.

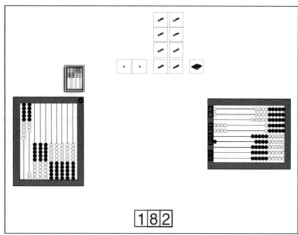

Sample set up for the Station game, showing 182 on the place-value cards, base-10 cards and abacuses.

EXPLANATIONS:

ACTIVITIES FOR TEACHING:	EXPLANATIONS:

The players sit at an available station. Tell the child to enter or make 82 with the material in front of him. Tell him to move to another open station and make 82.

Next tell him to add 1. [Materials will say 83.] Tell him to add 10. [Materials will say 93.] Tell him to add 100. [Materials will say 193.] (The child using side 1 will need to use a base-10 card for a hundred.) Ask: What is your sum? [193]

Before the next round, clear the materials. Repeat with entering 39, then adding 1, [40] adding 10, [50] and adding 100. [150] Remind him to trade when he can.

Clear and repeat with entering 108, then adding 1, [109] adding 10, [119] and adding 100. [219]

Clear and repeat with entering 2010, then adding 1, [2011] adding 10, [2021] and adding 100. [2121]

Worksheet 25. Give the child the worksheet. Explain that this worksheet is a little different from the Station Game. Here he will be adding 1, 10, and 100 to the same number.

Tell him he can use whatever materials he needs, if any. The problems and solutions are below:

Add 1		Add 10		Add 100	
4	**5**	4	**14**	4	**104**
67	**68**	67	**77**	67	**167**
99	**100**	99	**109**	99	**199**
200	**201**	200	**210**	200	**300**
238	**239**	238	**248**	238	**338**
493	**494**	493	**503**	493	**593**
790	**791**	790	**800**	790	**890**
906	**907**	906	**916**	906	**1006**
1010	**1011**	1010	**1020**	1010	**1110**
3025	**3026**	3025	**3035**	3025	**3125**

In conclusion. Ask the child: What year is this? What year will it be next year? What year will it be in 10 years? What year will it be in 100 years?

© Activities for Learning, Inc. 2013

Lesson 72: Adding 4-Digit Numbers

OBJECTIVES:
1. To learn to add 4-digit numbers on side 2 of the abacus

MATERIALS:
1. AL Abacus
2. Worksheet 26, Adding 4-Digit Numbers

ACTIVITIES FOR TEACHING:

Warm-up. Ask the child to say the days of the week and the months of the year. Then play the Comes Before game with the days and months.

Ask the child what number comes next: 200, 300, 400; [500] 155, 160, 165; [170] 530, 540, 550; [560] and 402, 401, 400. [399]

Ask: How many days are in a year? [365] How many days are in a leap year? [366]

Ask the child to count by tens to 400. [10, 20, 30, . . . , 400]

Ask the child to count by fives to 200. [5, 10, 15, . . . , 200]

Adding 4-digit numbers on side 2. Tell the child that today he will add 4-digit numbers on his abacus. Write the following in the vertical format:

$$\begin{array}{r} 4817 \\ +\ 2639 \\ \hline \end{array}$$

Ask the child to enter the first quantity on side 2 of the abacus as shown in the left figure. Explain: We will start adding with the ones. Adding 9 ones is shown in the right figure below.

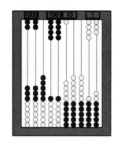   4817
                        + 2639

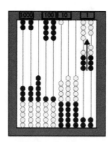   4817
                        + 2639

The first addend entered.   **Adding 9 ones.**

Ask: Do we need to trade? [yes] After the trade ask: What do we have now? [6 in ones place] Write a 6 in the ones places. Ask: Did anything else change? [added another ten] Say: Let's show it by writing a little 1 with the other tens. See the left figure on the next page.

EXPLANATIONS:

RightStart™ Mathematics Level B Second Edition   © Activities for Learning, Inc. 2013

ACTIVITIES FOR TEACHING:

Add the 3 tens. See the right figure below. Ask: How many tens do we have now? [5 tens] Do we need to trade? [no] Write the 5 tens.

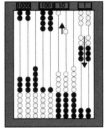 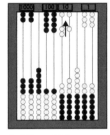

Trading the ones. Adding 3 tens.

```
      1              1
   4817           4817
 + 2639         + 2639
      6             56
```

Continue by adding the 6 hundreds. See the left figure below. Ask: Do we need to trade? [yes] After the trade ask: What do we have now? [4 in hundreds place] Write a 4 in the hundreds places. Ask: Did anything else change? [added another thousand] Where do we write it? [with the other thousand] See the right figure below.

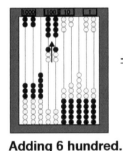 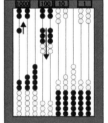

Adding 6 hundred. Trading hundreds.

```
      1             1 1
   4817           4817
 + 2639         + 2639
     56            456
```

Add the 2 thousands as shown below.

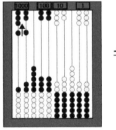 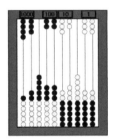

Adding 2 thousand. The final sum.

```
    1 1            1 1
   4817           4817
 + 2639         + 2639
    456           7456
```

Worksheet 26. Give the child the worksheet and ask him to do the first four problems using his abacus. The solutions are:

```
   1438            2948
 + 6381          + 5645
   7819            8593

   3454            4821
 + 5436          + 1481
   8890            6302
```

In conclusion. Ask: Which is easier to use to add, base-10 cards or the abacus?

EXPLANATIONS:

This activity is preparation for the standard paper and pencil addition algorithm. Therefore, it is vitally important to record the sum and any carry after each step.

LESSON 73: CONTINUING THE PATTERN

OBJECTIVES:
1. To connect evens with counting by 2s
2. To recognize counting patterns of 1s, 2s, 5s, and 10s
3. To continue a counting pattern

MATERIALS:
1. Worksheet 26, Adding 4-Digit Numbers
2. AL Abacus
3. Worksheet 27, Continuing the Pattern

ACTIVITIES FOR TEACHING:	EXPLANATIONS:

Warm-up. Ask the child to use his abacus to do the next two problems on the worksheet from the last lesson as shown below:

```
  5095        6476
+ 3564      + 2592
  8659        9068
```

Tell the child that you will say three numbers; he is to think about the pattern. Ask the child what number comes next: 8, 6, 4; [2] 25, 35, 45; [55] 10, 9, 8. [7]

Counting by 1s. Ask: When you count by 1s on the abacus, how many beads do you move over at a time? [1] Ask him to count by 1s, starting with 20; move over one bead at a time on the abacus. Stop at 40. [20, 21, 22, . . . , 40]

Counting by 10s. Next ask: When you count by 10s, how many beads do you move over at a time? [10] Then tell him: Count by 10s to 100, but start with 50. Move over 10 beads at a time. [50, 60, 70, . . . , 100]

Counting by 5s. Continue with counting by 5s: When you count by 5s, how many beads do you enter at a time? [5] Challenge him to count by 5s, starting with 35, and continuing to 100. [35, 40, 45, . . . , 100]

Counting by 2s. Now tell him we are going to count by 2s. How many beads do we enter at a time? [2] Start with 16 and continue to 40. [16, 18, 20, . . ., 40] Then ask: Did counting by 2s remind you of something else? [even numbers] Ask: Why is counting by 2s the same as saying the even numbers?

Naming the pattern. Tell the child that you are going to say 3 numbers and that he is to name the pattern. Start with:

        10   20   30   [10s]

Continue with the next pattern:

        30   32   34   [2s]

ACTIVITIES FOR TEACHING:	EXPLANATIONS:

Ask how he knew it was counting by 2s. If necessary, ask if he could use an abacus to show someone how to do it. [Enter 30; then see how many beads that are needed to make it 32, which is 2. Enter 2 more to see if you get 34.] See the figure below.

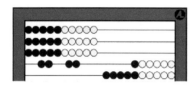

Finding the pattern for 30, 32, 34, by entering 30 and noting how many are needed to have 32.

Give the child one more pattern:

    35   40   45   [5s]

Write several patterns for the child to name:

    78   79   80   [1s]
    60   70   80   [10s]
    14   16   18   [2s]

Continuing the pattern. Write:

    40   50   60   ___   ___

and ask: What pattern do you see? [counting by 10s] What two numbers come next? [70, 80]

Repeat and ask the child for the next two numbers.

    14   15   16   ___   ___   [17, 18]
    15   20   25   ___   ___   [30, 35]

Worksheet 27. Give him the worksheet. The problems and solutions follow:

    7   8   9   **10**   **11**
    10   12   14   **16**   **18**
    30   40   50   **60**   **70**
    60   65   70   **75**   **80**
    24   26   28   **30**   **32**
    15   20   25   **30**   **35**
    86   87   88   **89**   **90**
    77   78   79   **80**   **81**
    76   78   80   **82**   **84**
    60   70   80   **90**   **100**
    35   40   45   **50**   **55**
    14   16   18   **20**   **22**

Let the child decide whether or not to use an abacus.

In conclusion. Name the next even number after these numbers: 64, [66] 98, [100] 222, [224] and 406. [408]

© Activities for Learning, Inc. 2013

Lesson 74: Review

OBJECTIVES:
1. To review concepts since the previous assessment

MATERIALS:
1. *Yellow is the Sun* book
2. Worksheet 28, Review
3. AL Abacus

ACTIVITIES FOR TEACHING:	EXPLANATIONS:

Warm-up. Read the book *Yellow is the Sun* to the child.
Patterning. Give the child the worksheet. Have him look at the patterns. Say:
  1. Circle the ABC pattern.

  2. Circle the increasing pattern.

Vertex and diagonals. Ask the child to draw a rectangle. Say:
  3. Put a dot at a vertex.
  4. Draw a diagonal line from that vertex.
[Many solutions are possible, one is shown above]
Greater than and equal symbols. For the next three problems, ask the child to insert the symbols to make the equation correct.
  5. 6 > 4
  6. 7 + 8 = 8 + 7
  7. 200 > 50 + 50
Strategies. Complete the following problems using the strategies learned in previous lessons.
  8. 79 + 5 = **84**
  9. 59 + 4 = **63**
 10. 38 + 4 = **42**
 11. 68 + 7 = **75**
 12. 47 + 6 = **53**
 13. 88 + 6 = **94**
	This lesson is a review of concepts learned so far. It is designed to prepare the child for the upcoming assessment lesson.
	
	The child may use the abacus when needed.

RightStart™ Mathematics Level B Second Edition   © Activities for Learning, Inc. 2013

ACTIVITIES FOR TEACHING:

Thousands. Ask the child to fill in the answers to the following questions:

14. How many 1s in 10? [10]

15. How many 10s in 100? [10]

16. How many 100s in 1000? [10]

Finding missing addends with part-whole circle sets. Ask the child to fill in the part-whole circle sets with the correct numbers. [Many solutions are possible.]

17.   18.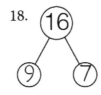

Adding three numbers. Ask the child to answer the following questions:

19. 3 + 5 + 5 = **13**

20. 2 + 7 + 8 = **17**

21. 10 + 2 + 3 = **15**

Adding multiples of ten. Have the child answer the following problems:

22. 18 + 40 = **58**

23. 35 + 60 = **95**

Days in a year. Ask:

24. How many days are in a year? [365]

25. How many days are in a leap year? [366]

Four digit addition.

26. 1438
    + 6381
    ──────
     7819

27. 2948
    + 5645
    ──────
     8593

28. 3454
    + 5436
    ──────
     8890

29. 4821
    + 1481
    ──────
     6302

EXPLANATIONS:

Lesson 75: Review Games

OBJECTIVES:
1. To review concepts using games

MATERIALS:
1. *Yellow is the Sun* book
2. AL Abacus
3. *Math Card Games* book
4. Place-value cards

ACTIVITIES FOR TEACHING:	EXPLANATIONS:
Warm-up. Read the book *Yellow is the Sun* to the child. Ask: What do you need with 8 to make 10? [2] What do you need with 8 to make 15? [7] What do you need with 6 to make 10? [4] What do you need with 3 to make 5? [2] What do you need with 9 to make 15? [6] Ask the child: What is 50 + 5? [55] What is 80 + 5? [85] What is 25 + 10? [35] What is 55 + 5? [60] Ask: On side 2 of the abacus, how many wires are there for the thousands? [2] How many wires for the hundreds? [2] How many wires for the tens? [2] How many wires for the ones? [2] How many wires are not used? [2] Ask the child: How many ones are in 1-ten? [ten] How many tens are in 1 hundred? [ten] How many hundreds are in 1 thousand? [ten] *Strategies.* Play the Addition Bingo game in the *Math Card Games* book, A50.	This lesson is a review of concepts learned so far through playing games. It is designed to prepare the students for the assessment in the next lesson. The child may use the abacus if needed.

RightStart™ Mathematics Level B Second Edition © Activities for Learning, Inc. 2013

ACTIVITIES FOR TEACHING:	EXPLANATIONS:

Thousands. Play the Bead Trading game in the *Math Card Games* book, A7.1.

Also play this more difficult version of Can You Find from the *Math Card Games* book, N43. Ask the child to lay out all the place-value cards. When cards are asked for, he picks them up and stacks them, but does not set them aside. Below are some suggested numbers:

1. Can you find 400?
2. Can you find 43?
3. Can you find 1004?
4. Can you find 570?
5. Can you find 6209?

Addition. Play the Mental Addition game found in the *Math Card Games* book, A57.

Lesson 76: Assessment 2

OBJECTIVES:
1. To assess concepts since the previous assessment

MATERIALS:
1. *Yellow is the Sun* book
2. AL Abacus
3. Worksheet 29, Assessment 2

ACTIVITIES FOR TEACHING:

Warm-up. Read the book *Yellow is the Sun* to the child.

Patterning. Show the child the following patterns on his worksheet. Have the child read and answer the following questions:

1. Circle the ABC pattern.

2. Circle the increasing pattern.

Vertex and diagonals. Ask the child to draw a square.
3. Now ask him to put a dot at a vertex.
4. From that vertex, ask the child to draw a diagonal line.

[Many solutions are possible, one is shown above]

Greater than and equal symbols. For the next 3 problems, ask the child to insert the symbols to make the equation correct.

5. 6 + 8 ⊜ 8 + 6
6. 300 ⊙ 60 + 60
7. 7 ⊙ 5

Strategies. Complete the following problems using the strategies learned.

8. 89 + 5 = **94**
9. 49 + 4 = **53**
10. 48 + 4 = **52**
11. 78 + 7 = **85**
12. 37 + 6 = **43**
13. 78 + 6 = **84**

EXPLANATIONS:

This lesson is an assessment of concepts learned so far.

The child may use the abacus where needed.

ACTIVITIES FOR TEACHING:

Thousands. Ask the child to fill in the answers to the following questions:

14. How many 1s in 10? [**10**]
15. How many 10s in 100? [**10**]
16. How many 100s in 1000? [**10**]

Finding missing addends with part-whole circle sets. Ask the child to fill in the part-whole circle sets with the correct numbers. [Many solutions are possible.]

17.
18.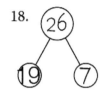

Addition. Ask the child to answer the following questions.

19. 5 + 5 + 5 = **15**
20. 3 + 6 + 9 = **18**
21. 11 + 1 + 4 = **16**

Adding Multiples of ten. Have the child answer the following problems.

22. 28 + 40 = **68**
23. 35 + 50 = **85**

Days in a year. Ask:

24. How many days are in a week? [7]
25. How many days are in a year? [365]
26. How many days are in a leap year? [366]

Four digit addition.

27. 1488
    + 3631
    5119

28. 4298
    + 4565
    8863

29. 4534
    + 3654
    8188

30. 2148
    + 4181
    6329

EXPLANATIONS:

© Activities for Learning, Inc. 2013

Lesson 77: Hours on a Clock

OBJECTIVES:
1. To begin learning the positions of the hour numbers on a clock

MATERIALS:
1. Worksheet 26, Adding 4-Digit Numbers
2. AL Abacus
3. Geared clock
4. Clock without Numbers (Appendix p. 9)
5. Sets of hour number cards
6. *Math Card Games* book, C2

ACTIVITIES FOR TEACHING:	EXPLANATIONS:

Warm-up. Ask the child to use his abacus to do the last two problems on Worksheet 26 used in a previous lesson, as shown below:
 	
    7744   8163
  + 1967   + 337
    9711   8500
 	
Review the partitioning of 15 by drawing a part-whole circle set and writing 15 as the whole. Write 5 as one part and ask the child for the other part. [10] Erase the parts; write another part, and ask the child to find the corresponding part. [8 & 7, 9 & 6]
 	
Ask the child to count by tens to 75 on the abacus, but start with 5. Enter 5, add two fives making 15, add two more fives to make 25, and so forth. [5, 10, 15, . . . , 75]
 	
Ask the child to say the days of the week and the months of the year. Then play the Comes Before game with the days and months.
 	
The hands on the clock. Give the child the geared clock and give him some time for free discovery. Explain that the *hour hand*, the shorter hand, tells us the hour. Further explain that the numbers 1 to 12 that we see on clock are the hour numbers. Ask: What color is the hour hand on your clock? [red] What color are the hour numbers? [red]
 	
Point out the *minute hand* and say: The minute hand is the longer hand and it tells parts of an hour, called minutes. There are 60 minutes in each hour. Ask: What color is the minute hand on your clock? [blue] What color are the minute numbers? [blue]
 	
Numbers around a clock. Point to the number at the top and say: Hours start at the top. Read this number. [12] Then point to the 1 and tell him to read it. [1] Continue around the clock. [1, . . . , 11]
	
	The terms *hour hand* and *minute hand* are more descriptive of their roles than are the immature names of *little hand* and *big hand*.
	
	Clock colors may vary with models.

ACTIVITIES FOR TEACHING:	EXPLANATIONS:

Show him the Clock without Numbers, which has 12 marks, and the hour cards. Ask him: How many hour numbers do we usually see on an clock? [12]

Give one set of hour cards to the child. Ask the child to take the 1 card to place it in the first position after the star. Then point to the 2 position and have the child lay the 2 card down. See the figure below. Continue until all hour cards are placed around the clock.

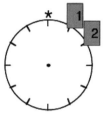

Placing the hour cards around the clock.

Arm positions. Ask the child to stand facing the clock. Point to the 12 and ask him to raise either arm like they are pointing to the 12. Then ask him move to the 1 position. Continue to 12. See the figures below.

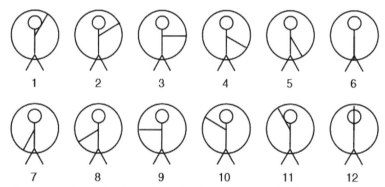

Arm positions for learning the hours on a clock.

Hour Memory game. Have the child play the Hour Memory game found in the *Math Card Games* book, C2. Tell him to play it twice and then play the variation.

In conclusion. Ask: What number is at the top of the clock? [12] What number is at the bottom of the clock? [6]

Lesson 78: Hours and Half-Hours

OBJECTIVES:
1. To review the term *half*
2. To learn the tem *o'clock*
3. To tell time to the hour and half-hour

MATERIALS:
1. Sums Practice 1, found after math journal
2. AL Abacus
3. *Math Card Games* book, C4 and C5
4. Geared clock
5. Dry erase board
6. Worksheet 30, Hours and Half-Hours

ACTIVITIES FOR TEACHING:	EXPLANATIONS:

Warm-up. Ask the child to use his abacus to do the first two problems on Sums Practice 1 as shown below:
 	
  9599   2563
+ 106   + 3861
  9705   6424
 	
Ask: What number is at the top of the clock? [12] What number is at the bottom of the clock? [6]
 	
Ask the child to count aloud by 5s to 100. [5, 10, 15, . . . , 100]
 	
Ask: What day comes after December 10th? [December 11th] What day comes after January 4th? [January 5th] What day comes after January 31st? [February 1st] What day comes after March 31st? [April 1st]
 	
Ask him to say the hours on a clock while using his arm positions.
 	
Placing the Hour Card game. Have the child play the Hours Memory game found in the *Math Card Games* book, C4. Play it twice.
 	
Secret Hour Cards game. Next tell him to play Secret Hour Cards game found in the *Math Card Games* book, C5.
 	
The o'clocks. Set the clock to 1:00 and tell the child that the time is one o'clock. Explain that *o'clock* means the beginning of the hour and that hours begin when the minute hand is at the top of the clock. Ask him to set the clock to one o'clock. Continue for 2:00 and other o'clocks.
 	
Set the clock to various o'clock times and ask the child to read them.
 	
Writing the o'clocks. Write 1:00 and tell the child: This is how we write one o'clock. Repeat for 2:00.
 	
Write 4:00 and ask the child to read it. Repeat for 12:00 and 8:00.
	These two games continue to work on placement of the hour numbers around the clock.
	
	If still more work is needed for learning the placement of the hour numbers, play games C6, C7, C8, or C9.
	
	The hands on these clocks can be turned either by turning the minute hand or by turning the knob in the back of the clock.

ACTIVITIES FOR TEACHING:	EXPLANATIONS:

Half-hour. Ask the child to watch the clock and see what happens to the minute hand when you move the hour hand from 10:00 to 11:00. [The minute hand moves all the way around.] Repeat for 11:00 to 12:00.

Tell him to stand and move one of his arms around in a circle, starting at the top. Then tell him to do it again, but stop halfway. See the figures below.

  Making a whole circle and making a half circle.

Start at 12:00 on the clock ask the child to tell you to stop when the minute hand is halfway around. Then ask: What happened to the hour hand? [halfway between 12 and 1] Tell him we say the time is 12:30. Repeat starting at 1:00. Ask him to set the clock for 1:30, 2:30, and 3:30.

Write 4:30 and ask the child: Where are the hands for this time? [hour hand halfway between 4 and 5 and minute hand straight down] Repeat for 9:30 and 11:30.

Drawing hands. Draw a clock on the dry erase board. Show the child how to draw the hands on a clock: Start at the number and draw to the center. Also show him how to draw an arrow: start at the point and draw a short line away from the end of the line on both sides. See the figures below.

Steps for drawing the hands on a clock.

When drawing clock hands, be sure to emphasize starting at the outside and drawing toward the center.

Write 5:00 and ask the child to draw the hands for the clock. Repeat for 6:30 and 11:00.

Worksheet 30. Give the child worksheet. The hands to be written in are: **10:00, 6:00, 8:30, 3:30.**

The numbers to be written in are: **4:30, 12:00, 9:00, 12:30.**

In conclusion. Tell the child: At midnight both hands are straight up. What time is that? [12:00] Say: There are 30 minutes in half an hour. How many minutes are in a whole hour? [60]

© Activities for Learning, Inc. 2013

Lesson 79: Minutes on the Clock

OBJECTIVES:
1. To begin learning the location of the minutes on a clock

MATERIALS:
1. Sums Practice 1, found after math journal
2. AL Abacus
3. Geared clock
4. Clock with Minutes (Appendix p. 10)
5. Sets of minute number cards
6. *Math Card Games* book, C10, C11, and C12

ACTIVITIES FOR TEACHING:	EXPLANATIONS:

Warm-up. Ask the child to use his abacus to do the next two problems on Sums Practice 1 as shown below:
 	
   7932   2787
 + 1452   + 5633
   9384   8420
 	
Say: There are 60 minutes in an hour. How many minutes are in a half hour? [30]
 	
Ask: What number is at the top of the clock? [12] What number is at the bottom of the clock? [6]
 	
Ask the child to count by fives to 75. [5, 10, 15, . . , 75]
 	
Ask the child: What are the names of the two hands on a clock [hour and minute] and what they tell? [The hour tells the hour; the minute hand tells the number of minutes after the hour.]
 	
Minute Cards around the Clock game. Explain to the child that he will work with the minute numbers, the usually invisible numbers on a clock. Show him the clock. Tell him that the little marks around the clock are minutes. The thicker marks are shared with the hour hand.
 	
Give the child the Clock with Minutes and a set of minute cards. Tell him that the two dots before the number tells that it is a minute number.
 	
Play the Minute Cards around the Clock game from the *Math Card Games* book, C10. See the figures on the top of the next page.	

RightStart™ Mathematics Level B Second Edition

ACTIVITIES FOR TEACHING:

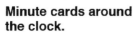

Minute cards around the clock.

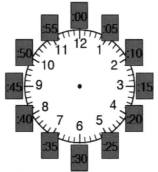

The clock completed.

When the child has all his cards in place, ask him to read them in order; tell him we read two zeroes (:00) as *o'clock* and we read the zero in front of the 5 as *oh*. [o'clock, oh 5, 10, 15, . . . , 55] Ask: What kind of counting does it sound like? [mostly, counting by 5s] Why do we count by 5s? [5 minutes between each number]

Arm positions. Ask the child to use arm positions while saying the minutes. See the figures below. Ask him to move to the 30 position, [straight down] to the 15 position, [to the right side] and to the 45 position. [to the left side]

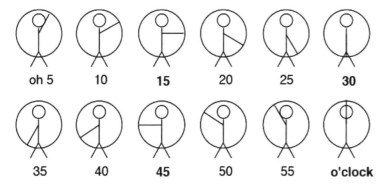

Minute Memory game. Ask the child to play the Minute Memory game, found in the *Math Card Games* book, C11.

Minute Solitaire. Tell the child to play the Minute Solitaire game, found in the *Math Card Games* book, C12. Tell him to use his clock for reference.

In conclusion. Ask: How many hour numbers does the clock show? [12] Where do the minutes start on the clock? [at the top] How many minutes in an hour? [60]

EXPLANATIONS:

A person learns the minutes' place easier by using a reference rather than by counting by 5s each time.

Lesson 80: More Minutes on the Clock

OBJECTIVES:
1. To continue learning the minutes numbers on a clock

MATERIALS:
1. Sums Practice 1
2. AL Abacus
3. Geared clock
4. Sets of minute number cards
5. Clock with Minutes (Appendix p. 10)
6. *Math Card Games* book, C13 and C14

ACTIVITIES FOR TEACHING:	EXPLANATIONS:

Warm-up. Ask the child to use his abacus to do the next two problems on Sums Practice 1 as shown below:
 	
    1655   7667
   + 7181   + 432
    8836   8099
 	
Ask: How many hour numbers does the clock show? [12] Where do the minutes start on the clock? [at the top] Say: There are 30 minutes in half an hour. How many minutes in an hour? [60]
 	
Ask the child to count using the clock hour numbers and arm motions. Repeat with the clock minute numbers.
 	
Ask him to name the ways to make 15. [10 + 5, 9 + 6, 8 + 7]
 	
Minute numbers. Ask the child to look at his geared clock. Ask: How many minutes are between the 12 and the 1? [5 minutes] How many spaces are between the 12 and 1? [5]
 	
Ask: How many groups of five are between the 12 and 2? [2] How many groups of five are between the 12 and 3? [3] How many groups of five are between the 12 and 4? [4]
 	
Explain that he can use his abacus to find the number of minutes. Tell him that to find the number of minutes at 2, enter 2 groups of five as shown on the next page in the left figure.
 	
Tell him: Use your abacus to find the number of minutes after the hour when the minute hand is at 3. [15] See the right figure on the next page. Tell him to check on his clock.	

RightStart™ Mathematics Level B Second Edition   © Activities for Learning, Inc. 2013

ACTIVITIES FOR TEACHING:

EXPLANATIONS:

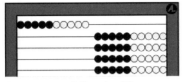 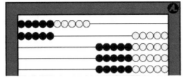

2 groups of five is 10.   3 groups of five is 15.

Repeat for 7 [35] and 8. [40]

Give the child a set of minute cards. Point to 6 on the Clock with Minutes. Ask the child to place the matching minute card near the 6. Then point to the 2 and have the child place the matching card near the 2. See the figure below.

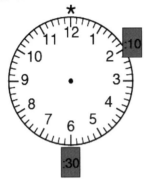

Placing the minute cards for the number at 6 and 2.

Continue asking for the numbers at random until all minute cards are placed around the clock.

Placing the Minute Card game. Play the Placing the Minute Card game found in the *Math Card Games* book, C13. Have him play it several times.

Secret Minute Cards game. Play the Secret Minute Cards game found in the *Math Card Games* book, C14.

In conclusion. Ask: Which is larger, an hour or a minute? [hour] How many minutes between the numbers on a clock? [5]

The basics of telling time are quite simple, but practice is necessary to obtain fluency.

© Activities for Learning, Inc. 2013

Lesson 81: Hours and Minutes

OBJECTIVES:
1. To continue learning the location of the minutes on a clock
2. To practice reading and setting a clock to the 5-minute marks

MATERIALS:
1. AL Abacus
2. Geared clock
3. Hour and minute number cards
4. Worksheet 31, Hours and Minutes

ACTIVITIES FOR TEACHING:	EXPLANATIONS:
Warm-up. Ask: Which is larger, an hour or a minute? [hour] How many minutes between the numbers on a clock? [5]	
Ask the child to say the clock hour numbers and use the arm motions. Repeat with the clock minute numbers.	
Say: There are 60 minutes in an hour. How many minutes are in a half hour? [30]	
Ask: What day comes after November 10th? [November 11th] What day comes after September 4th? [September 5th] What day comes after July 31st? [August 1st] What day comes after October 31st? [November 1st]	
Hours in a day. Give the child the clock. Ask: How many hours are there on a clock? [12] Tell him that every day the hour hand goes around twice, or two times. Ask: How many hours are in a whole day? [24 hours]	
Show him 12:00 on the clock and ask: What time is it? [12:00] Discuss that one 12:00 is called noon and that is around lunchtime, and the other 12:00 is called midnight. Ask: What are you usually doing at midnight? [sleeping]	
Choose another time that the child can relate to, such as 9:00. Ask: What are you doing at 9:00 in the morning? [perhaps eating breakfast] What are you doing at 9:00 in the evening? [perhaps getting ready for bed]	
Telling time on the clock. Give the child a set of hour clock cards and a set of minute cards. Set the clock for 2:30. Ask the child to match the hour card and the minute card and set them near the clock. See figure on top of next page.	

RightStart™ Mathematics Level B Second Edition © Activities for Learning, Inc. 2013

ACTIVITIES FOR TEACHING:	EXPLANATIONS:
	If there are fewer than 24 children, give some children two cards.

The clock set to 2:30.

Continue with the times below, which uses all the cards:

    8:05
    9:35
    4:00
    10:40
    6:15
    12:20
    11:50
    3:10
    1:25
    7:55
    5:45

Setting clocks. Ask the child to sets his clock to 1:05. Repeat for 2:15, 3:35, and 4:50.

Worksheet 31. Give the child the worksheet, where he draws in the hands and also write the time to the nearest 5 minutes.

The hands to be written in are:
    8:10   8:45   8:30   8:05

The numbers to be written in are:
    8:20   8:50   8:35   8:15

In conclusion. Ask: At which o'clock do the hands form a straight line? [6 o'clock] At which o'clock are the hands on top of each other. [12 o'clock]

© Activities for Learning, Inc. 2013

Lesson 82: Adding 4-Digit Numbers on Paper

OBJECTIVES:
1. To help the child discover how to add 4-digit numbers on paper

MATERIALS:
1. AL Abacus
2. Sums Practice 1
3. Worksheet 32, Adding 4-Digit Numbers on Paper
4. *Math Card Games* book, A9

ACTIVITIES FOR TEACHING:

Warm-up. Ask: Which is larger, an hour or a minute? [hour] At which o'clock do the hands form a straight line? [6 o'clock] At which o'clock are the hands on top of each other? [12 o'clock]

Ask the child to count using the clock hour numbers and arm motions. Repeat with the clock minute numbers.

Ask the child to count by tens on the abacus, but start with 5 up to 95. Enter 5, add two fives making 15, add two more fives to make 25, and so forth. [5, 10, 15, . . . , 95]

Ask the child to say the days of the week and the months of the year. Then play the Comes Before game with the days and months.

Sums greater than 9999. Ask the child to use his abacus to add the next problem on his Sums Practice 1, shown below:

```
  3378
+ 7865
```

```
   111
  3378
+ 7865
 11243
```

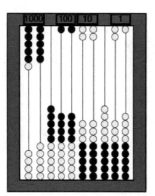

The sum is 11 thousand 243.

Ask: How many thousands are there? [11] Explain that he can pretend to trade, or just write down 11.

Adding without the abacus. Ask the child if he thinks he could do the last problem on that page without the abacus. Give only necessary help.

```
   111
  3568
+ 4636
  8204
```

EXPLANATIONS:

Be sure that the child knows most of his addition facts and are very proficient with adding 4-digit numbers on side 2 of the abacus.

ACTIVITIES FOR TEACHING:

EXPLANATIONS:

Help 1. Tell the child to imagine adding the ones on the abacus. Ask: What is 8 + 6? [14] Is there a trade? [yes] Where do you write the 4? [in ones column] Where do you write the trade? [above the tens column] What do you do next? [add tens] Continue if necessary.

Help 2. The child may respond with the following analysis. First ask him to add the number on the abacus and record the answer as usual. Then point to the ones column and ask: What is 8 + 6? [14] Where did you write the 4? Where did you write the 1? [with the tens]

Next point to the tens column and ask: How much are the tens, 1 + 6 + 3? [10] What do you write in the tens column? [0] Continue, or let the child explain the hundreds and thousands.

Practice. Write the following problem:

$$\begin{array}{r} 2563 \\ + 3594 \\ \hline \end{array}$$

and ask the child to tell you how solve.

$$\begin{array}{r} 11 \\ 2563 \\ + 3594 \\ \hline \mathbf{6157} \end{array}$$

Worksheet 32. Give the child the worksheet and challenge him to do them without the abacus. The problems and solutions follow:

$$\begin{array}{r} 4829 \\ + 3256 \\ \hline \mathbf{8085} \end{array} \qquad \begin{array}{r} 2467 \\ + 2165 \\ \hline \mathbf{4632} \end{array}$$

$$\begin{array}{r} 7215 \\ + 1835 \\ \hline \mathbf{9050} \end{array} \qquad \begin{array}{r} 4765 \\ + 4776 \\ \hline \mathbf{9541} \end{array}$$

$$\begin{array}{r} 2358 \\ + 5988 \\ \hline \mathbf{8346} \end{array} \qquad \begin{array}{r} 8794 \\ + 3695 \\ \hline \mathbf{12489} \end{array}$$

Corners™ game. Play the Corners™ game found in the *Math Card Games* book, A9. Each player can start with a score of 1000 and add on from there.

In conclusion. Ask: What's the hardest thing to remember when adding 4-digit numbers?

© Activities for Learning, Inc. 2013

ENRICHMENT LESSON 83: ADDING VERY LARGE NUMBERS

OBJECTIVES:
1. To help the child discover individually how to add 4-digit numbers on paper

MATERIALS:
1. Worksheet 33-1, Adding Very Large Numbers
2. Worksheet 33-2, Adding Very Large Numbers
3. *Math Card Games* book, A9

ACTIVITIES FOR TEACHING:	EXPLANATIONS:
Warm-up. Ask: How many days are in a year? [365] How many days are in a leap year? [366]	
Ask the child to count aloud by tens to 300. [10, 20, 30, . . . , 300]	
Ask the child to count aloud by fives to 100. [5, 10, 15, . . . , 100]	
Tell the child that you will say three numbers; they are to think about the pattern. Ask the child what number comes next: 4, 6, 8; [10] 35, 40, 45; [50] 6, 5, 4. [3]	
Ask the child what number comes next: 200, 300, 400; [500] 155, 160, 165; [170] 530, 540, 550; [560] and 402, 401, 400. [399]	
Worksheets 33-1 and 33-2. These worksheets are for the child who wants to be challenged with adding larger numbers. Here the child adds the same number 10 times. The problems and solutions are as follows:	Many children enjoy the challenge of adding large numbers. Adding such numbers really enforces the trading aspect of place value.

Worksheet 33-1

```
   9        12345679
 + 9      + 12345679
  18        24691358
 + 9      + 12345679
  27        37037037
 + 9      + 12345679
  36        49382716
 + 9      + 12345679
  45        61728395
 + 9      + 12345679
  54        74074074
 + 9      + 12345679
  63        86419753
 + 9      + 12345679
  72        98765432
 + 9      + 12345679
  81       111111111
 + 9      + 12345679
  90       123456790
```

Worksheet 33-2

```
  25        98765432
+ 25      + 98765432
  50       197530864
+ 25      + 98765432
  75       296296296
+ 25      + 98765432
 100       395061728
+ 25      + 98765432
 125       493827160
+ 25      + 98765432
 150       592592592
+ 25      + 98765432
 175       691358024
+ 25      + 98765432
 200       790123456
+ 25      + 98765432
 225       888888888
+ 25      + 98765432
 250       987654320
```

RightStart™ Mathematics Level B Second Edition © Activities for Learning, Inc. 2013

ACTIVITIES FOR TEACHING:

The columns of numbers have a surprise near the end, providing, of course, no mistakes are made.

Ask the child to compare the beginning number with the final number. [It is 10 times greater; that is, the last number is the same as the first number with a zero annexed to it.]

Corners™ with scores in the thousands. Tell the child to play the Corners™ game, found in the *Math Card Games* book, A9, but each player starts with 1000 points and adds on from there.

In conclusion. Ask: If your score in a regular Corners™ game is 255, what would it be if you started with 1000 points? [1255]

EXPLANATIONS:

© Activities for Learning, Inc. 2013

Lesson 84: Solving "Take From" Problems

OBJECTIVES:
1. To solve "Take From" problems

MATERIALS:
1. Sums Practice 2
2. Worksheet 34, Solving "Take From" Problems
3. AL Abacus

ACTIVITIES FOR TEACHING:

Warm-up. Ask the child to do the first two problems on Sums Practice 2 without his abacus if possible:

```
  2841        1533
+ 7159      + 1336
 10000        2869
```

Ask the child to read the answers aloud. [ten thousand, and two thousand eight hundred sixty-nine]

Ask: How many days are in a year? [365] How many days are in a leap year? [366]

Tell the child that you will say three numbers; he is to think about the pattern. Ask: what number comes next: 5, 7, 9; [11] 125, 130, 135; [140] 17, 16, 15. [14]

Ask the child what number comes next: 100, 200, 300; [400] 145, 150, 155; [160] 630 640, 650. [660]

Worksheet 34. Give the child worksheet.

"Take From" problem 1. Ask the child to read the first story problem on his worksheet.

> Jay had 8 cherries and ate 3 of them. How many cherries does Jay have left?

Ask him to fill in the part-whole circle set on his worksheet. See the left figure below. Also ask him to write an addition equation. See below.

$3 + \underline{5} = 8$

or

$8 = 3 + \underline{5}$

Finding what remains.

Ask the child if he can also write a subtraction equation.

$8 - 3 = \underline{5}$

Tell him how to read it: 8 minus 3 equals 5. Demonstrate the procedure on the abacus. See the figure on the next page. Tell him to reread the problem to be sure it makes sense.

EXPLANATIONS:

Problems in which a given quantity is increased are easiest for children to solve. This type of problem is more challenging.

The term "take away" is bad English. For example, "Six take away four equals two," isn't a logical sentence. "Take away" is bad mathematically because subtraction is much more than removing. It is also comparing or finding a difference or adding up as in making change.

ACTIVITIES FOR TEACHING:	EXPLANATIONS:

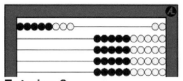 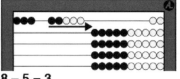

Entering 8. $8 - 5 = 3.$

Tell him to write the subtraction equation on his worksheet.

Problem 2. Ask the child to read the second problem on his worksheet.

   Kate's book has 16 pages. She read 10 pages. How many pages does she have left to read?

Ask the child to write the numbers in his part-whole circle set. Also ask him to write an addition and a subtraction equation. See below.

$16 = 10 + \underline{6}$ or
$10 + \underline{6} = 16$
$16 - 10 = \underline{6}$

Finding what remains.

Tell him to reread the problem to be sure it makes sense.

Problem 3. Ask the child to do the third problem in the same way.

   The Day family is traveling 20 miles to a camp. They have driven 15 miles. How many more miles do they need to drive?

$20 = 15 + \underline{5}$ or
$15 + \underline{5} = 20$
$20 - 15 = \underline{5}$

Problem 4. Ask the child to continue with the fourth problem.

   Alex had 12 eggs, which is a dozen. Alex dropped 3 eggs and they broke. How many eggs are not broken?

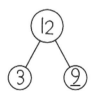

$12 = 3 + \underline{9}$ or
$3 + \underline{9} = 12$
$12 - 3 = \underline{9}$

In conclusion. Tell the child to make up a problem for you to solve.

© Activities for Learning, Inc. 2013

Lesson 85: Ten Minus a Number

OBJECTIVES:
1. To play the Go to the Dump game from the viewpoint of subtraction
2. To write subtract equations
3. To learn the 10 minus a number facts

MATERIALS:
1. Sums Practice 2
2. *Math Card Games* book, S1 and S2
3. Basic number cards*
4. AL Abacus
5. Math journal

ACTIVITIES FOR TEACHING:

Warm-up. Ask the child to do the next two problems on Sums Practice 2 without his abacus if possible:

```
  3293        6944
+ 6513      + 6482
  9806       13426
```

Ask the child to read the answers aloud. [nine thousand eight hundred six, and thirteen thousand four hundred twenty-six]

Ask: How many days are in a year? [365] How many days are in a leap year? [366]

Tell the child that you will say three numbers; he is to think about the pattern and say what number comes next. For example, say: 6, 8, 10; [12] 15, 20, 25; [30] 400, 500, 600; [700] 245, 250, 255; [260] 610, 620, 630. [640]

Say: 50 + 20 = 70 and 20 + 50 = 70. Ask: What do you notice about the equations? [The answers are the same.]

Tens Minus game. Play the Tens Minus game, found in the *Math Card Games* book, S1. Do not refer to the Go to the Dump game before they finish the game. Players need to think that a pair is the card number that matches 10 minus a card number in his hands.

After the game, ask: What other game did this game remind you of? [Go to the Dump]

Part-whole circle set. Draw a part-whole circle set and write 10 in the whole-circle and 7 in a left part-circle as shown below.

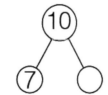

Finding missing part.

Ask: How do you find the missing part when you play Go to the Dump? [7 and what = 10] How do find the missing part when you play Tens Minus? [10 minus 7 = what]

EXPLANATIONS:

*Use half the deck of basic number cards for the two games; that is, 6 of each number from 0 to 10.

ACTIVITIES FOR TEACHING:	EXPLANATIONS:

Writing the 10 minus a number equations. Ask the child to enter 10 on his abacus. Then tell him to move 1 bead a little ways away as shown below. Ask him to say the subtraction equation [10 minus 1 = 9] and to write it in his math journal as shown on the next page.

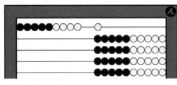

10 − 1 = 9.

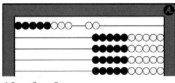

10 − 2 = 8.

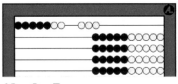

10 − 3 = 7.

1	0	−	1	=	9
1	0	−	2	=	8
1	0	−	3	=	7
1	0	−	4	=	6
1	0	−	5	=	5
1	0	−	6	=	4
1	0	−	7	=	3
1	0	−	8	=	2
1	0	−	9	=	1
1	0	−	1	0	=	0

The equations written in a math journal showing 10 minus a number.

Ask him to continue to 10 minus 10 = 0.

Ten as the Minuend game. Play the Ten as the Minuend game found in the *Math Card Games* book, S2. Use the same deck of cards as was used to play the Ten Minus game, but remove five of the 0 cards.

In conclusion. Ask: What is 10 minus 2? [8] What is 10 minus 8? [2] What is 10 minus 4? [6] What is 10 minus 6? [4] What is 10 minus 7? [3] What is 10 minus 3? [7]

The minuend is the starting number from which another number is subtracted. In 8 − 7, 8 is the minuend.

LESSON 86: SUBTRACTION AS THE MISSING ADDEND

OBJECTIVES:
1. To solve subtraction problems by adding on
2. To write the corresponding subtraction equations

MATERIALS:
1. Sums Practice 2
2. AL Abacus
3. Worksheet 35, Subtraction as the Missing Addend

ACTIVITIES FOR TEACHING:	EXPLANATIONS:
Warm-up. Ask the child to do the next two problems on Sums Practice 2 without his abacus: 　　3625　　　6856 　　+ 8375　　+ 984 　　12000　　 7840 Ask the child to read the answers aloud. [twelve thousand, and seven thousand eight hundred and forty] Ask: What is 10 minus 4? [6] What is 10 minus 6? [4] What is 10 minus 2? [8] What is 10 minus 8? [2] What is 10 minus 3? [7] What is 10 minus 7? [3] Ask the child to count by tens to 185, starting with 15. Enter 15 on the abacus, add two fives making 25, add two more fives to make 35, and so forth. [15, 25, 35, . . . , 185] Ask the child to say the days of the week and the months of the year. Then play the Comes Before game with the days and months. ***Problem.*** Read the following problem to the child: 　　Nine children are getting on a bus. Six children are already on the bus. How many more children must still get on the bus? [3] Ask the child to write the quantities he knows in a part-whole circle set. See the left figure on the next page. Draw a box in the right part-circle as shown. Explain that sometimes people use a box to show the missing number. Write addition and subtraction equations using the box: 　　　$6 + \Box = 9$ 　　　$9 - 6 = \Box$ Have the child enter 6 on the abacus and ask: What is missing to get to 9? [3] See the right figure on the next page.	 Researcher Karen Fuson found that children can understand subtraction easier by adding on, or counting up from the known part to the whole rather than counting down the known amount from the whole. Sometimes in primary mathematics, a box is used to indicate an unknown number. It is used in this lesson to make children familiar with it in the event they see it on a test.

RightStart™ Mathematics Level B Second Edition　　　　© Activities for Learning, Inc. 2013

ACTIVITIES FOR TEACHING:	EXPLANATIONS:

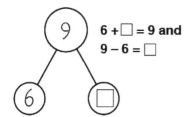 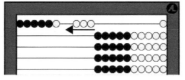

Adding on 3 to find 6 + □ = 9.

Ask: Did you find the part or the whole? [part] Also ask the child to write the addition and subtraction equations.

$$6 + 3 = 9$$
$$9 - 6 = 3$$

Practice. Change the number of children getting on the bus to 13 and the number that are already on the bus to 9.

Enter 9 on the abacus and ask: What is missing to get to 13? [4] Add 1 to get to 10 and 3 more to get to 13. See the right figure below.

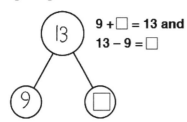 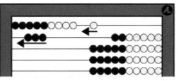

Solving the missing addend problem by adding up.

Ask the child to write the addition and subtraction equations:

$$9 + 4 = 13$$
$$13 - 9 = 4$$

Worksheet 35. This worksheet provides practice using missing addends to solve both missing addend and subtraction equations. The problems and solutions are as follows:

8 + 2 = 10	5 + 3 = 8	80 + 10 = 90
28 + 2 = 30	35 + 5 = 40	20 + 7 = 27
69 + 4 = 73	7 + 4 = 11	9 + 6 = 15
10 − 6 = 4	10 − 5 = 5	13 − 8 = 5
9 − 8 = 1	12 − 9 = 3	29 − 5 = 24
11 − 9 = 2	22 − 20 = 2	48 − 45 = 3
80 − 79 = 1	34 − 30 = 4	91 − 85 = 6
16 − 13 = 3	60 − 57 = 3	36 − 26 = 10

In conclusion. Ask: 6 plus what equal 10? [4] What is 10 minus 6? [4] Ask: 18 plus what equal 20? [2] What is 20 minus 18? [2]

© Activities for Learning, Inc. 2013

Lesson 87: Subtracting by Going Back

OBJECTIVES:
1. To practice subtraction by going back

MATERIALS:
1. Sums Practice 2
2. Dry erase board
3. AL Abacus
4. *Math Card Games* book, S9
5. Math journal

ACTIVITIES FOR TEACHING:

Warm-up. Ask the child to do the last two problems on Sums Practice 2 without his abacus:

```
  2999        3751
+ 2468      + 9356
  5467       13107
```

Ask the child to read the answers aloud. [five thousand four hundred sixty-seven, and thirteen thousand one hundred seven]

Ask: 7 plus what equal 10? [3] What is 10 minus 7? [3] 16 plus what equal 20? [4] What is 20 minus 16? [4]

Ask: What is 10 minus 4? [6] What is 10 minus 6? [4] What is 10 minus 2? [8] What is 10 minus 8? [2] What is 10 minus 3? [7] What is 10 minus 7? [3]

Ask the child to count by tens to 215 starting with 25. Enter 25, add two fives making 35, add two more fives to make 45, and so forth. [25, 35, 45, . . . , 215]

Ask the child to say the days of the week and the months of the year. Then play the Comes Before game with the days and months.

Subtraction as going back. Give the child the following problem:

> Sam has a cat that was 13 years old. How old was the cat last year? [12 years old]

Discuss the solution and ask the child to write the subtraction equation. [13 – 1 = 12] Ask a him to demonstrate it on the abacus. See figure below.

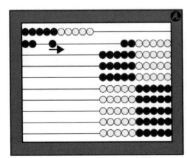

Subtracting by going back, 13 – 1 = 12.

EXPLANATIONS:

ACTIVITIES FOR TEACHING:	EXPLANATIONS:

Problem 2. Give the child the following problem:

Last year Sara grew 2 inches. Now she is 40 inches tall. How tall was Sara last year? [38 inches]

Ask the child to show it on the abacus. Ask: What does subtracting 40 – 2 remind you of? [Counting by 2s backward]

Subtracting 1 and 2. Ask the following:

What is 19 – 1? [18]   What is 35 – 1? [34]
What is 50 – 1? [49]   What is 100 – 1? [99]

Next ask:

What is 12 – 2? [10]   What is 34 – 2? [32]
What is 43 – 2? [41]   What is 15 – 2? [13]
What is 81 – 2? [79]   What is 39 – 2? [37]

Subtracting 5 and 10. Ask the child to try to do the following mentally. Then ask him to check his answers on side 1 of the abacus:

What is 100 – 10? [90]

What is 90 – 5? [85]

What is 85 – 10? [75]

Subtracting 15. Tell the child that to subtract 15, he first subtracts the 10 and then the 5:

What is 60 – 15? [45]

What is 40 – 15? [25]

What is 75 – 15? [60] See the figure below.

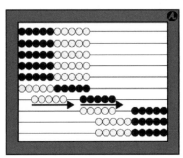

Subtracting 15 by subtracting 10 and then 5.

Zero Corners™ game. Play the Zero Corners™ game, from the *Math Card Games* book, S9. Here the players start with a score of 100. The child can use side 1 of his abacus to calculate scores and write them in his math journal.

In conclusion. Ask: What is 10 minus 1? [9] What is 100 minus 1? [99] What is 1000 minus 1? [999] Ask if he is ready for a really hard one: What is 10,000 minus 1? [9999]

© Activities for Learning, Inc. 2013

Lesson 88: Subtracting Consecutive Numbers

OBJECTIVES:
1. To learn the term *difference*
2. To learn the term *consecutive*
3. To subtract consecutive, consecutive even, and consecutive odd numbers by going up

MATERIALS:
1. Sums Practice 3
2. Worksheet 36, Subtracting Consecutive Numbers

ACTIVITIES FOR TEACHING:	EXPLANATIONS:

Warm-up. Ask the child to do the first two problems on Sums Practice 3 without his abacus:
 	
  7284   9999
 + 1794   +   1
  9078   10000
 	
 Ask him to read the answers aloud. [nine thousand seventy-eight, and ten thousand]
 	
Ask: What is 10 minus 1? [9] What is 100 minus 1? [99] What is 1000 minus 1? [999] What is 10,000 minus 1? [9999]
 	
Tell him to say the even numbers from 20 to 60. Then tell him to say the odd numbers from 61 to 91.
 	
The term difference. Tell the child that the answer after subtracting is called the *difference*. It means what's left. Ask: What is the difference for 10 − 8? [2]
 	
Subtracting the same number. Ask him: What is 9 − 9? [0] What is 3 − 3? [0] What is 123 − 123? [0] So, what is the difference when you subtract the same number? [always get 0]
 	
The term consecutive. Explain to the child that things following in order are called *consecutive*. For example, June and July are consecutive months; C and D are consecutive letters in the alphabet; and 3 and 4 or 121 and 122 are consecutive numbers.
 	
Ask: Are September and October consecutive months? [yes] Are January and June consecutive months? [no] Are 19 and 29 consecutive numbers? [no] Are 4 and 6 consecutive even numbers? [yes] Are 7 and 9 consecutive even numbers? [no] Are 7 and 9 consecutive odd numbers? [yes]
 	
Subtracting consecutive numbers. Tell the child: Let's subtract 19 − 18. Draw a part-whole circle set and ask: Where do we write the 19? [whole-circle] Where do we write the 18? [part-circle] See the figure on the next page. Ask: What is the easiest way to find the difference? [going up from 18 to 19] What is the difference? [1]	

RightStart™ Mathematics Level B Second Edition

ACTIVITIES FOR TEACHING:	EXPLANATIONS:

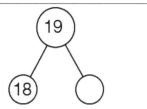 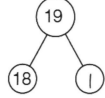

Subtracting consecutive numbers, 19 − 18 = 1.

Ask: What is 9 − 8? [1] What is 24 − 23? [1] What is 80 − 79? [1] What is 100 − 99? [1] Ask: What is the difference when you subtract consecutive numbers? [1]

Subtracting consecutive even numbers. Draw another part-whole circle set and write 18 in the whole-circle and 16 in the part-circle. See the left figure below.

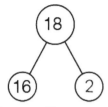 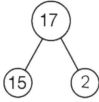

Consecutive even numbers.   **Consecutive odd numbers.**

Ask: What is special about 16 and 18? [even numbers] What is the difference? [2] What is 26 − 24? [2] What is 64 − 62? [2] Ask him to think of more examples. Ask: What is the difference when subtracting consecutive even numbers? [2]

Subtracting consecutive odd numbers. Write 17 and 15 in the part-whole circle set as shown above on the right. Ask: What are these numbers? [odd] What is the difference? [2] What is 17 − 15? [2] What is 13 − 11? [2] What is 73 − 71? [2] What is the difference when you subtract consecutive odd numbers? [2]

Worksheet 36. Give the child the worksheet. The problems and solutions are as follows:

>   17 − 16 = **1**
>   84 − 82 = **2**
>   35 − 33 = **2**
>   41 − 39 = **2**
>   73 − 72 = **1**
>   60 − 58 = **2**
>   36 − 35 = **1**
>   31 − 30 = **1**
>   88 − 86 = **2**
>   18 − 17 = **1**

In conclusion. Ask: What kind of numbers will give you a difference of 1 when you subtract them? [consecutive numbers] What kind of numbers will give you a difference of 2 when you subtract them? [consecutive even or consecutive odd numbers]

© Activities for Learning, Inc. 2013

LESSON 89: SUBTRACTING FROM 9 AND 11

OBJECTIVES:
1. To subtract from 9 and 11

MATERIALS:
1. Sums Practice 3
2. Geared clock
3. AL Abacus
4. *Math Card Games* book, S3 and S5

ACTIVITIES FOR TEACHING:	EXPLANATIONS:

Warm-up. Ask the child to do the next two problems on Sums Practice 3 without his abacus:

$$\begin{array}{r} 4675 \\ + 5948 \\ \hline \mathbf{10623} \end{array} \qquad \begin{array}{r} 7329 \\ + 6438 \\ \hline \mathbf{13767} \end{array}$$

Ask the child to read the answers aloud. [ten thousand six hundred twenty-three, and thirteen thousand seven hundred sixty-seven]

Ask the child: What is 8 – 6, [2] 9 – 8, [1] 5 – 1, [4] 9 – 2, [7] 6 – 6, [0] and 7 – 5? [2]

Set the hands of the geared clock to 6:10. Ask the child what time it will be when the minute hand goes all the way around. [7:10] Move the hands to 7:10.

Then ask where the minute hand would be when it moves half way around. [on the number 8] Move the hands to the 7:40 position and ask the child to read the time.

Ask the child to set his clock for 9:25 and 8:20.

Subtracting from 11. Ask the child: What is 10 – 3? [7] Then ask: What must 11 – 3 be? [8] Ask why it is one more. Show both on the abacus, using the first and third wires as shown below. By subtracting from the 10, it becomes obvious why 11 – 3 must be 1 more.

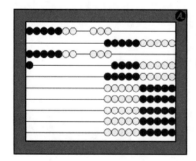

Comparing 11 – 3 with 10 – 3.

Ask the child: What is 10 – 5, [5] and what is 11 – 5? [6]
Continue with: What is 10 – 2, [8] and what is 11 – 2? [9]
Also ask: What is 11 – 9, [2] and what is 11 – 8? [3]

ACTIVITIES FOR TEACHING:

Subtracting from 9. Ask the child how he could find 9 minus a number if he knows what 10 minus a number is. [one less] Ask: What is 10 – 4? [6] What would 9 – 4 be? [5] Ask why it is one less. Ask the child to show both on the abacus, using the first and third wires as shown below.

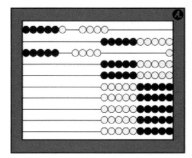

Comparing 9 – 4 with 10 – 4.

Ask the child: What is 10 – 7, [3] and what is 9 – 7? [2] Also ask: What is 9 – 3, [6] 9 – 5, [4] 9 – 2, [7] and what is 9 – 6? [3]

Nine as the Minuend game. Play the Nine as the Minuend game, found in the *Math Card Games* book, S3.

One or Eleven as the Minuend game. Play the One or Eleven as the Minuend game, found in the *Math Card Games* book, S5.

In conclusion. Give the child the following problems:

Forty-nine people attended a reunion. Six were babies. How many were not babies? [43]

Ronnie planted 31 bean plants. Seven were purple beans and the rest were green beans. How many were green beans? [24]

EXPLANATIONS:

Lesson 90: Subtracting with Doubles and Near Doubles

OBJECTIVES:

1. To subtract with doubles and near doubles

MATERIALS:

1. Sums Practice 3
2. Geared clock
3. Math balance
4. AL Abacus
5. Math journal
6. *Math Card Games* book, S19

ACTIVITIES FOR TEACHING:

Warm-up. Ask the child to do the next two problems on Sums Practice 3 without his abacus:

```
  8662        9267
+  359      + 6184
  9021       15451
```

Ask the child to read the answers aloud. [nine thousand twenty-one, and fifteen thousand four hundred fifty-one]

Ask the child: What is $7 - 5$, [2] $8 - 7$, [1] $4 - 1$, [3] $10 - 3$, [7] $5 - 5$, [0] and $8 - 6$? [2]

Set the hands of the geared clock to 5:35. Ask the child: What time it will be when the minute hand goes all the way around. [6:35] Move the hands to 6:35.

Then ask where the minute hand would be when it moves half way around. [on the number 1] Move the hands to the 7:05 position and ask the child to read the time.

Ask the child to set his clock for 4:15 and 8:55.

Doubles with the math balance. Tell the child to enter 12 on the left side of the math balance as shown below. Give the child 2 weights and tell him to make it balance by putting both weights on the same number.

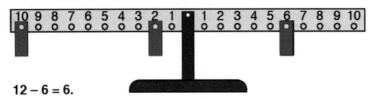

$12 - 6 = 6$.

Ask the child: What subtraction equation do you see with the math balance? [$12 - 6 = 6$] What is half of 12? [6]

Tell the child to enter 12 on side 2 of the abacus in the ones columns. Ask if they see the two 6s. See the figure below. Tell him to write the equation in his math journal.

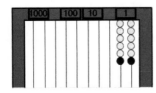

$12 - 6 = 6$

EXPLANATIONS:

ACTIVITIES FOR TEACHING:	EXPLANATIONS:

Repeat for 14, putting it on the math balance and the abacus. Ask the child to write the subtraction equation in his math journal.

$$14 - 7 = 7$$

Continue with 16 and 18. Also ask him to do 2, 4, 6, 8, and 10.

Near doubles. Ask the child to enter 13 on the math balance. Ask him if he can balance it by putting both weights on the same number. [No, both weights on 6 is too little and both weights on 7 is too heavy.] Then ask him to put the weights on consecutive numbers. See below.

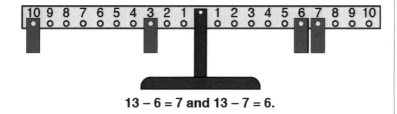

$13 - 6 = 7$ and $13 - 7 = 6$.

Ask the child to say the two equations.

$$13 - 6 = 7 \quad \text{and} \quad 13 - 7 = 6.$$

Tell him that sometimes people call these equations "near doubles."

Next tell him to enter 13 on his abacus as shown below. Ask him to write the equations in his math journal.

Repeat for 11, 15, and 17. Also ask him to do 3, 5, 7, and 9.

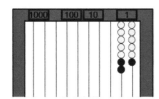

$13 - 6 = 7$ and
$13 - 7 = 6$.

Short Chain Subtraction Solitaire. Play the Short Chain Subtraction Solitaire game, found in the *Math Card Games* book, S19.

In conclusion. Ask: What is half of 10? [5] What is half of 12? [6] What is half of 18? [9] What is half of 14? [7] What is half of 16? [8]

LESSON 91: SUBTRACTING BY TAKING ALL FROM TEN

OBJECTIVES:
1. To focus on subtracting 9 and 8 using the Taking All From Ten strategy

MATERIALS:
1. Sums Practice 3
2. Geared clock
3. AL Abacus
4. Math journal
5. *Math Card Games* book, S6

ACTIVITIES FOR TEACHING:

Warm-up. Ask the child to do the last two problems on Sums Practice 3 without his abacus:

```
  7298        9337
+ 1953      + 2273
  9251       11610
```

Ask: What is half of 8? [4] What is half of 10? [5] What is half of 12? [6] What is half of 14? [7] What is half of 16? [8]

Ask the child: What is 10 − 6? [4] 11 − 6? [5] 10 − 7? [3] 11 − 7? [4] 10 − 3? [7] 11 − 3? [8]

Set the hands of the geared clock to 11:15 and ask the child to say the time. [11:15]

Then ask where the minute hand would be when it moves half way around. [on the number 9] Move the hands to the 11:45 position and ask the child to read the time.

Ask the child to set his clock for 9:25 and 8:20.

Subtracting 9. Have the child enter 14 on the abacus. Tell him to subtract the 9 from the 10, as shown in the figure below. Then ask: What is left? [1 and 4, or 5]

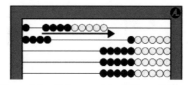

Subtracting 14 − 9 by subtracting 9 from the 10.

Tell the child to write the equation in his math journal.

14 − 9 = 5

EXPLANATIONS:

ACTIVITIES FOR TEACHING:	EXPLANATIONS:

Ask him to solve 17 − 9.

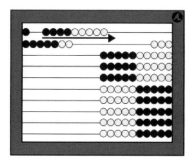

Subtracting 17 − 9 by subtracting 9 from the 10.

$17 - 9 = 8$

Tell him: We can call this strategy "taking all from ten."

Repeat for 12 − 9, [3] 15 − 9, [6] 16 − 9, [7] and 11 − 9. [2]

Subtracting 8. Ask the child: How could you use the Taking All From Ten strategy to find 17 − 8? [by subtracting 8 from the 10] Ask: What is left? [7 + 2 = 9] Ask the child to demonstrate it on the abacus. See the figure below.

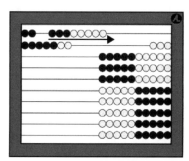

Subtracting 17 − 8 by subtracting 8 from the 10.

Ask the child to write the equation in his math journal.

$17 - 8 = 9$

Repeat for 16 − 8 [8] and 15 − 8. [7] Ask him to continue down to 11 − 8, [3] writing them all in his math journal.

Subtraction Memory game. Play the Subtraction Memory game, found in the *Math Card Games* book, S6. Use a 9 card for the number being subtracted. Play the game again with 8 as the number being subtracted.

In conclusion. Ask: How could you use this Taking All From Ten strategy for finding 12 − 7? [Take 7 from 10 and adding 3 + 2 = 5.] How could you use this strategy for finding 13 − 6? [4 + 3 = 7]

Do not teach a rule that subtracting 9 is 1 more than the number in the ones place. Let the child make that discovery and use it when it makes sense to him.

Lesson 92: Subtracting by Taking Part from Ten

OBJECTIVES:
1. To focus on subtraction facts using the Taking Part From Ten strategy

MATERIALS:
1. Sums Practice 4
2. Geared clock
3. AL Abacus
4. Worksheet 37, Subtracting by Taking Part from Ten

ACTIVITIES FOR TEACHING:

EXPLANATIONS:

Warm-up. Ask the child to do the first two problems on Sums Practice 4 without his abacus:

```
  1357        2137
+ 2468      + 6164
  3825        8301
```

Ask: How could you use the Taking All From Ten strategy from the previous lesson for finding 11 – 7? [Take 7 from 10 and adding 3 + 1 = 4.] How could you use this strategy for finding 14 – 6? [4 + 4 = 8]

Set the hands of the geared clock to 6:05 and ask the child to say the time. [6 oh-5] Ask him to set his clock for various times and state those times.

Taking Part From Ten strategy. Ask the child how he used the Taking All From Ten strategy he learned in the previous lesson to find 18 – 9. [subtracting the 9 from 10 leaving 1 and 8 which is 9]

Have him enter 18 on the abacus and ask if he could think of another way to subtract 9. Emphasize that he could remove 8 from the second row and 1 from the 10 as shown below.

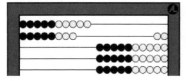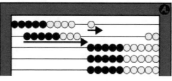

Subtracting 18 – 9 by removing 8 from the 8 and 1 more from the 10.

Enter 15 and ask the child how he could subtract 7, using the Taking Part From Ten strategy. [5 is subtracted from the 5 and 2 more from the 10, giving 8.] See the figures on the next page.

ACTIVITIES FOR TEACHING:	EXPLANATIONS:

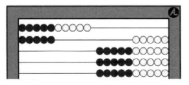 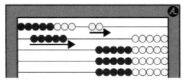

Subtracting 15 – 7 by removing 5 from the 5 and 2 more from the 10.

This time write

$$13 - 5 = \underline{} . \; [8]$$

Ask him how he could find the difference. [Take 3 from the 3 and 2 from the 10.]

The difference is what remains after subtracting.

Repeat for

$$12 - 6 = \underline{} . \; [6]$$

Here he can think of subtracting 2 from the 2 and 4 more from the 10. Also repeat for 13 – 8, [5] 16 – 9, [7] 12 – 3, [9] and 14 – 7. [7]

Worksheet 37. Give the child the worksheet and ask him to do it using the Taking Part From Ten strategy. The problems and solutions are as follows:

13 – 4 = **9**
15 – 7 = **8**
13 – 6 = **7**
14 – 6 = **8**
16 – 7 = **9**
12 – 3 = **9**
13 – 7 = **6**
16 – 9 = **7**
12 – 4 = **8**
14 – 8 = **6**
13 – 5 = **8**
12 – 7 = **5**
15 – 6 = **9**
13 – 8 = **5**
12 – 5 = **7**
14 – 5 = **9**
15 – 8 = **7**
12 – 6 = **6**
14 – 7 = **7**

In conclusion. Ask: How could you use this Taking Part From Ten strategy for finding 13 – 7? [Take 3 from the 3 and 4 from the ten to get 6.] How could you use this strategy for finding 15 – 6? [Take 5 from the 5 and 1 from the 10 to get 9.]

© Activities for Learning, Inc. 2013

Lesson 93: Finding the Difference

OBJECTIVES:
1. To learn the term *difference*
2. To solve compare problems

MATERIALS:
1. Sums Practice 4
2. Geared clock
3. AL Abacus
4. *Math Card Games* book, S13

ACTIVITIES FOR TEACHING:

Warm-up. Ask the child to do the next two problems on Sums Practice 4 without his abacus:

```
  1398        3149
+ 1406      + 7788
  2804       10937
```

Ask: How could you use the Taking Part From Ten strategy for finding 14 − 7? [Take 4 from the 4 and 3 from the ten to get 7.] How could you use this strategy for finding 17 − 7? [Take 7 from the 7 to get ten.]

Ask: How could you use the Taking All From Ten strategy for finding 12 − 7? [Take 7 from 10 and adding 3 + 2 = 5.] How could you use this strategy for finding 13 − 6? [4 + 3 = 7]

Set the hands of the geared clock to 4:15 and ask the child to say the time. [4:15] Ask him to set his clock for various times and state those times.

Finding differences on the abacus. Enter 4 and 6 on the top two wires of the abacus. See the left figure below. Ask the child: What is the *difference* in quantity between the 4 and 6? [2]

Ask: Did you add 4 and 6 to find the difference? [no] What did you do? [subtract] Ask him to put the numbers in a part-whole circle set. See the right figure below. Explain that the larger number goes in the whole-circle. The smaller number and difference go in the part-circles. Ask the child to write the equations.

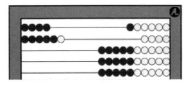

Find the difference between 4 and 6.

$6 - 4 = \underline{2}$ or
$4 + \underline{2} = 6$

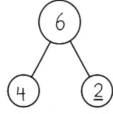

Larger number on top; smaller number and difference in part-circles.

EXPLANATIONS:

ACTIVITIES FOR TEACHING:	EXPLANATIONS:

Repeat for difference between 9 and 2. See figures below.

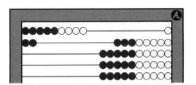

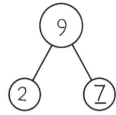

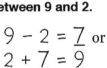

Find the difference between 9 and 2.

The difference is 7.

$9 - 2 = \underline{7}$ or
$2 + \underline{7} = 9$

Problem. Read the following problem to the child:

Mikayla has a book with 36 pages and Nathan has a book with 50 pages. Whose book has more pages and how many more? [Nathan, 14 more pages]

Draw a part-whole circle set and ask: Which number goes in the whole-circle? [50] What number goes in a part-circle? [36] See the left figure below. Ask: Whose book has more pages? [Nathan] How many more? [14] Ask the child to write the equation.

$50 - 36 = \underline{14}$ or $36 + \underline{14} = 50$

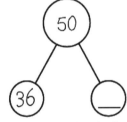 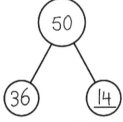

The part-whole circle set for a compare problem.

Harder Difference War game. Play the Harder Difference War game from the *Math Card Games* book, S13.

A child needing an easier game could play Difference War, S12.

In conclusion. Ask the child: When you add, what do you call the answer? [sum] When you subtract, what do you call the answer? [difference]

© Activities for Learning, Inc. 2013

LESSON 94: SOLVING COMPARE PROBLEMS

OBJECTIVES:
1. To solve compare problems

MATERIALS:
1. Sums Practice 4
2. AL Abacus
3. Geared clock
4. Worksheet 38, Solving Compare Problems

ACTIVITIES FOR TEACHING:

Warm-up. Ask the child to do the next two problems on Sums Practice 4 without his abacus:

```
  9385       2925
+   99     + 1464
  9484       4389
```

Ask the child: When you add, what do you call the answer? [sum] When you subtract, what do you call the answer? [difference]

Ask the child to recite all the doubles from 1 + 1 to 10 + 10 using his abacus. [1 + 1 = 2, 2 + 2 = 4, . . . , 10 + 10 = 20]

Ask: What is 43 + 20 ? [63] What is 20 + 43? [63] Ask the child: What do you notice about the equations? [The answers are the same.]

Set the hands of the geared clock to 8:05 and ask him to say the time. [8 oh-5] Ask him to set his clock for various times and state those times.

Worksheet 38. Give the child the worksheet.

Compare problem 1. Ask the child to read the first story problem on his worksheet.

> Jamie walked 9 blocks. Kim walked 3 blocks farther. How far did Kim walk?

Ask him: What are we trying to find, a part or a whole? [whole] What is the 9? [a part] What is the 3? [a part or a difference] Ask him to fill in the part-whole circle set on his worksheet. Also ask him to write the equation. See below.

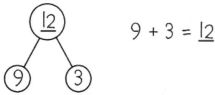

Finding the distance Kim walked.

EXPLANATIONS:

ACTIVITIES FOR TEACHING:	EXPLANATIONS:

Ask the child to share his addition equations. Then ask: Does it make sense that Kim walked 12 blocks? [yes]

Problem 2. Ask the child to read the second problem on his worksheet.

> The difference between two numbers is 7. The larger number is 13. What is the smaller number?

Ask: What is the largest number? [13] Where do you write it? [in the whole-circle] What is the 7? [a part or difference] Ask him to fill in the part-whole circle set on his worksheet. Also ask him to write an addition and a subtraction equation. Ask the child to share his results. See below.

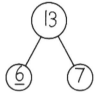

$13 - 7 = \underline{6}$ or
$7 + \underline{6} = 13$

Finding the smaller number.

Tell him to reread the problem to be sure it makes sense.

Problem 3. Ask the child to do the third problem in the same way.

> In a certain year, February had 3 fewer days than January. January has 31 days. How many days did February have?

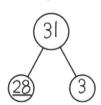

$31 - \underline{28} = 3$ or
$31 - 3 = \underline{28}$

Problem 4. Ask the child to continue with the fourth problem.

> West Park has 8 trees. North Park has 14 trees. How many fewer trees does West Park have than North Park?

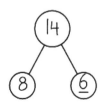

$14 - 8 = \underline{6}$ or
$8 + \underline{6} = 14$

In conclusion. Tell the child to make up a problem and solve it.

© Activities for Learning, Inc. 2013

Lesson 95: Addition and Subtraction Equations

OBJECTIVES:
1. To compare addition and subtraction
2. To recognize what is an equation
3. To introduce the unequal sign, ≠
4. To compose equations from numbers

MATERIALS:
1. Sums Practice 4
2. Geared clock
3. Worksheet 39, Addition and Subtraction Equations

ACTIVITIES FOR TEACHING:

Warm-up. Ask the child to do the last two problems on Sums Practice 4 without his abacus:

$$\begin{array}{r} 2976 \\ +2976 \\ \hline 5952 \end{array} \qquad \begin{array}{r} 3751 \\ +4216 \\ \hline 7967 \end{array}$$

Ask the child: When you add, what do you call the answer? [sum] When you subtract, what do you call the answer? [difference]

Ask the child to recite all the doubles from 1 + 1 to 10 + 10 using his abacus. [1 + 1 = 2, 2 + 2 = 4, . . . , 10 + 10 = 20]

Ask: What is 82 + 10? [92] What is 10 + 82? [92] Ask the child: What do you notice about the equations? [The answers are the same.]

Set the hands of the geared clock to 4:05 and ask him to say the time. [4 oh-5] Ask him to set his clock for various times and state those times.

Comparing addition and subtraction. Tell the child to think of ways that addition and subtraction are different. Ask the following:

1. In addition you end with more than you started; what happens in subtraction? [you have less]

2. In addition you start with the parts; where do you start in subtraction? [with the whole]

3. In addition you are putting things together; what happens in subtraction? [you are taking them apart]

4. In writing addition equations, you use "+" and call it plus; what do you use in subtraction? ["–"] What do you call it? [minus]

Recognizing what is an equation. Write 6 + 9 = 15 and ask: Is this an equation? [yes]

EXPLANATIONS:

Mathematically, the first question is valid only when applied to positive integers. Since that is the range of numbers at this stage of instruction, the answer is valid.

Primary mathematics has experienced some confusion over what constitutes an equation. For a while, equations were lumped into that non-mathematical catch-all, "number sentence," which included inequalities.

An equation must have an equal sign, designating that the two sides are equal.

ACTIVITIES FOR TEACHING:	EXPLANATIONS:

Continue with 4 + 7 + 15 and ask: Is this an equation? [no] Why not? [It does not have an equal sign.]

Write 9 = 9 and ask: Is this an equation? [yes]

Write 13 − 4 = 9 and ask: Is this an equation? [yes]

The is-not-equal sign. Draw a left turn sign as shown in the left figure below. Explain that it tells a driver to turn left. Then draw the do not turn left sign and ask: Do you know what this sign means? [Do not turn left.]

 Turn left symbol.    Do not turn left symbol.

The "do not" slash in many signs may be either forward or backward. However, the slash in an is-not-equal sign in mathematics is only forward.

Draw the equal sign. Tell him there is an is-not-equal (unequal) sign. Draw it as shown below on the right.

= Equal sign.   ≠ Is-not-equal sign.

Write the following equation: 4 __ 2 + 2.

Ask: Could this be an equation? [yes] Ask the child to write the equal sign on the line. [4 = 2 + 2]

Write the following equation: 1 + 1 __ 3.

Ask: Could this be an equation? [no] Ask the child to write the is-not-equal sign on the line. [1 + 1 ≠ 3]

Making equations. Write

      5 __ 1 __ 6

and tell him to make an equation using +, −, and = signs. [5 + 1 = 6] Explain that he needs to try different signs until he finds one that works. Repeat for

      3 __ 8 __ 5   [3 = 8 − 5]

Worksheet 39. Give the child the worksheet. The problems and solutions are below:

    3 + 2 = 1 + 4
    5 + 2 + 2 ≠ 10
    14 ≠ 10 − 4
    16 − 2 ≠ 14 + 2
    102 = 102
    4 + 3 = 7
    2 = 10 − 8
    3 + 3 = 7 − 1
    16 = 10 + 3 + 3 or 16 − 10 = 3 + 3
    8 + 0 = 9 − 1 or 8 − 0 = 9 − 1

The problems on the second half of this worksheet are like puzzles. A child may need to try several solutions before finding one that works. Encourage the child to persevere.

In conclusion. Ask: Why are equations called equations? [Both sides are equal.]

© Activities for Learning, Inc. 2013

LESSON 96: CONTINUING PATTERNS IN THE HUNDREDS

OBJECTIVES:
1. To recognize patterns in the hundreds and continue them

MATERIALS:
1. Sums Practice 5
2. Math journal
3. Worksheet 40, Continuing Patterns in the Hundreds

ACTIVITIES FOR TEACHING:	EXPLANATIONS:

Warm-up. Ask the child to do the first two problems on Sums Practice 5 without his abacus:

```
  3286        5599
+ 9041      + 1217
 12327        6816
```

Ask: Why are equations called equations? [Both sides are equal.]

Ask the child: When you add, what do you call the answer? [sum] When you subtract, what do you call the answer? [difference]

Ask him to say the days of the week and the months of the year.

Ask the child to mentally add 25 + 25, [50] 105 + 80, [185] 49 + 32, [79, 81] and 76 + 76. [146, 152]

Identifying a pattern. Write the following example and ask the child: Is the pattern increasing (getting larger) or decreasing (getting smaller)?

    216   217   218   [increasing]

Next ask: By how much is each number increasing? [1] What two numbers come next?

    216   217   218   ___   ___   [219, 220]

Repeat for:

    197   199   201   [increasing]

Ask: By how much is each number increasing? [2] What two numbers come next?

    197   199   201   ___   ___   [203, 205]

Repeat for:

    342   341   340   [decreasing]

Ask: By how much is each number decreasing? [1] What two numbers come next?

    342   341   340   ___   ___   [339, 338]

RightStart™ Mathematics Level B Second Edition

ACTIVITIES FOR TEACHING:	EXPLANATIONS:

Practice. Ask the child to name the next two numbers for:

    560   570   580   ____ ____ [590, 600]
    770   760   750   ____ ____ [740, 730]
    180   185   190   ____ ____ [195, 200]

Problem. Give the child this problem:

Cody had 92 head of cattle on Monday. On Tuesday 10 baby calves were born. How many head of cattle did he have altogether on Tuesday? [102] On Wednesday 10 more baby calves were born. How many head of cattle did he have altogether on Wednesday? [112] The same number of baby calves were born on Thursday and Friday. How many head of cattle did Cody have on Friday? [132]

Ask the child what numbers he was counting by. [10s] Ask the child to write the five numbers in his math journal.

    92   102   112   122   132

Worksheet 40. Give the child the worksheet. The solutions are below:

350	360	370	**380**	**390**
690	700	710	**720**	**730**
200	205	210	**215**	**220**
896	897	898	**899**	**900**
480	490	500	**510**	**520**
797	798	799	**800**	**801**
198	199	200	**201**	**202**
425	430	435	**440**	**445**
890	895	900	**905**	**910**
870	880	890	**900**	**910**
490	495	500	**505**	**510**
502	501	500	**499**	**498**
200	300	400	**500**	**600**
302	402	502	**602**	**702**
200	225	250	**275**	**300**

In conclusion. Ask: What does increasing mean? [get larger] What does decreasing mean? [get smaller]

© Activities for Learning, Inc. 2013

Lesson 97: Higher Even and Odd Numbers

OBJECTIVES:
1. To help child discover the pattern for determining even and odd numbers

MATERIALS:
1. AL Abacus
2. Math journal
3. Worksheet 41, Higher Even and Odd Numbers
4. **Crayons**

ACTIVITIES FOR TEACHING:	EXPLANATIONS:
Warm-up. Ask: What are the next two numbers in the pattern 540, 550, 560? [570, 580] What are the next two numbers in the pattern 230, 235, 240? [245, 250] What are the next two numbers in the pattern 205, 200, 195? [190, 185]	

Ask: What does increasing mean? [get larger] What does decreasing mean? [get smaller]

Ask the child: When you add, what do you call the answer? [sum] When you subtract, what do you call the answer? [difference]

Ask him to say the days of the week and the months of the year.

Ask the child to mentally add 99 + 6, [105] 36 + 58, [86, 94] 85 + 15 [95, 100] and 28 + 57. [78, 85]

Review of even numbers. Ask the child: Is 8 is an even number or an odd number? [even] How do you know? [with 8 objects, each one has a partner] Ask the child to demonstrate it with the abacus.

Write Even and Odd above two columns in his math journal as shown below. Ask the child to write the numbers 1 to 10 in the correct columns. See the left chart below.

Even	Odd		Even	Odd	
2	1		2	1	Charts for finding even and odd patterns.
4	3		4	3	
6	5		6	5	
8	7		8	7	
10	9		10	9	
			16	29	
			52	73	

ACTIVITIES FOR TEACHING:	EXPLANATIONS:

Even or odd. Ask the child to decide if 16 is even or odd. [even] One way is shown below. Ask the child to write 16 in the correct column in his math journal. Repeat for 29. [odd]

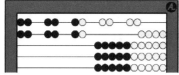
16 is even.

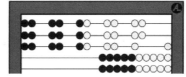
29 is odd.

Next ask the child to think of a few different numbers greater than 10 but less than 100, find out if it is even or odd, and record it in the correct column. When all his numbers are recorded, ask him if he sees a pattern. [Numbers ending in 0, 2, 4, 6, and 8 are even; the others are odd.] Ask him why that is so. [Ten is always even and ones can be even or odd.]

Practice. Ask the child to say whether the following numbers are even or odd:

 32 [even] 63 [odd] 14 [even] 32 [even]
 17 [odd] 89 [odd] 60 [even] 19 [odd]

The words even and odd. Ask: How many letters are in the word even? [4] Is it even or odd? [even] How many letters are in the word odd? [3] Is it even or odd? [odd]

Some children may find this intriguing.

Problems. Give the child the following problems:

A young child counted all the shoes in the family's mudroom. The child counted 11 shoes. Do you think the answer is correct if no shoes are missing? [no]

There are 17 mittens in a box. Do you think there are any missing? [Yes, at least 1 mitten must be missing.]

Worksheet 41. Give him the worksheet, which has two hundreds charts. He is to color the even numbers in one and the odd numbers in the other. The patterns are shown below.

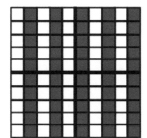
Even numbers colored.

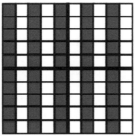
Odd numbers colored.

The child could use one chart and color evens and odds different colors.

In conclusion. Ask: Is the number of members in the family even or odd? Is the number of people in the room right now even or odd?

© Activities for Learning, Inc. 2013

Lesson 98: Pages in Books and Reading Years

OBJECTIVES:

1. To discover that in books and in periodicals, right pages are odd-numbered and left pages are even-numbered
2. To find a certain page in a book
3. To learn two ways of reading years

MATERIALS:

1. Sums Practice 5
2. **Several books with at least 50 numbered pages**
3. Dry erase board
4. *Math Card Games* book, S9

ACTIVITIES FOR TEACHING:	EXPLANATIONS:

Warm-up. Ask the child to do the next two problems on Sums Practice 5 without his abacus:

$$\begin{array}{r} 6474 \\ + 1593 \\ \hline 8067 \end{array} \qquad \begin{array}{r} 4637 \\ + 6513 \\ \hline 11150 \end{array}$$

Ask: What does increasing mean? [get larger] What does decreasing mean? [get smaller]

Ask: What are the next two numbers in the pattern 720, 730, 740? [750, 760] What are the next two numbers in the pattern 150, 155, 160? [165, 170] What are the next two numbers in the pattern 325, 315, 305? [295, 285]

Ask the child to mentally add 89 + 6, [95] 28 + 69, [88, 97] 80 + 25 [105] and 69 + 89. [149, 158]

Pages in books. Give the child a book and tell him to open it to any page with a number on it. Ask him to write down the page number from the right hand side on his dry erase board. Tell him to do this for other right hand pages. Then ask him to look at the numbers and ask: Is the page number even or odd? [odd]

Repeat for page numbers on the left page. [even]

Practice. Ask the child: Do you think page 27 is on the left side or on the right side? [right] Ask him to find that page and see if he is correct.

Repeat for page 1, [right] page 16, [left] page 25, [right] page 39, [right] and page 48. [left] Use higher numbers if the book has enough pages.

Copyright dates. Ask the child to find the title page at the very front of his book. Tell him that the title page looks very much like the cover, and often it is in black and white.

ACTIVITIES FOR TEACHING:	EXPLANATIONS:
Now ask him to turn to the next page, which usually has very small print. Tell him to find the word *Copyright*. Write it for him as follows: Copyright © Tell him that the © in the circle, ©, means copyright. Explain that the year listed after it tells the year the book was published. Ask him to write the copyright year for other books. ***Reading years in the 1900s.*** Point to a year in the 1900s, such as 1994, and ask the child to read it like an ordinary number. [one thousand nine hundred ninety-four] Explain: With years we usually think in hundreds, so we think "nineteen hundred ninety-four," but we skip saying "hundred." Instead, we say "nineteen ninety-four." Point to other years and ask the child to say them. ***Reading years in the 2000s.*** Write the following years: 2000 2001 2002 2003 2004 2005 2008 2009 Tell the child: Most people read these years as "two thousand," "two thousand one," "two thousand two," and so on. Write 2010 and tell the child: We can call it "two thousand ten," but many people say, "twenty ten." Both are correct. Write 2011 and ask him: How can you say it? [two thousand eleven, or twenty eleven] Repeat for the current year. ***Year problems.*** Pointing to the copyright year list written earlier, ask: Which book has the oldest published date? Which book has the newest date? How many years apart were they published? ***Zero Corners™ game.*** Play the Zero Corners™ game, from the *Math Card Games* book, S9. Use the starting scores given in the game instructions. ***In conclusion.*** Ask: What year is this? What year was last year? What year will it be next year?	 Less often the year 2001 is read as "twenty oh-one."

© Activities for Learning, Inc. 2013

Lesson 99: Greater Than or Less Than Symbols

OBJECTIVES:
1. To learn the term *opposites*
2. To learn to write the < symbol
3. To use the > and < symbols

MATERIALS:
1. Sums Practice 5
2. **A sticky note** to cover the < and > symbols
3. *Math Card Games* book, S13
4. Worksheet 42, Greater Than or Less Than Symbols

ACTIVITIES FOR TEACHING:	EXPLANATIONS:

Warm-up. Ask the child to do the next two problems on Sums Practice 5 without his abacus:
 	
   2358   1997
  + 3397   + 2786
   5755   4783
 	
 Ask: What year is this? What year was last year? What year will it be next year?
 	
 Ask: What comes next in this pattern: book, pencil, paper, book, pencil? [paper] What type of pattern is this? [simple]
 	
 Ask the child to give the sums for the following: 49 + 8, [57] 85 + 9, [94] 55 + 10, [65] 93 + 7, [100] 66 + 2, [68] and 25 + 9. [34]
 	
 Opposites. Ask: What is the opposite of cold? [hot] What is the opposite of subtract? [add] What is the opposite of equal? [is not equal] What is the opposite of greater than? [less than]
 	
 Less than symbol. Tell the child that there is a math symbol for "less than." Write 3 and 5 with a space between him. Follow the steps given in the figures below.
 	
   3   5   Decide which number is less.
 	
   3• 5   Draw one dot in the middle by the lesser number.
 	
   3•:5   Draw two dots near the greater number.
 	
   3<5   Connect the dots, starting at the larger number.
 	
 Ask: Did making the less than symbol seem a lot like making the greater than symbol? [yes] Explain that making the symbols is about the same, but reading them is a little harder.
	
	 The greater than symbol was introduced in lesson 47.

ACTIVITIES FOR TEACHING:	EXPLANATIONS:

Reading the > and < symbols. Write 10 < 20 and cover the < symbol with the sticky note. Then slowly uncover it in the direction we read as shown below.

10 ☐ 20
10 ◁] 20
10 < 20

Ask: What did you see first, the small part or the large part? [small] So, we read it as "is less than." Ask him to read the whole statement. [ten is less than twenty]

Now write 12 > 6 as shown below. Cover and uncover the > symbol in the same way as above.

12 ☐ 6
12 ▷] 6
12 > 6

Ask: What did you see first, the small part or the large part? [large] So, we read it as "is greater than." Ask him to read the whole statement. [twelve is greater than 6]

Practice. Give him several examples to read:

  8 > 4   2 < 3   8 < 80   1000 > 100   2 > 0

Harder Difference War game. Play the Peace Variation of the Harder Difference War game from the *Math Card Games* book, S13. For the Peace Variation, the player with the lower difference takes the cards.

Worksheet 42. Give the child the worksheet. Tell him the right side of the worksheet is like playing a war or peace game. The problems and solutions are shown below:

104 < 140   9 + 4 < 10 + 4
76 > 67   24 + 85 = 85 + 24
213 < 231   25 + 10 = 30 + 5
1024 > 124   100 + 7 > 106
6009 > 609   7 + 7 = 8 + 6
550 < 5500   19 + 16 > 15 + 15
517 < 715   14 + 14 < 50

In conclusion. Ask the child: What odd number is less than 93, but greater than 90? [91] What even numbers are less than 55, but greater than 49? [50, 52, and 54]

© Activities for Learning, Inc. 2013

LESSON 100: INTRODUCING AREA

OBJECTIVES:
1. To understand area as "taking up space"
2. To learn the term *area*

MATERIALS:
1. Sums Practice 5
2. One set of tangrams
3. Tiles
4. Worksheet 43, Introducing Area

ACTIVITIES FOR TEACHING:	EXPLANATIONS:

Warm-up. Ask the child to do the last two problems on Sums Practice 5 without his abacus:

    5075   8342
   + 3873   + 6394
    8948   14736

Ask: How many sides does a quadrilateral have? [4] Have the child show parallel lines with his arms. Have the child show perpendicular lines with his arms.

Ask the child: 11 = 5 + what? [6] 11 = 7 + what? [4] 11 = 9 + what? [2] 11 = 6 + what? [5] 11 = 4 + what? [7]

Have the child solve the following problem:

   There are 20 black or white dogs playing in the grass. In the group, 7 dogs are black. How many of the dogs are white? [13 white dogs]

Ask: What are the next two numbers in the pattern 320, 330, 340? [350, 360] What are the next two numbers in the pattern 190, 185, 180? [175, 170] What are the next two numbers in the pattern 885, 895, 905? [915, 925]

Ask: What does increasing mean? [get larger] What does decreasing mean? [get smaller]

Making a square. Give the tangrams to the child. Ask him to find the two small triangles and the square as shown below. Ask: Are the small triangles congruent? [yes] How do you know? [They fit exactly on top of each other.] Now tell him to make a square using the small triangles. See the figures below.

  Two small triangles congruent with the tangram square.

Ask: Is your new square congruent with the tangram square? [yes] Does your new square take up the same amount of space as your tangram square? [yes]

Making a medium triangle. Now tell him to make a triangle using both small triangles. See the figures on the next page.

Young children seem to understand area at an intuitive level.

This lesson is concerned with the basic concept of area, not with any calculations. Area is a fundamental concept of mathematics; even elementary mathematics uses the area of circles and squares to model fractions.

RightStart™ Mathematics Level B Second Edition   © Activities for Learning, Inc. 2013

ACTIVITIES FOR TEACHING:	EXPLANATIONS:

   Two small triangles congruent with the medium triangle.

Ask: Is your new triangle congruent with the medium triangle? [yes] Do your small triangles take up the same amount of space as your medium triangle? [yes]

Explain that two shapes that take up the same space on a flat surface have the same *area*.

Making a parallelogram. Tell the child to make a parallelogram with the small triangles. See below. Ask: Is your parallelogram congruent with the tangram parallelogram? [yes]

   Two small triangles congruent with the tangram parallelogram.

Equal areas. Tell the child to find the three tangram pieces that he could make with the two small triangles. [medium triangle, square, parallelogram] See below. Ask: Do they have equal areas? [yes] Are they congruent? [no]

    Equal areas, but not congruent.

Squares. Tell the child to make a square with the medium triangle and the two small triangles. Also ask him to make a square with four tiles. See below. Ask: Do they have equal areas? [yes] Are they congruent? [yes]

These problems are like puzzles. A child may need to try several solutions before finding one that works. Encourage the child to persevere.

   Equal areas and congruent.

Worksheet 43. Give the child the worksheet. The problems and solutions follow:

△ ≠ △

◸ + ◸ = □

◿ + ◺ = △

□ = △

▱ = ◸ + ◺

□ ≠ □

▭ = ⊞

✚ = ⊠

Because the two smaller triangles are equal to the square (second problem) and to the large triangle (third problem), the square is equal to the large triangle (fourth problem).

On this worksheet, the tiles are shown lightly shaded.

In conclusion. Ask: If two figures are congruent, are the areas equal? [yes]

© Activities for Learning, Inc. 2013

Lesson 101: Halves and Fourths

OBJECTIVES:
1. To introduce halves and fourths through dividing
2. To divide paper strips and squares into halves and fourths
3. To divide squares into fourths two ways to make an octagon

MATERIALS:
1. Geared clock
2. Dry erase board
3. Worksheet 44, Halves and Fourths
4. **Scissors and glue**

ACTIVITIES FOR TEACHING:	EXPLANATIONS:
Warm-up. Ask the child: When counting by 5s, what comes after 10, [15] 25, [30] 65, [70] 90, [95] and 105. [110]	
Set the clock to various times and ask the child to read it.	
Ask the child to mentally add 4 + 6 + 2, [12] 5 + 5 + 7, [17] 30 + 3 + 6, [39] 10 + 10 + 6, [26] and 1 + 6 + 6. [13]	
Dividing-by-2 problems. Ask the following problem:	
Kelly has 2 pet rabbits. On Monday Kelly has 8 carrots to divide equally between the rabbits. How many carrots does each rabbit get? [4]	
Ask the child how he solved the problem; then show him how to write it mathematically:	
$$\frac{8 \text{ carrots}}{2} = 4 \text{ carrots}$$	
Read it as: 8 (carrots) divided by 2 equals 4 (carrots).	
Continue with the problem:	
On Tuesday Kelly has 6 carrots to divide between the rabbits. How many carrots does each rabbit get? [3]	
Ask the child to write the solution:	It is not important where or whether they write the word carrot.
$$\frac{6 \text{ carrots}}{2} = 3 \text{ carrots}$$	
Kelly is almost out of carrots. On Wednesday Kelly has 2 carrots for the rabbits. How much does each rabbit receive? [1]	
Ask the child to write the solution:	
$$\frac{2 \text{ carrots}}{2} = 1 \text{ carrot}$$	
On Friday Kelly has only 1 carrot left. After dividing it, how much did each rabbit receive? [one half]	
Ask the child to write the first part and complete it:	
$$\frac{1 \text{ carrot}}{2} = \frac{1}{2}$$	
Read it as: 1 (carrot) divided by 2 equals one half (carrot).	

RightStart™ Mathematics Level B Second Edition © Activities for Learning, Inc. 2013

ACTIVITIES FOR TEACHING:	EXPLANATIONS:
Worksheet 44. Give the child the worksheet and scissors. Tell him to follow the instructions.	The instructions are to cut apart the five rectangles.

Dividing strips into fourths. Tell the child to set aside the two squares. Tell him to keep one strip whole and write 1 on it. Then ask him to fold a second strip in half and cut on the fold. Ask: What is each piece called? [one half] Tell him to write $\frac{1}{2}$ on each piece. See below.

Then ask him to take the last strip, to fold it in half twice, and to cut it on the folds. Explain: You cut that strip into 4 equal parts, so we call each piece, one fourth. Show him how to write it, $\frac{1}{4}$. Ask him to write it on each piece.

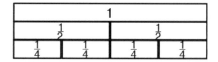 Three strips, showing whole, 2 halves, and 4 fourths.

Ask the child the following:
  Show the strip that is the whole.
  Show the whole two other ways. [2 halves, 4 fourths]
  Show one half. [a half piece]
  Show it another way. [2 fourths]
  How many fourths are in a whole? [4]
  How many halves are in a whole? [2]
  How many fourths are in a half? [2]

Making an octagon. Ask the child to fold one of the squares into fourths by folding it in half twice. Ask him to fold the other square into fourths by folding on the diagonals as shown below.

Next place one square upon the other by lining up the fold lines. Place a small amount of glue at the center of the bottom square and press the two squares together. Lastly, cut off the eight extending triangles or fold four flaps forward and four flaps backward.

Tell him it is called an octagon. Often times, the child will want to write STOP across it to resemble a stop sign.

Making an octagon from two squares.

In conclusion. Tell him to look at the octagon. Then ask: How many sets of parallel lines do you see? [4] How many sides does an octagon have? [8]

© Activities for Learning, Inc. 2013

Lesson 102: Fourths and Quarters

OBJECTIVES:
1. To find a fourth of a square and a circle
2. To learn the term *quarter*
3. To learn a quarter hour

MATERIALS:
1. Sums Practice 6
2. Two sets of tangrams
3. Worksheet 45*, Fourths and Quarters
4. Scissors

ACTIVITIES FOR TEACHING:

Warm-up. Ask the child to do the first two problems on Sums Practice 6. He will first need to put the numbers into columns. The solutions are:

```
  7833        584
+ 1209      + 8732
  9042       9316
```

Ask the child to solve the following problem:

There are 43 songbirds. Some are wrens and 23 are meadowlarks. How many are wrens? [20 wrens]

Ask the child: What odd number is less than 83, but greater than 80? [81] What even numbers are less than 65, but greater than 59? [60, 62, and 64]

Ask: What is 50 + 15? [65] What is 75 + 10? [85] What is 35 + 15? [50]

Making a large square. Give the child two sets of tangrams. Tell him to make larger triangles with the two large triangles of each set. See the left figure below. Then ask him to combine the larger triangles to make a large square. See the second figure below.

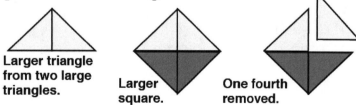

Larger triangle from two large triangles.   Larger square.   One fourth removed.

Now ask the child to remove one half of the square. Ask: How much was removed? [two triangles] What fraction is left? [one half] Tell him to put it back. Repeat for the other color of tangrams.

Next, ask the child to remove one fourth of the square. [1 triangle] See the third figure above. Tell him to put it back. Ask him to remove one fourth with a different color.

Worksheet 45. Give the child the worksheet and scissors. Tell him to cut out the circle.

EXPLANATIONS:

*Be sure the back of this worksheet is clean because both sides will be used.

RightStart™ Mathematics Level B Second Edition © Activities for Learning, Inc. 2013

ACTIVITIES FOR TEACHING:

Dividing the circle into halves and fourths. Tell the child to fold the circles in half, being careful to fold on one of the marks. See the left figure below. Ask: What do we call each of the folded parts? [half]

Circle folded in halves.   Circle folded into fourths.

Ask: How could you divide your circle into four equal parts? [Fold in half again.] See the right figure above. Ask: What do we call each of the folded parts? [a fourth] Tell him to write $\frac{1}{4}$ in each fourth on the back (blank side) of the circle.

Tell him that one fourth has another name. It is also called one *quarter*. Ask: How many quarters are in a whole? [4] How many quarters in a half? [2] What is another word for quarter? [fourth]

Right angles. Ask the child: How many right angles do you see at the center of the circle? [4]

Tell him: Think about the tangram pieces. Without looking, how many right angles are there on all of them? [9] Give him quiet time to think; then ask if necessary: Do the triangles have a right angle? [yes] How many triangles are there? [5] Do the other shapes have right angles? [square, 4; parallelogram, 0] Tell him to look at the tangrams to check.

Quarter hour. Ask him to stand and move one of his arms around in a circle, starting at the top. Then tell him to start at the top again, but to stop a quarter of the way. Tell him to continue with two more quarters. See below.

Making the four quarters of a circle.

Making a clock. Tell the child to use the side of the circle with the marks and to write the numbers around the edge like a clock. Then ask: What numbers are on the quarter hours? [3, 6, 9, and 12] How many minutes are in a quarter hour? [15]

In conclusion. Ask: What are the two names for one half of a half? [one fourth and a quarter] How many quarters in a whole? [4] How many quarters in a half? [2]

EXPLANATIONS:

This tangram question is a good place for the children to practice spatial reasoning.

© Activities for Learning, Inc. 2013

Lesson 103: Finding Quarter Parts

OBJECTIVES:
1. To apply that a quarter is half of a half
2. To find a quarter of 12 objects and a quarter of 100

MATERIALS:
1. Sums Practice 6
2. **4 identical transparent containers with straight sides**
3. **A pitcher of water, preferably colored with food coloring to make it more visible**
4. Tiles
5. AL Abacus

ACTIVITIES FOR TEACHING:

Warm-up. Ask the child to do the next two problems on Sums Practice 6. He will first need to put the numbers into columns. The solutions are:

$$\begin{array}{r} 4638 \\ +3219 \\ \hline 7857 \end{array} \qquad \begin{array}{r} 1420 \\ +3710 \\ \hline 5130 \end{array}$$

Ask the child to count by 10s to 100 [10, 20, 30, . . . , 100] and to count by 5s to 100. [5, 10, 15, . . . , 100]

Ask: How many eggs are a dozen eggs? [12] How many doughnuts are a dozen doughnuts? [12] How many roses are in a dozen roses? [12]

Ask the child to mentally add 37 + 32, [67, 69] 37 + 33, [67, 70] 100 + 77, [170, 177] and 68 + 68. [128, 136]

Ask: What are the two names for one half of a half? [one fourth, a quarter] How many quarters in a whole? [4] How many quarters in a half? [2]

Finding half of the water. Set out two identical containers and fill one of them with water from the pitcher. Ask the child to pour half of the water into the other container. Pouring back and forth from one container to the other may be necessary. Ask him if he agrees that half of the water is in each container.

Then ask: Which container has more water? [neither] Where is the whole [the amount in both containers] and where are the parts? [each container] Point to the one of the containers and ask: How much of the whole amount is in this container? [half] Repeat for the other container. [half] Ask: What do two halves make? [whole]

EXPLANATIONS:

The whole amount of water.

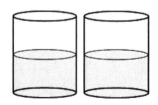

One half of the water poured into each of two containers.

ACTIVITIES FOR TEACHING:	EXPLANATIONS:

A quarter of the water. Set out two more containers. Ask the child to find half of each of the halves. See the figure below. Ask: What is one half of one half? [a quarter or one fourth] Ask: What do two quarters equal? [a half] What do two halves equal? [whole] How many quarters are in a half? [2] How many halves are in a whole? [2] How many quarters are in a whole? [4]

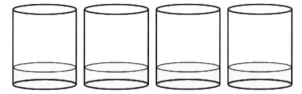

One quarter of the water poured into each of 4 containers.

Ask: How could you get three quarters? [Pour three of the one quarters together] Will three quarters be more or less than a whole? [less] Ask the child to make three quarters. Then ask: How much do you need with the three quarters to make a whole? [one quarter]

A quarter of 12. Tell the child to take 12 tiles. Ask for another name for twelve. [dozen] Ask him to find a quarter of the tiles. [3] Ask him to explain how he did it. [find half twice]

Then ask: How much is half of 12? [6] How much is 1 quarter of 12? [3] How much is 2 quarters of 12? [6] How much is 3 quarters of 12? [9] How much is 4 quarters of 12? [12] How much is a half dozen? [6]

Ask: How many months are in a year? [12] How many months are in half a year? [6] What is a quarter of a year? [3 months]

A quarter of 100. Tell the child to find a quarter of 100 on the abacus. Finding half is shown in the left figure below. There are two ways to find the quarter.

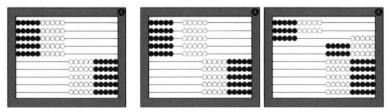

One half of 100 = 50. Two ways for finding one fourth of 100.

Ask: What is one quarter of 100? [25] What is two quarters of 100? [50] What is three quarters of 100? [75]

In conclusion. Ask: What is another word for quarter? [a fourth] Which is more, one half or two quarters? [same] Which is more, one half or three quarters? [three quarters]

© Activities for Learning, Inc. 2013

Lesson 104: Measuring with Centimeters

OBJECTIVES:
1. To measure in centimeters
2. To collect information and categorize it
3. To learn the term *data*

MATERIALS:
1. Sums Practice 6
2. Worksheet 46, Measuring with Centimeters
3. Centimeter cubes
4. One set of tangrams

ACTIVITIES FOR TEACHING:

Warm-up. Ask the child to do the last two problems on Sums Practice 6. The solutions are:

```
  7129        4233
+ 1516       + 726
  8645        4959
```

Ask: What is another word for quarter? [a fourth] What are the two names for one half of a half? [one fourth, a quarter] How many quarters in a whole? [4] How many quarters in a half? [2]

Ask: Which is more, one half or two quarters? [same] Which is less, one half or three quarters? [one half]

Ask the child to solve the following problem.

There are 15 butterflies flying by the flowers. In the group, 6 butterflies are yellow. How many of the butterflies are not yellow? [9 butterflies]

Ask the child to mentally add 47 + 32, [77, 79] 47 + 22, [67, 69] 100 + 87, [180, 187] and 67 + 60. [127]

Tangram lengths. Give the child the tangrams. Ask: Are all edges of your tangram pieces the same length? [no] Explain: In this lesson you are going to find out how many different lengths the edges of the tangram pieces have. You will also find out which length is the most common and which is the least common.

Worksheet 46. Give the child the worksheet and the centimeter cubes. Show him a centimeter cube and explain that the distance along an edge is 1 centimeter.

Ask him to measure the longest side of the large triangle in centimeters. Demonstrate as shown below in the left figure. Ask: How many centimeters long is it? [10 cm]

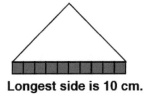
Longest side is 10 cm.

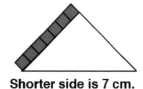
Shorter side is 7 cm.

EXPLANATIONS:

According to Clements & Sarama, researchers found that children are often confused when asked to measure with various non-standard units. Only, after they are familiar with the concept of measurement, will they be able to understand the need for standard measurements.

ACTIVITIES FOR TEACHING:	EXPLANATIONS:

Next ask him to measure the side of the large triangle. [7 cm] Repeat for the other side. [7 cm] See the right figure on the previous page.

Point to the first figure from the worksheet. Ask the child what each side measured; write it on the corresponding side of the figure. Tell him that we write cm for centimeter. See the left figure below.

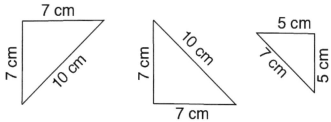

The lengths of the sides of the first 3 tangram pieces.

Tell the child the worksheet shows all the tangrams pieces. Tell him to measure the sides using the centimeter cubes and write the lengths for the first three triangles on their worksheet. See figures above.

Some children will realize that shapes may be identical and measuring them again is unnecessary. Other children will want to measure everything, which is necessary for them.

Measuring the square. Tell the child to measure a side of the square. Ask: Does it measure 3 cm? [too little] Does it measure 4 cm? [too much] Tell him: The side measures 3 and a part of a another centimeter. What part is it? [one half] Tell them: We say it is 3 and one half centimeters. Show them to how write $3\frac{1}{2}$ cm.

Although fractions are not common within the metric system, they are permissible.

Do the same thing with the last three pieces. Answers are shown below.

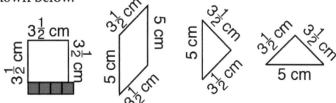

The lengths of the sides of the last 4 tangram pieces.

Worksheet Question 2. Explain to the child that he has a lot of information, called *data*; now he can organize it in the chart. First, his is to count the number of sides having 10 cm and write it below the box saying 10 cm. Next he is to find the number of sides that are 7 cm long and write it below the 7 cm. Do the same thing with the last two lengths. The solutions are:

      10   7   5   3
       2   5   6 $10\frac{1}{2}$

Worksheet Question 3. Here he is to tell what he learned about the lengths.

In conclusion. Ask: Are you surprised there are only four different lengths?

© Activities for Learning, Inc. 2013

LESSON 105: GRAPHING

OBJECTIVES:
1. To collect data
2. To tabulate the data
3. To construct graphs from the data
4. To read information from the graphs

MATERIALS:
1. Sums Practice 7
2. Worksheet 47-1 and 47-2, Graphing
3. **Crayons or colored pencils**

ACTIVITIES FOR TEACHING:	EXPLANATIONS:

Warm-up. Ask the child to do the first two problems on Sums Practice 7. The solutions are:
 	
    1865   2883
  + 3408   + 56
    5273   2939
 	
Ask: Which is greater, 72 + 4 or 72 + 10? [72 + 10] Which is greater, 32 or 30 + 2? [same] Which is greater, 10 minus 3 or 10 minus 5? [10 minus 3] Which is greater, one half of 10 or one half of 20? [one half of 20]
 	
Review the symbols < and > by writing the following and asking the child which symbol to use: 3 + 4 ○ 10, [<] 31 ○ 13? [>] and 29 + 5 ○ 29 + 10. [<]
 	
Collecting data. Tell the child that he is going to collect data about the number of pockets his family has. Then he will make a graph to show the results.
 	
Worksheet 47-1. Give the child the worksheet. For the first question, see the top figure on the next page. Tell him: Count the pockets you have and remember the number. Then tell him: After each person says the number of pockets they have, find the correct rectangle and write their name in it. Ask each family member in turn to give the number of pockets.
 	
Question 2. Ask: How can you find the number of people having no pockets? [by counting the number of names in the first rectangle] Ask him to write that number in the first rectangle. See the second figure on the next page. Continue by asking: How can you find the number of people having 1 pocket? [counting] Tell him to complete the row.
	
	Graphs are a visual way to display data, or numerical information. There are three steps:
	  1. Collect the data
	  2. Tabulate the data
	  3. Graph the data.

ACTIVITIES FOR TEACHING:

1. Write the name of each person in the correct box.

People having 0 pockets. Anna, Tracy, Jon	People having 1 pocket.
People having 2 pockets.	People having 3 pockets.
People having 4 pockets.	People having >4 pockets.

Question 1.

2. Write the total number of people for each number of pockets.

0 pockets	1 pocket	2 pockets	3 pockets	4 pockets	>4 pockets
3					

Question 2.

Then ask: Who has the fewest pockets? Who has the most pockets? How many people have four (use an actual number) pockets?

Question 3. Tell him to look at the chart near the bottom of the worksheet. See the figure below.

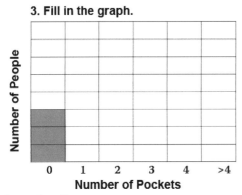

Question 3.

Ask: How many people have no pockets? Tell him to color that many boxes in the first column, starting from the bottom. (3 are colored in with this example.) Ask him to complete the chart.

Question 4. Ask: What number of pockets is most common? What number of pockets is least common?

Worksheet 47-2. This worksheet is similar to the first worksheet, but uses the number of letters in the family members' first names.

In conclusion. How many people have more than 5 letters in their names? [Add results of last two columns.]

EXPLANATIONS:

Encourage the children to work as independently as possible for the second worksheet.

© Activities for Learning, Inc. 2013

LESSON 106: MEASURING WITH INCHES

OBJECTIVES:
1. To become aware that different units give different measurements
2. To learn to write *cm* for centimeter
3. To learn to write *in.* for inches

MATERIALS:
1. Sums Practice 7
2. Tiles and Centimeter cubes
3. One set of tangrams
4. AL Abacus
5. Worksheet 48, Measuring with Inches
6. **A business card, if available**

ACTIVITIES FOR TEACHING:

Warm-up. Ask the child to do the next two problems on Sums Practice 7. The solutions are:

```
  283        79
  255       234
 + 60      + 81
  598       394
```

Ask: How much is 33 + 10? [43] How much is 54 + 10? [64] How much is 87 + 10? [97] How much is 61 + 10? [71] How much is 98 + 10? [108]

Ask: Which is greater, 72 + 4 or 72 + 10? [72 + 10] Which is greater, 32 or 30 + 2? [same] Which is greater, 10 minus 3 or 10 minus 5 [10 minus 3] Which is greater, one half of 10 or one half of 20? [one half of 20]

Review the symbols < and > by writing the following and asking the child which symbol to use: 2 + 4 ○ 10, [<] 21 ○ 12 [>] and 39 + 5 ○ 39 + 10. [<]

Inches. Give the child the tiles, centimeter cubes, and tangrams. Show a tile and explain that the edge of a tile is 1 inch long. Tell him to measure the longest side of the large triangle. [4 in.] See figure below.

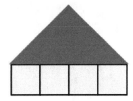

Measuring in inches with tiles.

Problem. Ask the child the following problem.

Find all the sides of the tangram pieces that measure 2 in. [6 sides]

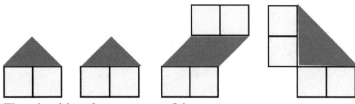

The six sides that measure 2 in.

EXPLANATIONS:

Even if you do not use inches in everyday life, this activity helps the child understand that the measurement of an object depends upon the unit of measurement.

RightStart™ Mathematics Level B Second Edition © Activities for Learning, Inc. 2013

ACTIVITIES FOR TEACHING:	EXPLANATIONS:

Measuring a line. Ask the child to use the tangram pieces and make the longest line he can. See below. Then ask him to measure it in inches using the tiles. [18 in.]

The longest line with the tangram pieces.

Ask: If you put your line next to another line, how long would the new line be? [36 in.]

Now ask him to make the shortest line using all the tangram pieces. See the figure below. Ask him to measure it. [13 in.]

The shortest line with the tangram pieces.

Ask: What is the difference in length between the longest line you made and the shortest line you made? [5 in.]

Measuring the abacus. Explain that what we measure with is called a *unit*. Give the child the following problem:

Jason measured a side of a plastic AL Abacus and found it was 19. What were Jason's units, centimeters or inches? [centimeters] Which side did he measure? [the shorter side]

Continue with:

Jessica measured the length of 10 AL Abacus beads. She found it was 4. What were Jessica's units, centimeters or inches? [inches]

Worksheet 48. Explain that this worksheet has figures of things that were measured, but they are missing the units, centimeter or inches. Tell him that people usually write *cm* for centimeter and *in.* for inches. He can measure the real objects, or the pictures, and write either cm or in.

The first object is a business card. If available, show one to the children.

Yes, *in.* needs a period, but *cm* does not.

The solutions are as follows:
    2 in., $3\frac{1}{2}$ in.   2 in., 5 cm
    7 cm, 10 cm   8 cm, 3 cm
    10 cm, 4 in.
    15 cm, 6 in.

In conclusion. Ask: When you measure an object with centimeters and with inches, which unit will give the higher number? [centimeters]

© Activities for Learning, Inc. 2013

Lesson 107: Paper Measuring Problems

OBJECTIVES:
1. To practice measuring in inches
2. To solve measuring problems
3. To add two halves

MATERIALS:
1. Sums Practice 7
2. **A sheet of plain paper, $8\frac{1}{2}$" by 11",** for each child
3. Tiles

ACTIVITIES FOR TEACHING:	EXPLANATIONS:

Warm-up. Ask the child to do the last two problems on Sums Practice 7. The solutions are:

```
   688          97
  3874         852
  + 52       +9460
  ────       ─────
  4614       10409
```

Ask: When you measure an object with centimeters and with inches, which unit will give the higher number? [centimeters]

Ask the child to solve the following problem.

> Ann and John are driving home from the lake. It takes 40 minutes to get home. They have driven 15 minutes already. How many minutes until they arrive home? [25 minutes]

Ask: How much is 43 + 10? [53] How much is 41 + 10? [51] How much is 72 + 10? [82] How much is 33 + 10? [43] How much is 91 + 10? [101]

Review the symbols < and > by writing the following and asking the child which symbol to use: 2 + 7 ○ 11, [<] 52 ○ 25 [>] and 44 + 5 ○ 44 + 10. [<]

Measuring a sheet of paper. Give the child the piece of paper. Tell the child: Use the tiles and find out how long a piece of paper is. [11 in.] Then ask him: Now measure the width of the same sheet of paper. [$8\frac{1}{2}$ in.] Write both dimensions for the child to see.

This paper size is the standard in North America.

Problem 1. Give the child the following problem to solve on a pieces of paper:

> A little insect walked around the edge of the piece of paper. How far in inches did it walk? [39 in.]

$8\frac{1}{2}$ by 11 in. piece of paper.

ACTIVITIES FOR TEACHING:	EXPLANATIONS:
Give him a few minutes to work on his own before working with him. Observe how the child is solving the problem. Ask him to explain his work. One way to write it is: $$8\tfrac{1}{2} + 11 + 8\tfrac{1}{2} + 11 = 39 \text{ in.}$$ If he has difficulty with adding this equation, ask: What is one half and one half? [1]	The simplest solution is to lay out tiles along all four edges, count them and adding one more for the two halves. A more sophisticated solution is to double the sides already measured, getting 22 and 17 and adding them together.

Problem 2. Give him the following problem:

What is the size of the largest square you could make with the piece of paper? [$8\tfrac{1}{2}$ in. on each side] How far does the insect walk to go around this square? [34 in.]

Problem 3. Continue with:

How many fewer inches did the insect walk around the square than the whole piece of paper? [5 in.]

Ask him to write the equation. [39 − 34 = 5 in.]

Problem 4. Tell him to fold the paper in half so the two short edges are touching. See the figure below.

 Paper folded in half.

Continue with the next problem:

Two insects wanted to travel from one corner of the folded sheet of paper to the opposite corner. One insect, called A, walked along the two sides.

The other insect, called B, walked on the diagonal from one corner to the opposite corner. Which insect walked farther? [A] How much farther? [4 in.]

$$A \text{ walked: } 5\tfrac{1}{2} + 8\tfrac{1}{2} = 14 \text{ in.}$$
$$B \text{ walked: } 10 \text{ in.}$$
$$14 - 10 = 4 \text{ in.}$$
A walked 4 in. farther

Problem 5. Give him the following problem:

What is the size of the largest square you could make with the folded piece of paper? [$5\tfrac{1}{2}$ in. on each side] How far does the insect walk to travel around this square? [22 in.]

How much shorter is a side of this square than the square in Problem 2? [$8\tfrac{1}{2} - 5\tfrac{1}{2} = 3$ in.]

In conclusion. Ask: What is one half plus one half? [1] What is 2 and one half plus 9 and one half? [12]

Lesson 108: Making Rectangles with Tiles

OBJECTIVES:
1. To practice measuring in inches
2. To solve measuring problems

MATERIALS:
1. Sums Practice 8
2. Tiles
3. 4-in-1 ruler
4. Worksheet 49, Making Rectangles with Tiles

ACTIVITIES FOR TEACHING:	EXPLANATIONS:

Warm-up. Ask the child to do the left column on Sums Practice 8. The sums are:
    7   3   1   2   10   6   5   8   4   9
 Ask: What is one half plus one half? [1] What is 3 and one half plus 5 and one half? [9]
 	
 Ask the child to solve the following problem.
 	
     There are 14 swings on a swing set. Some children are swinging on the swings. Three swings are empty. How many children are swinging? [11 children swinging]
 	
 Ask: When you measure an object with centimeters and with inches, which unit will give the lower number? [inches]
 	
 Use the symbols < and > by writing the following and asking the child which symbol to use: 4 + 5 ○ 11, [<] 63 ○ 36 [>] and 65 + 5 ○ 60 + 15. [<]
 	
 Introducing the ruler. Give the child the tiles and the ruler. Ask him to line up 10 tiles. Ask: How long is your row? [10 in.] Show him how to place the ruler below the row of tiles as shown below with the first tile starting at the zero.
 	
 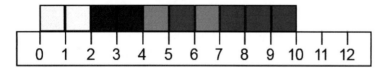
 Tiles lined up against the ruler.
 	
 Tell him: Look at the number on your ruler that is at the end of your row. What does it say? [10] The ruler tells you how many tiles long your row is! Tell him: Add 2 more tiles to your row. How many tiles does your row have now? [12] What does your ruler say? [12]
 	
 Ask him to subtract 4 tiles from the row. What is the difference according to the ruler? [8]
	
	Be sure the child is using the inch scale.

ACTIVITIES FOR TEACHING:	EXPLANATIONS:

Worksheet 49. Give the child the worksheet. Tell him to look at the figure shown on the left. Ask: Do you see the square? Tell him to make the square with 8 tiles.

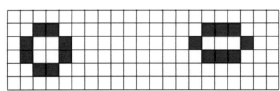

A square made with 8 tiles.   A another rectangle made with 8 tiles.

Rotating the rectangle 90 degrees is not a new rectangle. Thus, the two rectangles below are the same.

Making another rectangle with 8 tiles. Tell him to take 8 more tiles. He can use the ruler to help count 8 rectangles. Ask him to make another rectangle. See the right figure above. Tell him to draw the rectangle on the worksheet.

The children do not need to draw each individual tile.

Ask: How many inches is the distance around your square? [8 in.] What is the distance around the other rectangle? [8 in.] How many tiles could you fit in the rectangles? [4 in the square and 3 in the rectangle]

Finding the number of squares that will fit inside requires spatial reasoning as well as a basis for calculating area.

Making rectangles with 16 tiles. Tell the child: Make as many different rectangles as you can with 16 tiles. [4 are possible]

Then tell him to draw them on the worksheet. Inside each rectangle he writes the number of tiles that could fit. The solutions are below. Ask: How many inches would a bug walk around each rectangle? [16 in.]

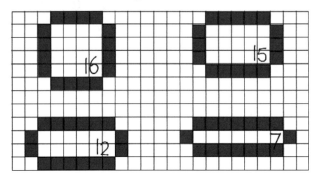

The possible rectangles made with 16 tiles.

Measuring other objects. He is also to measure in inches three things in the room and record them on the worksheet.

In conclusion. Ask: What does a ruler tell you? [how long something measures] Can you use the same place on the ruler to measure the number of centimeter cubes? [no]

© Activities for Learning, Inc. 2013

Lesson 109: Geometry Solids

OBJECTIVES:
1. To identify prisms and pyramids
2. To identify shapes by touch

MATERIALS:
1. Sums Practice 8
2. Geometry solids
3. Geometry panels*, 1 set
4. **A ball, a funnel, a cylindrical can**
5. **A brown paper bag**

ACTIVITIES FOR TEACHING:

Warm-up. Ask the child to do the right column on Sums Practice 8. The sums are:

   3   7   5   1   2   6   4   9   10   8

Ask: What does a ruler tell you? [how long something measures] Can you use the same place on the ruler to measure the number of centimeters? [no]

Ask: When you measure an object with centimeters and with inches, which unit will give the higher number? [centimeters]

Ask: What is one half plus one half? [1] What is 3 and one half plus 5 and one half? [9]

Prisms. Give the geometry solids to the child. Ask: How many solids have curved faces or sides? [5] Tell him to set those aside. Then tell him to find and set aside the pyramid, the figure whose sides meet at a point.

Triangular prisms. Set out the four panel prisms in a row as shown to the right in the first row. Explain: Prisms have congruent figures at each end. Pick up the panel triangular prism and point out the two triangles. Ask the child to find the solid prism with triangles at each end.

Rectangular prisms. Next pick up the panel cube. Ask: What congruent shape is at both ends? [square] Tell him to find the three solid prisms with rectangles at each end. See the figures below.

    Three rectangular prisms.

Explain that one of the prisms is very special because all its faces are congruent. What is the name of that prism? [cube] Ask him to find it. [first figure above]

Tell him another one of the solid prisms is a little special because its end faces are squares. Ask him to find it. [second figure on the previous page]

EXPLANATIONS:

*Before the lesson, make the following figures (shown below) from the geometry panels:
1. triangular prism
2. cube
3. pentagonal prism
4. hexagonal prism
5. triangular pyramid (tetrahedron)
6. square pyramid
7. pentagonal pyramid
8. hexagonal pyramid.

The prisms: 1. triangular, 2. cube, 3. pentagonal, 4. hexagonal.

The pyramids: 5. triangular, 6. square, 7. pentagonal, 8. hexagonal.

ACTIVITIES FOR TEACHING:	EXPLANATIONS:
Ask him to find the solid prism that has end faces that are rectangles that are not squares. [third figure on the previous page]	
Repeat for the panel pentagonal prism. Explain that we do not have a solid pentagonal prism	
Show the panel hexagonal prism; tell him to find the solid prism with hexagon faces. Ask: How many rectangles (squares) does it have between the two faces? [6]	
Then tell him to find the solid prism with octagon faces. Explain that you do not have a panel octagon prism. How many rectangles does it have between the two faces? [8]	
Pyramids. Show the four panel pyramids. Explain that pyramids have a figure at one end and a point at the other end. Its sides are triangles. Show him the base of the panel triangular pyramid and ask: What figure is it? [triangle]	
Next point out the panel rectangular (square) pyramid. Ask: What figure is at the base? [square or rectangle] How many triangles does it have between the point and the base? [4]	
Repeat for the panel pentagonal and hexagonal pyramids. Then ask: How many triangular sides does your wooden pyramid have? [4]	Some geometry sets have square pyramids, and some sets have triangular pyramids.
The remaining solids. Tell the child to get out the solids with curved parts. Show him a ball. Remind him that its mathematical name is *sphere*. Ask him to find the solid spheres. Then ask him to find the solid that is half a sphere, called the *hemisphere*.	
Show him a funnel and ask him to find the solid *cone*. Repeat for a can and ask him to find the two solid *cylinders*.	

Stereognostic game 1. Give the child the paper bag. Ask him to carefully place all 12 solids into the bag. Then for each solid listed below, say its name, and ask him to find and remove it from the bag without looking:
    sphere   2 cylinders   triangular prism
    cube   hemisphere   2 rectangular prisms
    cone   pyramid   2 prisms
	The *stereognostic* sense is the ability to identify an object strictly by touch.

Stereognostic game 2. For this game the child starts with all the solids in the bag. He feels a solid and says its name. Then he removes it and verifies it by looking.	
In conclusion. Ask: Which figure is round all over? [sphere] Which figures have circles on a face? [cylinder, hemisphere, and cone]	

© Activities for Learning, Inc. 2013

Lesson 110: Building with Cubes

OBJECTIVES:
1. To build cubes and pyramids
2. To practice measuring in centimeters
3. To practice interpreting figures as 3D objects

MATERIALS:
1. Sums Practice 9
2. **A book about pyramids**
3. Centimeter cubes
4. 4-in-1 ruler
5. Worksheet 51, Building with Cubes

ACTIVITIES FOR TEACHING:	EXPLANATIONS:
Warm-up. Ask the child to do the right column on Sums Practice 9. The sums are: 6 3 10 7 9 8 4 9 2 5 Ask the child to count by tens, starting at 85 and ending at 185. [85, 95, 105, . . . , 185] Ask: Which figures have circles on a face? [cylinder, hemisphere, and cone] Which figure is round all over? [sphere] Ask: What is one half plus one half? [1] What is 7 and one half plus 1 and one half? [9] Ask: When you measure an object with centimeters and with inches, which unit will give the lower number? [inches] **Book on pyramids.** Read to the child a book about pyramids, especially the Egyptian pyramids. **Building cubes.** Give the centimeter cubes to the child. Ask: What shape is this? [cube] What does each side measure? [1 cm] Tell the child to use the centimeter cubes to make a larger cube that is 2 cm on a side. See the second figure below. Cube 1 cm on a side. Cube 2 cm on a side. Cube 3 cm on a side. **Measuring the number of cubes.** Ask: How many centimeter cubes did you need to make the 2-centimeter cube? [8] Tell him to use the centimeter scale on his ruler to measure as shown on the next page. Tell him to make a cube that is 3 cm on a side. Suggest he uses his ruler to make the edges straight. See the third figure above. Ask him to use his ruler and find out how many cubes were needed. [27]	

RightStart™ Mathematics Level B Second Edition

ACTIVITIES FOR TEACHING:	EXPLANATIONS:

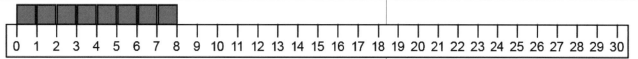

Centimeter cubes lined up against the ruler.

Building pyramids. Tell the child he can build pyramids with his cubes. Tell him to make square prisms 1 cm high up to 5 cm on an edge. See the figures below.

Building the square prisms.

Show the child how to stack the prisms to make the pyramids. Make the first pyramid, shown below on the left, by placing the 3-prism centered on the 5-square prism and place the last cube on top.

Pyramid made from 1-, 3-, and 5-square prisms. **Pyramid made from 1-, 2-, 3-, and 4-prisms.**

The pyramid on the left is easier to make.

The pyramid above on the right uses the 1-, 2-, 3-, and 4-square prisms. Tell the child that the ancient Egyptians made their pyramids like this and filled in the spaces with mortar to make the sides smooth.

Ask: Which pyramid uses more cubes and how many more? Tell him to use his rulers to measure. [Left pyramid has 35 cubes and right pyramid has 30 cubes, so left pyramid has 5 more.]

Looking directly at the front of the two pyramids gives the illusion that the right pyramid has more cubes because $1 + 2 + 3 + 4 = 10$; whereas, the left pyramid has $1 + 3 + 5 = 9$.

Worksheet 51. For this worksheet the child can use the cubes and ruler to find the number of cubes in each figure. The answers are below:

    a. 8   d. 8   g. 16   j. 14
    b. 8   e. 10   h. 10   k. 18
    c. 18   f. 10   i. 10   l. 14

In conclusion. Ask: Can you measure more centimeters or more inches on your ruler? [centimeters]

© Activities for Learning, Inc. 2013

Lesson 111: Mentally Adding with Sums over 100

OBJECTIVES:
1. To learn to add multiples of ten to 2-digit numbers with sums over 100 mentally

MATERIALS:
1. Sums Practice 9
2. AL Abacus
3. Worksheet 50, Mentally Adding with Sums over 100

ACTIVITIES FOR TEACHING:

Warm-up. Ask the child to do the left column on Sums Practice 9. The sums are:

   8   2   4   3   9   5   6   10   9   7

Ask: Which figure is round all over? [sphere] Which figures have circles on a face? [cylinder, hemisphere, and cone]

Ask: When you measure an object with centimeters and with inches, which unit will give the higher number? [centimeters]

Ask: What is one half plus one half? [1] What is 6 and one half plus 3 and one half? [10]

Adding tens. Tell the child to enter 84 on side 2 of the abacus. See the left figure below. Then tell him to enter 50 more. See the right figure below.

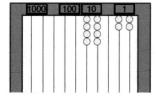
Entering 84.

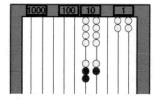
Adding 50.

Ask the child if he can read your answer before trading. Ask: How did you do it? [by seeing the 10 light-colored ten beads as 1 hundred] Then ask him to trade. See the figures below. Ask: What is 84 + 50? [134]

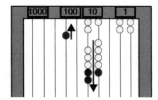
Trading 1 ten for 1 hundred.

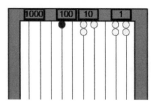
84 + 50 = 134.

EXPLANATIONS:

ACTIVITIES FOR TEACHING:

EXPLANATIONS:

Practice. Now ask the following: What is 96 + 10? [106] Tell the child to try first without an abacus, then check with their abacus. Repeat for 61 + 70, [131] 75 + 70, [145] 59 + 60, [119] and 47 + 80. [127]

Problem 1. Read the following problem to the child:

Ninety Canadian geese land on Long Lake. Two minutes later 60 more geese land. How many geese landed on the lake. [150 geese]

Encourage the child to solve the problem in his head. Then ask him to check the solution on his abacus. Ask: Does the 2 minutes have anything to do with the number of geese? [no]

Extend the problem as follows:

Suppose 93 geese landed first and 60 more landed five minutes later. How many geese would there be? [153]

Problem 2. Read the following problem to the child:

On the first day of August, 40 caterpillars broke out of their chrysalises to become butterflies. On the second day of August, 80 more caterpillars broke out of their chrysalises and become butterflies. How many butterflies are there? [120]

Extend the problem as follows:

Someone miscounted. Actually 47 caterpillars emerged the first day and 80 on the second day. How many butterflies are there? [127]

Worksheet 50. This worksheet provides further practice. Again encourage the child to do them mentally but use the abacus to check. The solutions are below:

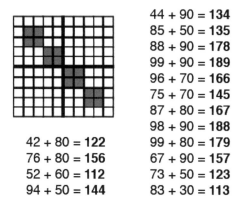

44 + 90 = **134**
85 + 50 = **135**
88 + 90 = **178**
99 + 90 = **189**
96 + 70 = **166**
75 + 70 = **145**
87 + 80 = **167**
98 + 90 = **188**

42 + 80 = **122**   99 + 80 = **179**
76 + 80 = **156**   67 + 90 = **157**
52 + 60 = **112**   73 + 50 = **123**
94 + 50 = **144**   83 + 30 = **113**

In conclusion. Ask the child to count by tens, starting at 95 and ending at 195. [95, 105, . . . , 195]

© Activities for Learning, Inc. 2013

Lesson 112: Pennies, Nickels, and Dimes

OBJECTIVES:
1. To review the names and value of penny, nickel, and dime
2. To add the value of several coins

MATERIALS:
1. Sums Practice 10
2. Coins: penny, nickel, dime
3. AL Abacus
4. *Math Card Games* book, M4
5. Worksheet 52, Pennies, Nickels, and Dimes

ACTIVITIES FOR TEACHING:

Warm-up. Ask the child to do the left column on Sums Practice 10. The sums are:

   7   5   6   8   7   9   6   8   9   10

Ask: Can you measure more centimeters or more inches on your ruler? [centimeters]

Ask the child to count by tens, starting at 75 and ending at 175. [75, 85, 95, . . . , 175]

Ask: Which figures have circles on a face? [cylinder, hemisphere, and cone] Which figure is round all over? [sphere]

Ask: What is one half plus one half? [1] What is 11 and one half plus 2 and one half? [14]

Penny, nickel, and dime. Give the pennies, nickels, and dimes to the child. Lay out the three coins in order as shown below. Point to the penny and say: This is a penny, worth 1 cent. Continue with a nickel saying: This is a nickel, worth 5 cents. Point to the dime and say: This is a dime, worth 10 cents.

Penny worth 1¢.   **Nickel worth 5¢.**   **Dime worth 10¢.**

Ask him to point to a penny. Continue with the nickel and dime. Ask: How much is the penny worth? [1 cent] (Be sure he includes the word *cent*.) Repeat for the nickel [5 cents] and dime. [10 cents]

Ask: Do you see any patterns? How is the penny different from the nickel and the dime? Discuss its copper color and the direction the heads face. [Only the penny faces right.] Ask: Which coin is the thickest? [nickel]

EXPLANATIONS:

Activities with coins gives children an opportunity to apply their knowledge of tens.

There are four skills to learning money:
1. Learning names and values of the coins
2. Adding the value of several coins
3. Choosing (fewest) coins to make a desired total
4. Starting at a value and choosing the fewest coins to reach a desired total (making change).

U.S. coins have several obstacles that make learning money difficult for children.
1. The size the dime is smaller than the penny or nickel.
2. The numerical value of the coins is not printed on the coin.
3. There is a 25¢ coin, but a $20 bill.

ACTIVITIES FOR TEACHING:	EXPLANATIONS:

Tell him: The coins gets larger in size as their value increases, or are worth more, except for the dime. Explain that the dime is smaller because it used to be made from silver, a very costly metal.

Entering the values on the abacus. Ask: What is the name of the coin that is worth 1 cent? [penny] Tell him to enter its value on the abacus. See the left figure below.

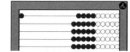 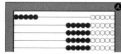 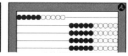

Penny worth 1¢.   Nickel worth 5¢.   Dime worth 10¢.

Ask: What is the name of the coin that is worth 5 cents? [nickel] Tell him to enter that amount on the abacus. See the second figure above. Ask: How many pennies does it take to equal 1 nickel? [5]

Ask: What is the name of the coin that is worth 10 cents? [dime] Tell him to enter that value on the abacus. See the third figure above. Ask: How many pennies does it take to equal 1 dime? [10] How many nickels equal 1 dime? [2]

Adding amounts. Tell the child to use his abacus if it helps him to answer the following:

　How much is 1 nickel and 2 pennies worth? [7 cents]
　How much is 1 nickel and 4 pennies worth? [9 cents]
　How much is 6 pennies and 1 nickel worth? [11 cents]
　How much is 3 nickels worth? [15 cents]
　How much is 4 dimes and 1 penny worth? [41 cents]
　How much is 3 dimes and 3 nickels worth? [45 cents]

Money War game. Play the Money War game found in the *Math Card Games* book, M4. Use only the penny, nickel, and dime cards.

Writing the ¢ sign. Show the child how to write 2¢. Explain that the cent sign looks like a "c" with a vertical line through it.

Worksheet 52. Give the child the worksheet. The solutions are below:

　　　7¢　　11¢　　15¢
　　　30¢　22¢　　15¢
　　　40¢　25¢　　30¢
　　　16¢　20¢　　16¢

In conclusion. Which is smallest in size; penny, nickel, or dime? [dime] Which is worth the most; penny, nickel or dime? [dime]

© Activities for Learning, Inc. 2013

Lesson 113: Coin Problems

OBJECTIVES:
1. To learn that 100 cents equals 1 dollar
2. To solve coin problems

MATERIALS:
1. Sums Practice 10
2. Coins: penny, nickel, dime
3. AL Abacus
4. Math journal
5. *Math Card Games* book, M6

ACTIVITIES FOR TEACHING:	EXPLANATIONS:
Warm-up. Ask the child to do the right column on Sums Practice 10. The sums are: 4 1 7 9 3 8 6 2 5 0 Ask the child to give the ways to make 11: 9 and what? [2] 8 and what? [3] 7 and what? [4] Continue to 1 and what? [10] Show the child a penny and ask him its name and what it is worth. [penny, 1 cent] Ask the child to enter that amount on the abacus. Next show the child a nickel and ask him its name and what it is worth. [nickel, 5 cents] Ask the child to enter that amount on the abacus. Which is smallest in size; penny, nickel, or dime? [dime] Which is worth the most; penny, nickel or dime? [dime] Show the child a square and ask: Is it a quadrilateral? [yes] Is it a parallelogram? [yes] Is it a triangle? [no] Is it a rectangle? [yes] Is it a square? [yes] ***Dimes.*** Give pennies, nickels, and dimes to the child. Ask: How many pennies are the same as one dime? [10] Then ask: How many nickels does it take to equal one dime? [2] Ask the child to find 1 dime and to enter its value on the abacus. [10] Ask him to find 3 dimes and to enter that value on his abacus. [30] Continue with 4 dimes, 7 dimes, and 10 dimes. With 10 dimes entered, tell the child one hundred cents is called *one dollar.* Ask: How many dimes make a dollar? [10] How many pennies are needed to make a dollar? [100] How many nickels are needed to make a dollar? [20]	

ACTIVITIES FOR TEACHING:

EXPLANATIONS:

Coin problem 1. Ask the child to use the coins and find all the ways to make 10¢. Solutions are:

   1 dime

   2 nickels

   1 nickel and 5 pennies

   10 pennies

Coin problem 2. Tell the child to write the answers to the next problem in his math journal.

   How many different ways can you make 20 cents using pennies, nickels, and dimes?

Tell him to use "p" for penny, "n" for nickel, and "d" for dime. Tell him to name the coins worth the most first. Also tell him there are nine solutions. The solutions are:

```
2 d
1 d 2 n
1 d 1 n 5 p
1 d 1 0 p
4 n
3 n 5 p
2 n 1 0 p
1 n 1 5 p
2 0 p
```

When he has completed writing his answers, ask:

   Which answer needed the fewest coins? [2 dimes]

   Which answer needed the most coins? [20 pennies]

   Which answer needed three kinds of coins? [1 dime, 1 nickel, and 5 pennies]

Make Sixteen Cents game. Play the Make Sixteen Cents game found in the *Math Card Games* book, M6.

In conclusion. Ask: How many pennies are in 1 dollar? [100] How many nickels are in 1 dollar? [20] How many dimes are in 1 dollar? [10]

© Activities for Learning, Inc. 2013

Lesson 114: Choosing Coins

OBJECTIVES:
1. To choose coins that are needed to make a given amount
2. To add the value of several coins
3. To use a chart to record ways to make 27¢

MATERIALS:
1. Sums Practice 11
2. Geared clock
3. Coins: penny, nickel, dime
4. AL Abacus
5. Math journal
6. Worksheet 53, Choosing Coins

ACTIVITIES FOR TEACHING:

Warm-up. Ask the child to do the left column on Sums Practice 11. The sums are:

   2 1 7 10 8 3 5 4 9 6

Ask: How many pennies are in 2 dollars? [200] How many nickels are in 2 dollars? [40] How many dimes are in 2 dollars? [20]

Ask the child to sing the song "Thirty Days has September." Ask the child to name the months with 31 days. [January, March, May, July, August, October, and December]

Ask the child to count the minutes on a clock with arm positions.

Set the clock to various 5-minute intervals and ask the child to state the times.

Finding the correct coins. Give the coins to the child. Tell him to lay out 3 dimes, 3 nickels, and 3 pennies. Ask: If you want to buy a balloon for 21¢, which coins do you need? [2 dimes and 1 penny] Tell him to check by entering the amount on the abacus. See below.

 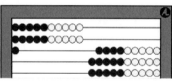

Buying the balloon problem for 21¢.

Repeat for 18¢ [3 nickels and 3 pennies or 1 dime, 1 nickel, and 3 pennies] and for 40¢. [3 dimes and 2 nickels]

Next tell him to lay out 5 of each coin and ask the child to make 25¢. [Many solutions are possible.]

Repeat for 62¢. [5 dimes, 2 nickels, and 2 pennies, or 4 dimes, 4 nickels, and 2 pennies]

EXPLANATIONS:

ACTIVITIES FOR TEACHING:

Making 27 cents. Draw the chart in the math journal as shown below on the left. Tell the child to find all the ways to make 27¢.

Dimes	Nickels	Pennies

Dimes	Nickels	Pennies
0	0	27
0	1	22
0	2	17
1	0	17
0	3	12
1	1	12
0	4	7
1	2	7
2	0	7
0	5	2
1	3	2
2	1	2

The blank chart. The ways to make 27¢.

Write the first few solutions the child finds. Then ask him to fill in the chart. It is not necessary to do it in any kind of order. The solutions are shown above on the right.

When it is finished, ask him: Which solution took the fewest number of coins? [2 dimes, 1 nickel, 2 pennies] Which solution took the most coins? [27 pennies] What is the difference in the number of coins for the solutions needing the most coins and the fewest coins? [27 − 5 = 22] Which solution needs exactly 10 coins? [1 dime, 2 nickels, 7 pennies]

Worksheet 53. Give the child the worksheet. He is to circle the coins needed to make the amounts. Some amounts have more than one answer.

Optional. When the child has finished the worksheet, ask him to add the value of all the coins in each rectangle and to write the sum under the amounts. Those answers are below:

    48¢   19¢
    43¢   48¢
    47¢   56¢
    52¢   26¢

In conclusion. Ask: When you add a bunch of coins, which ones do you add first? [probably dimes, then nickels, and pennies last]

EXPLANATIONS:

© Activities for Learning, Inc. 2013

Lesson 115: Counting Money with Quarters

OBJECTIVES:
1. To learn the value of a quarter and half-dollar
2. To count money using the four coins

MATERIALS:
1. Sums Practice 11
2. AL Abacus
3. At least five each of the following coins: quarter, dime, nickel, penny, one half-dollar
4. Worksheet 54, Counting Money with Quarters

ACTIVITIES FOR TEACHING:

Warm-up. Ask the child to do the right column on Sums Practice 11. The sums are:

   1   2   1   1   1   2   3   2   4   3

Ask the child to say whether the following numbers are even or odd: 7, [odd] 37, [odd] 72, [even] and 71. [odd]

Ask the child to mentally add 53 + 32, [83, 85] 53 + 19. [63, 72]

Ask: How many pennies are in 1 dollar? [100] How many nickels are in 1 dollar? [20] How many dimes are in 1 dollar? [10]

Ask: When you add a bunch of coins, which ones do you add first? [probably dimes, then nickels, and pennies last]

A half-dollar. Give the coins to the child. Ask him to lay a penny, nickel, and dime in a row. Ask him to add the other two coins as shown below.

1¢   5¢   10¢   25¢   50¢

Displaying the coins and their values.

Explain: The largest coin is a *half-dollar.* Hardly anyone uses them any more, so they are hard to find. Ask: What is a dollar worth? [100 cents] Tell him that the word *cent* comes from a Latin word meaning hundred. Ask: What is a half-dollar worth? [50 cents]

A quarter of a dollar. Tell him: The fourth coin in the row is a quarter. Ask him to use an abacus to find a quarter of a dollar. [25¢] See figures below for two ways of finding a quarter of a dollar.

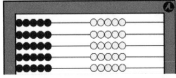 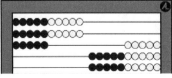

Two ways of seeing a quarter of a dollar.

EXPLANATIONS:

RightStart™ Mathematics Level B Second Edition   © Activities for Learning, Inc. 2013

ACTIVITIES FOR TEACHING:	EXPLANATIONS:

Ask: How many quarters equal one dollar? [4] How much is half of a dollar? [50¢] How much is 2 quarters? [50¢] How much is 4 quarters? [100¢, 1 dollar]

Ask: How many pennies does it take to equal 1 quarter? [25] How many nickels does it take to equal 1 quarter? [5]

Lay out four quarters and ask him to count by 25s. If necessary, help him by asking how much is 25 + 25, [50] then 50 + 25, [75] and 75 + 25. [100] Ask him to repeat counting by 25s. [25, 50, 75, 100]

Counting money. Show 1 quarter, 1 dime, and 1 nickel in no particular order. Ask the child how much the 3 coins are worth together. [40¢]

Some children may find it helpful to write the values of the coins beneath them.

Counting money: 25, 35, 40 or 25, 30, 40.

Ask the child to explain how he got his answers. Ask him what is the best order for adding the values in his mind. [Some children may think it is easier to add the nickel to the quarter to get 30 and then the add the dime. Others may want to add the dime to the quarter first and then the nickel.]

Repeat for 1 quarter, 3 dimes, and 1 nickel. [60¢]

Repeat for 2 quarters. [50¢]

Repeat for 2 quarters, 1 dime, and 3 pennies. [63¢]

Worksheet 54. Give the child the worksheet. Tell him to start with the largest coins first, adding the values in his head if he can. The solutions are below:

46¢   45¢   70¢
60¢   65¢   63¢
80¢   71¢   77¢

	Quarter	Dime	Nickel	Penny
29¢:	1	0	0	4
43¢:	1	1	1	3

In conclusion. Ask: Why is a half-dollar called a half-dollar? [It is half of a dollar.] Why is a quarter called a quarter? [It is a quarter of a dollar.] What is another name for a quarter? [one fourth]

© Activities for Learning, Inc. 2013

LESSON 116: USING THE FEWEST COINS

OBJECTIVES:
1. To making amounts with coins

MATERIALS:
1. Sums Practice 12
2. *Math Card Games* book, M8, M9,* M10
3. Coins
4. Dry erase board

ACTIVITIES FOR TEACHING:	EXPLANATIONS:

Warm-up. Ask the child to do the left column on Sums Practice 12. The sums are:
   4 8 9 9 9 6 10 9 5 10
 Ask: Why is a half-dollar called a half-dollar? [It is half of a dollar.] Why is a quarter called a quarter? [It is a quarter of a dollar.] What is another name for a quarter? [one fourth]
 	
 Ask him to count by 25s to 200 using an abacus. [25, 50, 75, . . . , 200]
 	
 Ask the child to solve the following problem:
    Julie has 23 crayons on her desk. She gets the remaining 12 crayons from the box. How many crayons were in the box? [35 crayons]
 	
 Make Fifty-One Cents game. Play the game Make Fifty-One Cents from the *Math Card Games* book, M8.
 	
 Make Seven-Five Cents game. Play the game Make Seven-Five Cents from the *Math Card Games* book, M9.
	*As an alternative to the suggested cards for M9, use the cards from a single multiplication envelope, such as the 3s, 4s, 6s, 7s, 8s, or 9s.
	
	 Another choice is to use at least 30 basic number cards, 1–9. Overlap two cards to form the number.

ACTIVITIES FOR TEACHING:	EXPLANATIONS:

Using the fewest coins. Give the coins to the child. Tell him that you will write and say an amount. He is to make the amount with his coins, using as few coins as possible.
 	
Start with 40¢. [quarter, nickel, dime] Ask the child to share the solution. Continue with the following:
 	
   16¢ [dime, nickel, penny]
   31¢ [quarter, nickel, penny]
   45¢ [quarter, 2 dimes]
   54¢ [half-dollar or 2 quarters, 4 pennies]
   42¢ [quarter, dime, nickel, 2 pennies]
   49¢ [quarter, 2 dimes, 4 pennies]
   67¢ [half-dollar or 2 quarters, dime, nickel, 2 pennies]
   78¢ [half-dollar, quarter, 3 pennies or 3 quarters 3 pennies]
   99¢ [half-dollar, quarter, 2 dimes, 4 pennies or 3 quarters, 2 dimes, 4 pennies]
 	
Make the Amount game. Play the game Make the Amount from the *Math Card Games* book, M10. The players can score with tally marks on the dry erase board.
 	
In conclusion. Ask: Which amounts need only one coin? [50¢, 25¢, 10¢, 5¢, and 1¢]
	Alternative solutions are given for this activity without half-dollars.

© Activities for Learning, Inc. 2013

Lesson 117: Making Change

OBJECTIVES:
1. To learn the term *change*
2. To learn to make change
3. To practice subtracting by adding on

MATERIALS:
1. Sums Practice 12
2. AL Abacus
3. Dry erase board
4. Geometry solids and **4 sticky notes***
5. Coins
6. *Math Card Games* book, M12

ACTIVITIES FOR TEACHING:

Warm-up. Ask the child to do the right column on Sums Practice 12. The sums are:

   8   3   8   10   7   10   5   9   8   8

Ask: Which amounts need only one coin? [50¢, 25¢, 10¢, 5¢, and 1¢]

Ask: Why is a half-dollar called a half-dollar? [It is half of a dollar.] Why is a quarter called a quarter? [It is a quarter of a dollar] What is another name for a quarter? [one fourth]

Ask him to count by 25s to 250 using an abacus. [25, 50, 75, . . . , 250]

Ask the child to solve this problem and to write the equation.

   Kayla had 16 flowers and gave 7 to Joe. How many does she have now? [16 – 7 = 9]

Buying the cylinder with 10¢. Show the cylinder with the price tag 6¢. Tell the child he is to be the buyer and tell him to use a dime to buy the cylinder.

Ask: What two coins do you need to pay for it? [nickel and penny] Ask him what coin he has. [dime] Ask: Is that enough money for him to pay for the cylinder? [yes] Explain: Since you offered too much money, you need to get some money back.

Explain that the money a person gets back when he buys something with too much money is called *change*. Ask: How much change will he get back? [4¢]

Draw two part-whole circle sets as shown on the next page. Write the words shown in the left circles. Ask: What does the price plus change equal? [money offered] What is the money offered minus the price? [change]

Ask: How much money is offered? [10¢] Write it in the whole-circle. See the right figure on the next page. What is the price? [6¢] What is the change? [4¢] Write as shown.

EXPLANATIONS:

*Place stick notes on the solids as follows:
1. 6¢ on a cylinder
2. 10¢ on the cone
3. 19¢ on the cube
4. 15¢ on hexagonal prism.

ACTIVITIES FOR TEACHING:	EXPLANATIONS:

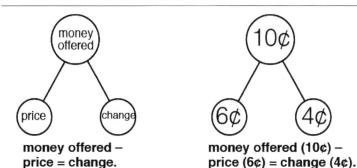

money offered −
price = change.

money offered (10¢) −
price (6¢) = change (4¢).

Buying the cone with 10¢. Ask the child to bring a dime. Tell him to buy the cone marked 10¢. Ask: How much change will you get? [none] Why? [It is an even trade—a 10¢ cone for 10¢.]

Buying the cube with 25¢. Ask the child to buy the cube for 19¢ with a quarter. Tell him to write the numbers in a part-whole circle set. See below. Give the child the change: a penny saying, 20, and a nickel, saying 25. Emphasize that you are adding on. See the abacus below.

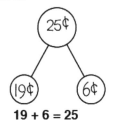

$19 + 6 = 25$

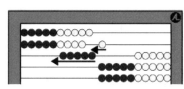

Adding on from 19 to 25.

Traditionally, change is counted up as the coins are given. Because cash registers today usually calculate the change, the cashier seldom counts the change. This lesson does not emphasize reciting the change.

Buying the prism with 25¢. Ask the child to buy a prism for 15¢, with a quarter. Ask the child: How do you go from 15 to 25? Remind him we need to use as few coins as possible, so we want to use a dime, not two nickels. See the figures below.

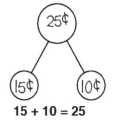

$15 + 10 = 25$

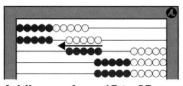

Adding on from 15 to 25.

Change from Twenty-Five Cents game. The game, Change from Twenty-Five Cents, is played like Change from Fifty Cents found in the *Math Card Games* book, M12.

In conclusion. Tell him about a child who thought cashiers gave a person money to pay him for buying something. Ask: Why does a person receive change? [They paid too much.]

For cards, use multiplication cards, 3, 6, 9, 12, 15, and 18 (from the 3s envelope) and 5, 10, and 20 (from the 5s envelope). For the money cards use 15 pennies, 7 nickels, and 6 dimes (removing 2 nickels, 8 dimes, the quarters and half-dollars from the complete money deck).

© Activities for Learning, Inc. 2013

Lesson 118: Adding with a Calculator

OBJECTIVES:
1. To learn to add on the calculator

MATERIALS:
1. Sums Practice 13
2. Casio SL-450S calculator
3. *Math Card Games* book, A9
4. Math journal

ACTIVITIES FOR TEACHING:

Warm-up. Ask the child to do both columns on Sums Practice 13. The sums are:

10	7	8	4	10	7	9	8	10	7
9	6	7	10	5	6	10	6	9	7

Ask the child to sing the song "Thirty Days has September." Ask him to name the months with 31 days. [January, March, May, July, August, October, and December]

Ask: How much more is needed with 65 to make 70? [5] How much more is needed with 92 to make 100? [8]

Ask the child to mentally add 24 + 24, [44, 48] 37 + 37, [67, 74] 99 + 2, [101] and 95 + 10. [105]

Ask the child the following problem:

> Little Bo Peep started out with 19 sheep in the morning on the day she lost all her sheep. Five of her missing sheep arrived home at 2:00. How many more sheep must still come home? [14]

Introducing the calculator. Give the child the calculator. If necessary, show him how to remove the cover from the front of the calculator and put it on the back. Tell him that when he puts the calculator away, the cover needs to be put back on the front of the calculator.

Casio SL-450S calculator.

Solar cell. Explain to the child that this calculator has no batteries. It uses a solar cell, which turns light into power. Tell him that the solar cell is the smaller rectangle on the front of the calculator, below the display. Ask him to watch what happens when he covers the solar cell. [The numbers on the display slowly fade away and disappear.]

EXPLANATIONS:

This Casio calculator has several advantages over a TI calculator for a young children. The constant key feature, which frequently causes errors for the unwary on other calculators, is not activated on a Casio until the operation sign is pressed twice. Also, this Casio shows 0 when first turned on.

ACTIVITIES FOR TEACHING:	EXPLANATIONS:

ACTIVITIES FOR TEACHING:

Simple adding. Ask the child to figure out 55 + 55 for himself. [110] Encourage discussion. After a few minutes, ask the child to explain how he did it. If necessary, demonstrate as follows:

    Press 55,

    Press the (+) key,

    Press 55,

    Press the (=) key. The answer will be seen as 110.

Tell him if he needs to start over, the (AC) key clears everything.

Days in a year. Ask him to use the calculator to find the number of days in a year. [365]

Ask: How many days in January? [31] Continue asking for the number of days in the remaining months as the child add the results on his calculator. As an intermediate check, the number of days in the first three months is 90.

Doubles Corners™ game. Play the Doubles Corners™ game, a variation of the Corners™ game found in the *Math Card Games* book, A9. In this variation, players lay down *two* cards per turn. Also use the rule that if no one can play, everyone takes an extra card. This can happen more than once. After a turn, a player takes cards only up to four.

For scoring, a player first adds together the scores from the two cards and then adds that mentally to his previous score written in his math journal. After he writes down the score, he can use his calculator to check his addition.

In conclusion. Ask the child: Were you faster than the calculator? Which was usually correct, you or the calculator?

EXPLANATIONS:

Encourage the child to learn about the calculator intuitively.

Intuition is a method of learning that is becoming increasingly more important in our technological world. To learn intuitively is to try new procedures by combining common sense with a willingness to take a risk. It implies the hope that what is learned is worth the inevitable frustration.

© Activities for Learning, Inc. 2013

Lesson 119: Introducing Multiplication as Arrays

OBJECTIVES:
1. To introduce multiplication
2. To learn the term *product*

MATERIALS:
1. Dry erase board
2. AL Abacus
3. Worksheet 55, Introducing Multiplication as Arrays

ACTIVITIES FOR TEACHING:	EXPLANATIONS:

ACTIVITIES FOR TEACHING:

Warm-up. Ask the child: Do you think you are faster than the calculator? Which was usually correct, you or the calculator?

Ask: Which amounts need only one coin? [50¢, 25¢, 10¢, 5¢, and 1¢]

Ask: Why is a half-dollar called a half-dollar? [It is half of a dollar.] Why is a quarter called a quarter? [It is a quarter of a dollar.] What is another name for a quarter? [one fourth]

Have the child write the equation for doubling 5 on his dry erase board. [5 + 5 = 10] Continue with writing the equation for doubling 4. [4 + 4 = 8]

Ask: What is half of 12? [6] What is half of 4? [2]

Beginning multiplication. Tell the child: Enter 6 on the first wire of your abacus. Now double it. See the left figure below. Ask: How much is it? [12] Say: So 6 taken 2 times is 12.

Then ask him to enter 6 on the first wire and then triple it. See the right figure below. Ask: How many times did you enter 6? [3] How much is entered? [18] How did you figure it out? Ask for several solutions. Tell him: The equation is: 6 taken 3 times equals 18.

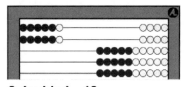
6 doubled = 12.

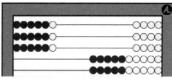
6 tripled = 18.

Tell him: This is *multiplication!* The answer to a multiplication problem is called the *product*.

Finding 9 taken 3 times. Tell the child to enter 9 taken 3 times. Tell him to find the product by using Take and Give. Remind him to use both hands, the way he traded on side 2 of the abacus.

EXPLANATIONS:

Sometimes 6 × 3 is thought of as "6 groups of 3." However, consistency with the other arithmetic operations requires a second look. When adding 6 + 3, we start with 6 and transform it by adding 3. When subtracting 6 − 3, we start with 6 and transform it by removing 3. When dividing 6 ÷ 3, we start with 6 and transform it by dividing it into 3 groups or into groups of 3s. Likewise, 6 × 3 means we start with 6 and transform it by duplicating it 3 times.

In the array (an arrangement of quantities in rows and columns) model, 6 × 3, 6 represents the horizontal quantity and 3 the vertical quantity. This is also consistent with the coordinate system; in (6, 3), the first number, 6, indicates the horizontal number and 3, the vertical number.

In Take and Give, beads from one row are given to another row, usually to make tens. To assure accurate trading, both hands should be used simultaneously. Several beads may be traded during a Take and Give operation.

ACTIVITIES FOR TEACHING:	EXPLANATIONS:

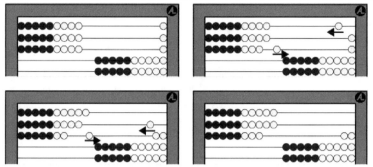

Using Take and Give to find 9 × 3.

When 5-year-olds were introduced to multiplication, they said, "Don't give us easy ones like 2 × 4, but give us hard ones like 9 × 9." They greatly enjoyed using Take and Give to find the answers.

Ask the child to say the equation. [9 taken 3 times equals 27.] Show him how the equation is written:

$$9 \times 3 = 27$$

Finding 8 taken 4 times. Tell him to enter 8 taken 4 times on the abacus. See below.

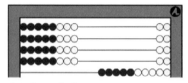

8 taken 4 times.

Note that the multiplication sign, ×, is not an "x," which is a variable in algebra. A good model for writing the multiplication sign is the diagonals in a square as shown here.

Ask him to think of as many ways as possible to find the product. [32] Some possibilities include:

1. The dark-colored beads are 2 tens, or 20, and the light-colored beads are 12; 20 + 12 is 32.
2. The first two rows are 16; 16 + 16 is 32.
3. Four 10s is 40; 40 − 8 is 32.
4. Take and Give ends up with 32.

Write the equation:

$$8 \times 4 = 32$$

Worksheet 55. Ask the child to do the top half of the worksheet. The solutions are:

5 × 2 = **10**	5 × 5 = **25**
8 × 2 = **16**	7 × 3 = **21**
10 × 5 = **50**	2 × 6 = **12**
4 × 2 = **8**	4 × 5 = **20**
6 × 4 = **24**	2 × 2 = **4**
3 × 3 = **9**	6 × 5 = **30**
4 × 3 = **12**	9 × 4 = **36**
6 × 10 = **60**	9 × 6 = **54**

This worksheet will be used again in the next lesson.

In conclusion. Ask: How much is 3 + 3? [6] Then ask: How much is 3 taken 2 times? [6]

© Activities for Learning, Inc. 2013

Lesson 120: Multiplication as Repeated Addition

OBJECTIVES:
1. To write multiplication equations

MATERIALS:
1. AL Abacus
2. Dry erase board
3. Worksheet 55, Introducing Multiplication as Arrays (from previous lesson)
4. Math balance

ACTIVITIES FOR TEACHING:	EXPLANATIONS:
Warm-up. Ask the child: How much is 3 + 3? [6] How much is 3 taken 2 times? [6] How much is 4 + 4? [8] How much is 4 taken 2 times? [8] How much is 9 + 9? [18] How much is 9 taken 2 times? [18]	
Ask: How much more is needed with 85 to make 95? [10] How much more is needed with 72 to make 80? [8]	
Ask the child to mentally add 25 + 25, [50] 50 + 50, [100] 99 + 4, [103] and 95 + 15. [105, 110]	
Ask: Which amounts need only one coin? [50¢, 25¢, 10¢, 5¢, and 1¢]	
Reading an array. Enter 5 × 7 on the abacus as shown below. Ask the child to read what is entered. [5 taken 7 times] Then ask him to find the product. [35]	Beginning multiplication is often modeled as repeated addition. A better model is using an array, which is easier to visualize and works for multiplying fractions.

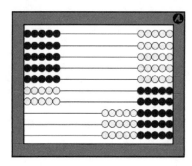

5 taken 7 times = 35

Writing multiplication equations. Show him how it is written:

$$5 \times 7 = 35$$

Explain that multiplication sign is made like the diagonals in a square. ⊠

Ask him to write the equation on his dry erase board.

Repeat for 6 × 5. [6 × 5 = 30]

ACTIVITIES FOR TEACHING:	EXPLANATIONS:

Worksheet 55. Ask the child to do the second half of the worksheet. The solutions are:

$5 \times 2 = 10$ $5 \times 5 = 25$
$8 \times 2 = 16$ $7 \times 3 = 21$
$10 \times 5 = 50$ $2 \times 6 = 12$
$4 \times 2 = 8$ $4 \times 5 = 20$
$6 \times 4 = 24$ $2 \times 2 = 4$
$3 \times 3 = 9$ $6 \times 5 = 30$
$4 \times 3 = 12$ $9 \times 4 = 36$
$6 \times 10 = 60$ $9 \times 6 = 54$
$6 \times 3 = 18$ $7 \times 2 = 14$ $7 \times 6 = 42$
$5 \times 7 = 35$ $10 \times 8 = 80$ $9 \times 8 = 72$

Multiplying with the math balance. Tell the child that he can check his solution on the worksheet with the math balance. Tell the child to think how he could enter 5×2. Ask him to do it. See below.

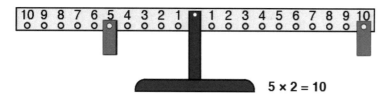

$5 \times 2 = 10$

Ask the child to do the next problem, 5×5, from the worksheet. See below.

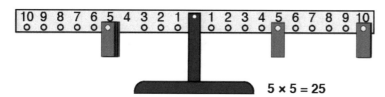

$5 \times 5 = 25$

Continue by asking him to do the next problem, 8×2, from the worksheet.

Continue as long as the child is interested.

Enter the following on the math balance and ask the child to say the equation. [$28 = 7 \times 4$]

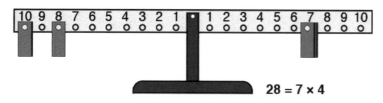

$28 = 7 \times 4$

In conclusion. Ask: What is multiplication?

To enter more than five weights on a peg, enter the amount over five on the back side of the peg.

© Activities for Learning, Inc. 2013

Lesson 121: More Calculator Activities

OBJECTIVES:
1. To learn skip counting with the constant feature
2. To multiply with the calculator
3. To subtract with the calculator

MATERIALS:
1. Casio SL-450S calculator
2. Worksheet 55, Introducing Multiplication as Arrays (from previous lesson)

ACTIVITIES FOR TEACHING:	EXPLANATIONS:
Warm-up. Ask the child: How much is 5 + 5? [10] How much is 5 taken 2 times? [10] How much is 6 + 6? [12] How much is 6 taken 2 times? [12] How much is 10 + 10? [20] How much is 10 taken 2 times? [20]	
Ask: How much more is needed with 95 to make 105? [10] How much more is needed with 82 to make 90? [8]	
Ask the child to mentally add 26 + 24, [46, 50] 49 + 51, [99, 100] 99 + 5, [104] and 94 + 10. [104]	
Name the amounts that can be made with only one coin. [50¢, 25¢, 10¢, 5¢, and 1¢]	
Counting by fives. Tell the child his calculator can count by fives. Tell him to:	
Press ⑤	
Press ⊕ ⊕ (A k appears on the left side of display.)	For other calculators, press the + once; most do not have the k indicator.
Press ⊜ ⊜ ⊜	
Ask: What is the calculator showing? [counting by 5s] Tell him to count as high as he wants.	
Tell him to start at 400 and count by fives, enter 400 and keep pressing the equals key. [405, 410, . . .]	
Ask the child to clear the calculator. Start at 1000 and count by fives.	
Tell him: Without changing anything, press 3 and =, [8] press 7 and =, [12] and then press 9 and =. [14] What did the calculator do? [added 5 to the numbers]	

ACTIVITIES FOR TEACHING:	EXPLANATIONS:

Counting by 2s. Challenge him: Can you figure out how to count by 2s on the calculator?

  Press ②

  Press ⊕ ⊕ (A k appears on the left side of display.)

  Press ⊜ ⊜ ⊜

Next ask him to enter 40. Ask: What number comes next when counting by 2s? [42] Ask him to check on the calculator. Repeat for 38, [40] and 98. [100]

After he has counted by 2s, tell him to enter 1 and press = over and over. Ask: What happened? [gives odds]

Multiplying on the calculator. Say: Try and find the product for 5 × 4 on your calculator. [20]

  Press ⑤ ⊗ ④ ⊜

Worksheet 55. Ask him to use his calculator to check some of the problems on the worksheet.

Days old problem. Give him the following problem to solve with a calculator:

  When a person turns 7 years old, how many days have they lived? [2555 plus 1 or 2 days for leap years]

Subtracting on the calculator. Write

$$56 - 19 + 19 = \_\_\_$$

and ask: What do you think the answer will be? Tell him to try it on the calculator. [56] Repeat for 87 + 34 − 34. [87]

Calculator puzzles. Write 4789 and tell the child to enter it on the calculator. Then ask: How could you change this number so the display will say 4780? You cannot clear the calculator or enter the number again. Ask him to think about how he could do it, and then try it on the calculator. [press ⊖ ⑨ ⊜]

Give him the following:

  Change 602 to 672.   [press ⊕ ⑦ ⓪ ⊜]

  Change 5785 to 785.   [press ⊖ ⑤ ⓪ ⓪ ⓪ ⊜]

  Change 2193 to 3193. [press ⊕ ① ⓪ ⓪ ⓪ ⊜]

  Change 1406 to 1006. [press ⊖ ④ ⓪ ⓪ ⊜]

  Change 7139 to 7449. [press ⊕ ③ ① ⓪ ⊜]

In conclusion. Say to the child: Name as many different things as you can that you can do on a calculator.

© Activities for Learning, Inc. 2013

LESSON 122: INTRODUCING DIVISION

OBJECTIVES:
1. To introduce division
2. To solve division problems

MATERIALS:
1. AL Abacus
2. Dry erase board
3. Math balance
4. Calculator

ACTIVITIES FOR TEACHING:	EXPLANATIONS:
Warm-up. Say: Name as many different things as you can that you can do on a calculator.	
Ask the child to build the stairs on the abacus. Then ask: How many beads are on the first row? [1] On the third row? [3] On the fifth row, [5] and so on. End by asking him to name the rows using ordinal numbers. [first, second, third, . . . , tenth]	
Ask: What is 4 taken 3 times? [12] What is 4 + 4 + 4? [12]	
Dividing problem. Give the child the following problem:	
Jacob has 12 flowers to plant. He wants to plant 4 in a row. How many rows can he plant? [3]	
If necessary, suggest he enter 12 on the abacus. Ask: How many do you need in each row? [4] Tell him to use Take and Give to find the answer. See the figures below.	

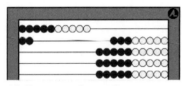
12 flowers altogether.

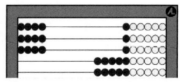
With 4 in a row, he can have 3 rows.

If necessary, remind the children to use both hands whenever using Take and Give. Also, more than 1 bead can be moved at a time.

Ask: How many rows can Jacob plant? [3] Tell him that the mathematical way to say it is: Twelve divided by 4 equals 3. Show him how to write the equation:

$$12 \div 4 = 3$$

Have him write it on the dry erase board.

Change the problem to:

Joy has 12 flowers to plant. She wants to plant 3 in a row. How many rows can she plant? [4]

Ask him to solve it on the abacus and to write the equation. See the figure on the next page.

The symbol, $\div$, is used primarily in elementary mathematics and on calculators.

RightStart™ Mathematics Level B Second Edition © Activities for Learning, Inc. 2013

ACTIVITIES FOR TEACHING:	EXPLANATIONS:

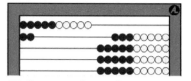 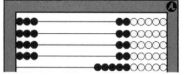

12 flowers altogether.   With 3 in a row, she can have 4 rows.

Ask him to write the equation:

$$12 \div 3 = 4$$

Change the problem to:

Jordan has 12 flowers to plant. He wants to plant 6 in a row. How many rows can he plant? [2] The equation is:

$$12 \div 6 = 2$$

Change the problem to:

Jessa has 12 flowers to plant. She wants to plant 2 in a row. How many rows can she plant? [6] The equation is:

$$12 \div 2 = 6$$

Dividing on the math balance. Explain that he can do division on the math balance. Say: Let's find out what is 12 divided by 4. Tell the child: Enter 12 on the left side. Now enter weights on the 4 until it balances. [3] See the figure below. Tell him to say the equation: 12 divided by 4 equals 3. Ask: Is that the same answer you found on your abacus? [yes]

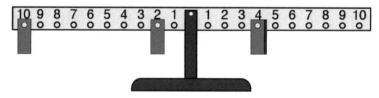

Showing 12 divided by 4 equals 3.

Use the math balance and repeat for 12 divided by 3, [4] 6, [2] and 2. [6]

Dividing on the calculator. Encourage the child to use the calculator to discover how to find 12 divided by 4. [3] Repeat for 3, 6, and 2.

In conclusion. Ask: What is 12 plus 2? [14] What is 12 minus 2? [10] What is 12 taken 2 times? [24] What is 12 divided by 2? [6]

Lesson 123: Beginning Fractions

OBJECTIVES:
1. To learn the names of the unit fractions
2. To compare unit fractions

MATERIALS:
1. Fraction charts
2. *Math Card Games* book, F2, F2.1

ACTIVITIES FOR TEACHING:	EXPLANATIONS:
Warm-up. Ask: What is 12 plus 2? [14] What is 12 minus 2? [10] What is 12 taken 2 times? [24] What is 12 divided by 2? [6] Ask the child: How much is 4 + 4? [8] How much is 4 taken 2 times? [8] How much is 6 + 6? [12] How much is 6 taken 2 times? [12]	
Assembling the fraction chart. Give the child the fraction charts, both the whole and the separate pieces. Ask him to put the pieces together like a puzzle as shown below. (He should *not* build it on top of the whole chart.) 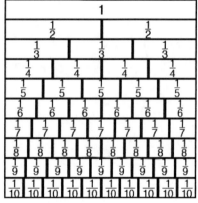 The fraction chart.	It is important to introduce children to fractions early in their mathematical development. The younger child has little difficulty with the concept that ¼ is less than ½. On the other hand, an older child first encountering fractions feels certain that 4 is always greater than 3. The linear fraction model provides a child with a better representation of fractions than circles, including improper fractions. Comparing fractions is much easier with linear pieces. It is essential that all the fraction pieces be the same color. A fraction piece should be identified by its length, not its color.
The fraction stairs. Tell the child to find only one piece of each size and turn them face down. Then tell him to build the fraction stairs by placing the longest piece at the bottom, the next longest piece on top, keeping edges even, followed by the next longest piece, and so on. See the figure on the right. 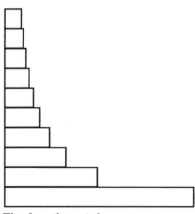 The fraction stairs.	The mathematical name of the fraction stair curve is *hyperbola*.

RightStart™ Mathematics Level B Second Edition © Activities for Learning, Inc. 2013

ACTIVITIES FOR TEACHING:	EXPLANATIONS:

Ask: Could you climb those stairs? Are they like the stairs on the abacus? [no] How are they different? [The steps get smaller the higher you climb.]

Naming the fractions. Ask the child: Build the stairs again, but this time face up and the longest piece is on top. See below. Tell him: These are the *unit* fractions.

A unit fraction is a fraction having 1 as the numerator, such as ⅓.

Note that this model, shown below, parallels how fractions are written. The fraction $\frac{1}{2}$ means 1 ÷ 2. The top piece, 1, is divided into the 2 pieces below. The bottom edge of the 1 piece is the dividing line.

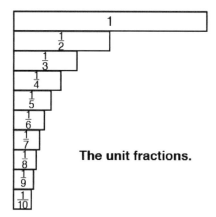

The unit fractions.

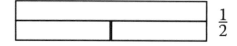

The fraction names. Explain: Except for one half and one quarter, we use ordinal number names for naming fractions. Ask: Can you find one half? Can you find one fourth? What is another name for one fourth? [one quarter] Can you find one sixth? Can you find one eighth? Where is one tenth? Can you find one seventh?

Tell the child: Read the unit fraction names from top to bottom. [one, one half, one third, . . . , one tenth]

Many other languages distinguish between ordinal number words and fraction words by different suffixes, making it easier for students to understand what a fraction is.

Speakers of British English rarely use the term one fourth; they say *one quarter*.

Comparing unit fractions. Ask him the following:

1. Which is more, one half or one fourth? [one half]
2. Which is more, one third or one? [one]
3. Which is more, one third or one quarter? [one third]
4. Which is more, one eighth or one fourth? [one fourth]
6. Which is more, one sixth or one seventh? [one sixth]

Avoid teaching a rule such as: The greater the number, the smaller the fraction. Such rules prevent real understanding.

A child who had learned that rule was asked, "Which is greater, $\frac{3}{7}$ or $\frac{1}{7}$?" He replied incorrectly with "$\frac{1}{7}$." He was not thinking about fractions, but about the rule.

Fraction Memory game. Play the Fraction Memory game found in the *Math Card Games* book, F2. The object of this game is to match a fraction piece with the written symbol on a fraction card.

Unit Fraction War game. Next play the Unit Fraction War game found in the *Math Card Games* book, F2.1. Here players compare unit fractions while referring to their fraction charts.

In conclusion. Ask: How many halves in a whole? [2] What is another name for one fourth? [one quarter] Which is less, one half or one? [one half]

© Activities for Learning, Inc. 2013

Lesson 124: Unit Fractions

OBJECTIVES:
1. To compare unit fractions
2. To understand fractions as division

MATERIALS:
1. Fraction charts

ACTIVITIES FOR TEACHING:	EXPLANATIONS:
Warm-up. Ask the child: How many halves in a whole? [2] What is another name for one fourth? [one quarter] Which is less, one half or one? [one half]	
Ask: What is 12 plus 2? [14] What is 12 minus 2? [10] What is 12 taken 2 times? [24] What is 12 divided by 2? [6]	
Ask them: How much is 10 + 10? [20] How much is 10 taken 2 times? [20] How much is 20 + 20? [40] How much is 20 taken 2 times? [40] How much is 30 + 30? [60] How much is 30 taken 2 times? [60]	
Ask the child: How much more is needed with 75 to make 105? [30] How much more is needed with 72 to make 90? [18]	
Ask the child to mentally add 16 + 24, [36, 40] 48 + 52, [98, 100] 90 + 40, [130] and 94 + 40. [134]	
Working with halves. Give the child the fraction pieces and tell him to spread them out face down. Then say: Find the longest piece. Now find a piece that is half as long. [the $\frac{1}{2}$ piece] Tell him to set it below the longest piece, as shown below.	

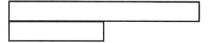

The 1-piece and a half piece.

Ask: How many one-half pieces do you need to make a whole? [2] Ask him to find the other one-half piece and set it under the 1-piece. Ask: How many pieces is the 1 divided into? [2] Tell him: Turn over one of the smaller pieces and see the symbol, $\frac{1}{2}$. It means 1 divided, or broken, into 2 equal parts.

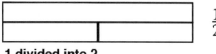

1 divided into 2.

ACTIVITIES FOR TEACHING:	EXPLANATIONS:

Working with thirds. Now ask him: Find three fraction pieces that divide the 1-piece into 3 equal parts. Tell him to set it under the 1 as shown below. Then ask him to turn over a smaller piece and see what it says. [one third] Ask: What does it mean? [1 divided into 3 equal parts.]

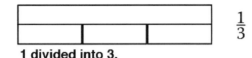
1 divided into 3.

Working with fourths. Repeat the activity with fourths. See figure below. Ask: What does each smaller piece say? [one fourth] What does it mean? [1 divided into 4 equal parts.]

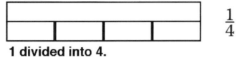
1 divided into 4.

The whole fraction chart. Ask the child to turn the pieces over and build the fraction chart as shown below.

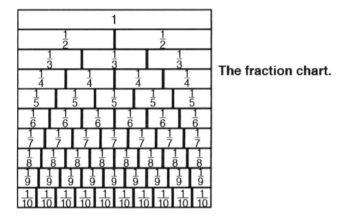
The fraction chart.

Ask him to answer the following while using the chart:

1. Where are the thirds? [third row]
2. How many fourths are equal to one whole? [4]
3. How many eighths are in a whole? [8]
4. How many tenths are in 1? [10]
5. Which is more, one third or one fourth? [one third]
6. Which is more, one sixth or one fourth? [one fourth]
7. Which is less, one tenth or one ninth? [one tenth]
8. How many thirds are in a whole? [3]
9. How many fourths are in a half? [2]

In conclusion. Ask: What does one half mean? [something divided into two equal parts] What does one fourth mean? [something divided into four equal parts]

Lesson 125: Fractions of Twelve and Eight

OBJECTIVES:
1. To find a fraction of 12
2. To find a fraction of 8

MATERIALS:
1. Fraction charts
2. Centimeter cubes
3. Math journal

ACTIVITIES FOR TEACHING:

Warm-up. Ask the child: What does one half mean? [something divided into 2 equal parts] What does one fourth mean? [something divided into 4 equal parts]

Ask: How many halves in a whole? [2] What is another name for one fourth? [one quarter] Which is less, one half or one? [one half]

Ask: What is 10 plus 2? [12] What is 10 minus 2? [8] What is 10 taken 2 times? [20] What is 10 divided by 2? [5]

Part of the fraction chart. Give the child the fraction pieces and the centimeter cubes. Tell him to find the 1, the halves, thirds, and fourths (the first four rows). Then tell him to build the chart with those pieces as shown below.

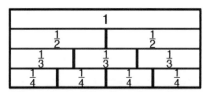
First part of the fraction chart.

A fraction of 12. Tell him to put 12 centimeter cubes on the 1-piece. Tell him: Take 12 more cubes and put equal amounts on each half. How many will go on each half? [6]

Tell him to take 12 more cubes and put equal amounts the on the thirds. How many cubes will go on each third? [4] Tell them to do the fourths. [3 on each fourth]

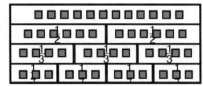
Finding fractions of 12.

Ask: What is one half of 12? [6] What is one third of 12? [4] What is one fourth of 12? [3]

EXPLANATIONS:

Sometimes children, after using circle models, think that a half of something means there will be only two pieces. This lesson shows otherwise.

ACTIVITIES FOR TEACHING:

Writing the fraction equation. Show the child how to write "one half of 12 is 6":

$$\frac{1}{2} \text{ of } 12 = 6$$

Tell him to write the three equations in the math journal. See below.

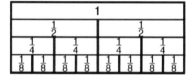

The fraction of 12 equations.

A fraction of 8. Tell the child to find the 1, the halves, fourths, and eighths fraction pieces. Tell him to build the chart with those pieces. See the left figure below.

The fraction whole, halves, quarters, and eighths.   **Finding fractions of 8.**

Tell him to put 8 centimeter cubes on the 1-piece. Tell him: Take 8 more cubes and put half on each half. Tell him to do the fourths and eights. See the figure above on the right. Ask: How many cubes will go on each fourth? [2] How many cubes will go on each eighth? [1]

Ask the child to write the three equations as shown below:

$$\frac{1}{2} \text{ of } 12 = 6$$
$$\frac{1}{3} \text{ of } 12 = 4$$
$$\frac{1}{4} \text{ of } 12 = 3$$
$$\frac{1}{2} \text{ of } 8 = 4$$
$$\frac{1}{4} \text{ of } 8 = 2$$
$$\frac{1}{8} \text{ of } 8 = 1$$

Writing the fraction of 8 equations.

In conclusion. Ask: What is half of 20? [10] What is a quarter of 20? [5] What is half of 4? [2] What is a fourth of 4? [1] What is an eighth of 4? [one half]

EXPLANATIONS:

© Activities for Learning, Inc. 2013

Lesson 126: Comparing Fractions by Weighing

OBJECTIVES:
1. To become aware of weight
2. To introduce the term *heavier*
3. To compare fractions through weighting

MATERIALS:
1. Fraction charts
2. Math balance, four weights *, **two 4-inch (10 cm) paper cups,** and **two rubber bands**
3. *Math Card Games* book, F7
4. **Objects for weighing**, optional

ACTIVITIES FOR TEACHING:

Warm-up. Ask the child: Ask: What is half of 12? [6] What is a quarter of 12? [3] What is half of 4? [2] What is a fourth of 4? [1] What is an eighth of 4? [one half]

Ask the child: Is 1 plus 1, adding or subtracting? [adding] Is 9 and 2 more, adding or subtracting? [adding] Is 10 minus 1, adding or subtracting? [subtracting] Is taking 2 from 8, adding or subtracting? [subtracting]

Ask: After adding on the abacus, will your answer be greater or less? [greater] After subtracting, will your answer be greater or less? [less]

Weighing fraction pieces. Give the child the fraction chart and tell him to assemble it.

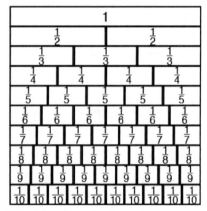

The fraction chart.

Hang a cup from each 10-peg on the math balance as shown on the next page. Tell the child: This is now a scale and we will not be using the numbers. What do you think will happen if we put two weights in each cup? [balances] Tell him to try it. Ask: Which is *heavier*, three weights or two weights? Tell him to try it. [3 weights]

EXPLANATIONS:

*To prepare the math balance to be used as a scale, punch holes in two paper cups and insert a rubber band in the holes as shown above. Instead of the rubber bands, twist ties or two paper clips per side will also work.

Clear plastic cups allow the children to see the contents of the cups more easily, but use only cups with plastic code 1. The code is found in the recycling triangle, usually on the bottom. A cup with plastic code 6 is brittle and often breaks when making the hole, leaving sharp edges.

ACTIVITIES FOR TEACHING:	EXPLANATIONS:

The math balance converted to a scale.

Ask: How many fraction halves does it take to equal the 1? [2] What do you think will happen if we put the 1-piece in one cup and the two halves in the other cup? Which is heavier? Place the 1-piece in one cup and have the child place the two halves in the other cup.

If necessary, move the little white weights on the underside of the yellow arm to adjust the balance.

Tell the child to hold the one third in one hand and a one half with the other hand. Before the child places the pieces in the cups, ask: Which will be more? Then tell him to try it. [one half is more]

Since the 1-piece is difficult to keep in the cup, slip it in the rubber band loop.

Make the following comparisons of which is heavier:
1. One half or two fourths [equal]
2. One fourth or one eighth [one fourth]
3. Two fourths or four eighths [equal]
4. One third or two sixths [equal]
5. Two thirds or three fourths [three fourths]
6. Three sevenths or one third [three sevenths]
7. One third plus one sixth or one half [equal]
8. Five tenths or four sevenths [four sevenths]
9. One half or three ninths [one half]
10. One half or three sixths [equal]

Fraction War. Play the Fraction War game found in the *Math Card Games* book, F7. The players will need the 1s, halves, fourths, and eighths fraction pieces.

Comparing other objects with the scale, optional.
Ask him to compare other small objects with the scale, such as a piece of Styrofoam and a piece of plastic or metal.

In conclusion. Ask: Which is heavier, one half of something or one third of the same thing? [one half] Which is heavier, one sixth of something or one fifth of the same thing? [one fifth]

© Activities for Learning, Inc. 2013

Lesson 127: Lines of Symmetry

OBJECTIVES:
1. To make symmetrical patterns
2. To learn the term *reflection*
3. To learn the term *line of symmetry*

MATERIALS:
1. Dry erase board
2. Geoboard and rubber bands
3. Tiles
4. Geometry reflector
5. Two sets of tangrams

ACTIVITIES FOR TEACHING:

Warm-up. Ask the child: Which is heavier, one half of something or one third of the same thing? [one half] Which is heavier, one sixth of something or one eighth of the same thing? [one sixth]

Ask: What is half of 8? [4] What is two quarters of 8? [4] What is a quarter of 8? [2] What is a fourth of 8? [2]

What is half of 20? [10] What is half of 5? [2 and one half] What is one third of 30? [10]

The physical Mirror game. Tell the child to pretend he is a mirror. Stand across the child and move your arms or make facial expressions for the child to copy. Be sure he moves his right arm in response to your left arm.

Then tell the child you will be the mirror. Give him a minute or so, and then reverse roles.

The Mirror game with tiles. Give the child the tiles and a geoboard.

Using the geoboard and tiles, demonstrate with the child sitting across from you. Place a rubber band across a center row of the geoboard as shown below. Explain that the rubber band will be the mirror.

Start by placing a tile anywhere on your side of the geoboard. The child places a tile of the same color in the mirrored position. See the figures below.

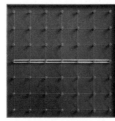 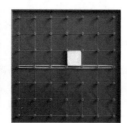 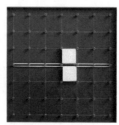

Rubber band as the mirror. **A tile.** **The tile and its reflection.**

EXPLANATIONS:

ACTIVITIES FOR TEACHING:

Next ask the child to take a turn placing a tile. Place the reflection of the tile on your side. A complex arrangement is shown below on the left. After making such an arrangement, ask: Where are half of the tiles? [on one side of the line of symmetry] Where is the other half? [on the other side]

A complex design.   **Using the geometry reflector.**

Ask the child to play the Mirror game with tiles again.

The geometry reflector. Give him the geometry reflector (see the right figure above). Tell him to place the reflector on the rubber band. Explain that he can see the reflection and the actual tiles. Say: The rubber band makes the *line of reflection*.

Other lines of reflections. Tell the child he can play the Mirror game using a vertical line of reflection. He can even use a geoboard diagonal. See the figures below.

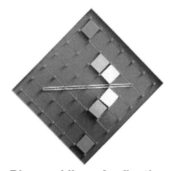

Vertical line of reflection.

Diagonal line of reflection.

The Mirror game with tangrams.
Give him one set of tangrams and you take the other set. Take turns building a symmetrical design. The figure on the right shows an example. Adjoining edges need not meet.

In conclusion. Ask: Does a person's face have a line symmetry? [yes] Does a circle have a line of symmetry? [yes] Does a calendar have a line of symmetry? [no]

A symmetrical design made with tangrams.

EXPLANATIONS:

The geometry reflector is a mirror that also allows the objects behind it to be seen. When it is placed on a line of symmetry, the reflection and the actual objects will coincide.

While the beveled edge gives better reflections for images on paper, it makes little difference for this lesson.

© Activities for Learning, Inc. 2013

Lesson 128: Finding Symmetry

OBJECTIVES:
1. To find lines of symmetry
2. To introduce *planes of symmetry*

MATERIALS:
1. Tangrams
2. Rubber bands (from the geoboards)
3. Four tally sticks
4. Geometry reflector
5. Dry erase board
6. Geometry solids

ACTIVITIES FOR TEACHING:	EXPLANATIONS:

Warm-up. Ask the child: When a design has a line of symmetry, what fraction of the design is on each side of the line of symmetry? [one half]

Ask him: How many sides does an equilateral triangle have? [3] What is special about an equilateral triangle? [All sides are equal.] A side of a certain equilateral triangle is 11 cm; what is the distance around the whole triangle? [33 cm]

Tell him: It is 8 cm around all the sides of a square. What is halfway around the square? [4 cm] What is a quarter of the way around the square? [2 cm] What is the length of a side of the square? [2 cm]

Lines of symmetry in the tangram pieces. Give the child the tangrams, rubber bands, and tally sticks.

Ask him to find a large triangle. Then tell him: Show its line of symmetry, using either the narrow edge of the tally stick or a rubber band. Then check it with the reflector. See the left figure below. Tell him to draw the triangle and its line of symmetry on a dry erase board.

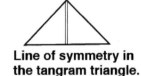
Line of symmetry in the tangram triangle.

Lines of symmetry in a square.

Ask: Do the other triangles have a line of symmetry? [yes]

Ask: Can you find four lines of symmetry in the square? Suggest he use the reflector to see them. See the four right figures above.

Ask: How many lines of symmetry can you find in the tangram parallelogram? [none] How many lines of symmetry are there in all of the tangram pieces? [9, (5 for triangles and 4 for square)]

RightStart™ Mathematics Level B Second Edition

ACTIVITIES FOR TEACHING:	EXPLANATIONS:

Lines of symmetry in an equilateral triangle. Tell the child to take three tally sticks and make an equilateral triangle. See the left figure below. Tell him to use another tally stick turned to the narrow edge to show the three lines of symmetry. See the next three figures below. Tell him to draw them on the dry erase board.

An equilateral triangle and its three lines of symmetry.

Planes of symmetry in a cylinder. Give him the geometry solids.

Tell him to find a cylinder. Next tell him to put a rubber band around the cylinder as shown in the left figure below.

Planes of symmetry in a cylinder.

Ask: When you put the reflector on the rubber band on the circle and along the side, do they look like lines of symmetry? [yes] If your reflector were a saw and you sawed through the cylinder where the rubber band is, would the two halves be reflections? [yes] What is the shape you would see? [rectangle] Tell him: We can't call the rubber band a *line* of symmetry because it is not a line. It is a *plane of reflection.* A plane is a flat surface.

Now tell him: Move the rubber band and put it around the curved side of the cylinder (see the right figure above) to make another plane of reflection. Tell him to check it with the reflector. Ask: If you sawed through the cylinder, what shape is the plane of reflection? [circle]

Plane of symmetry in a cone. Help the child to place a wider rubber band around the cone. See the figure on the right. Ask: If you sawed along the rubber band, would the two halves be reflections? [yes] What is the shape of the plane of reflection? [triangle]

Plane of reflection in a cone.

In conclusion. Say: Name some objects that have a line or plane of symmetry. [for example: chair, star, scissors, pencil, ball]

© Activities for Learning, Inc. 2013

Lesson 129: Tangram and Geoboard Figures

OBJECTIVES:
1. To review types of quadrilaterals
2. To copy tangram figures to the geoboard
3. To introduce the term *trapezoid*
4. To review halves, fourths, and quarters of a circle
5. To make symmetrical designs

MATERIALS:
1. Tangrams
2. Geoboard
3. Geometry reflector

ACTIVITIES FOR TEACHING:

Warm-up. Ask the child: Does a sphere have a line of symmetry or a plane of symmetry? [plane of symmetry] Does a circle have a line of symmetry or a plane of symmetry? [line of symmetry]

Ask him: Does a square have a line of symmetry or a plane of symmetry? [line of symmetry] Does a cube have a line of symmetry or a plane of symmetry? [plane of symmetry]

Ask: Does a rectangle have parallel lines? [yes] Does a rectangle have perpendicular lines? [yes] Are right angles parallel lines or perpendicular lines? [perpendicular lines] How many right angles does a rectangle have? [4]

Quadrilaterals. Give the tangrams and geoboard to the child.

Ask: How many sides does a quadrilateral have? [4] Tell him to construct the following quadrilaterals using at least two tangram pieces and then to make it on the geoboard. Some solutions are shown below.

1. A square.
2. A rectangle that is not a square.
3. A parallelogram that is not a rectangle.

EXPLANATIONS:

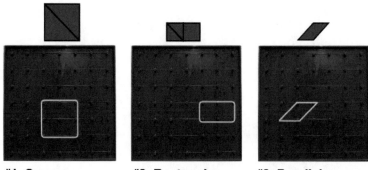

#1. Square.   #2. Rectangle.   #3. Parallelogram.

See more on the next page.

ACTIVITIES FOR TEACHING:

4. A quadrilateral having only one set of parallel lines and a right angle. Tell him it is a *trapezoid*.
5. A quadrilateral having only one set of parallel lines and no right angles. Tell him it is also a trapezoid.
6. A quadrilateral with no parallel lines.

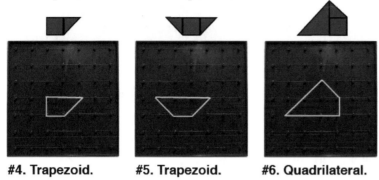

#4. Trapezoid. #5. Trapezoid. #6. Quadrilateral.

Halves and fourths of a circle. Tell the child to turn his geoboard over and see the circle. Then tell him to place a rubber band around one fourth of the circle. See the left figure below. Tell him to do another quarter next to his first quarter. See the right figure below. Ask: What is another name for two quarters or two fourths? [one half]

One fourth, or one quarter, of a circle.

Two fourths, or one half, of a circle.

Symmetrical designs. Tell the child to make symmetrical designs with either the tangrams or on the geoboard and to check them with the geometry reflector. A few examples are shown below:

Symmetrical designs.

In conclusion. Ask: How many sides does a quadrilateral have? [4] Name some special quadrilaterals. [square, rectangle, parallelogram, trapezoid]

EXPLANATIONS:

The North American definition of a *trapezoid* as having exactly one set of parallel lines is equivalent to the British *trapezium*.

© Activities for Learning, Inc. 2013

ENRICHMENT LESSON 130: INTRODUCING ANGLES

OBJECTIVES:
1. To become aware of angles
2. To introduce the terms *90 degrees* and *45 degrees*

MATERIALS:
1. One set of tangrams
2. Goniometer
3. Items with right angles: centimeter cubes, math balance weights, tiles, geometry solids, fraction halves or fourths
4. **Piece of paper**
5. Tiles

ACTIVITIES FOR TEACHING:	EXPLANATIONS:
Warm-up. Ask the child to find the line of symmetry on their body. [face, body, hands, feet]	
Ask the child: Which is heavier, one half of something or one fourth of the same thing? [one half] Which is heavier, one tenth of something or one fifth of the same thing? [one fifth]	
Ask: What does one half mean? [something divided into 2 equal parts] What does one fourth mean? [something divided into 4 equal parts]	
Ask: What is 10 + 10? [20] What is 10 doubled? [20] What is half of 20? [10] What is 20 doubled? [40] What is half of 40? [20] What is 25 doubled? [50] What is half of 50? [25] What is 50 doubled? [100] What is half of 100? [50]	
Right angles on tangram pieces. Give the child the tangrams and tell him to find a large triangle. Ask: Where is the right angle? Do all your triangles have a right angle? [yes] How many right angles does the square have? [4] How many right angles does the parallelogram have? [0]	This lesson on angles is designed to give children an appreciation of angles.
The goniometer. Give the child the goniometer (GON ee om i ter); see the left figure below. Tell him that the goniometer measures the space between two edges, or lines, at their vertex.	The children are not expected to read the numbers on the goniometer.
Lay the goniometer flat on a surface and demonstrate how to open it by holding the bottom part with your right hand and gently opening the top part with your left hand. Tell him to place a large triangle at the center to make it exactly a right angle. See the right figure below.	
	If the two parts of the goniometer come apart, they can be snapped back together. Align the part with the bump on top of the other and press down.

The goniometer.

ACTIVITIES FOR TEACHING:	EXPLANATIONS:

Measuring right angles. Tell the child: A right angle has another name; it is sometimes called a *90-degree angle*. Tell him to use the goniometer and check the four angles in the tangram squares. Also, tell him to hold on to the circle part of the goniometer to keep it from moving.

Tell him to check the 90-degree angles in other items, such as centimeter cubes, math balance weights, tiles, geometry solids, fraction halves or fourths, 45 triangle, and 30-60 triangle.

Measuring 45-degree angles. Now tell him to place the smaller angles of two tangram triangles in the goniometer, as shown below on the left. Ask: Do the two angles equal 90 degrees? [yes] What is the size of one angle? [half of 90 = 45 degrees]

Two smaller angles equal to 90 degrees.

The goniometer set to 45 degrees.

Ask him to measure other angles in the tangram pieces. Also ask him to measure the smaller angles in the triangles. [45 degrees]

Fold a piece of paper in half at a corner. Ask the child to check it with the goniometer. Is it 45 degrees? [yes] See the left figure below.

Ask the child to make a square with four tiles. Tell him to place the medium triangle on it as shown below on the right. Ask: Do you see the diagonal? [yes] What angle is it? [45 degrees]

Corner of piece of paper folded in half.

Diagonal in square made with four tiles.

In conclusion. Ask: What is half of a right angle? [45] Name the angles in a tangram triangle. [90, 45, 45]

© Activities for Learning, Inc. 2013

Lesson 131: Number and Operations in Base Ten Review

OBJECTIVES:
1. To review the number and operations in base ten topics

MATERIALS:
1. Place-value cards
2. Tiles
3. Dry erase board
4. AL Abacus
5. Math journal

ACTIVITIES FOR TEACHING:

Representing numbers. Ask the child to write the number 101 in his math journal, each digit in a separate rectangle. Continue writing in the columns up to 120.

Ask the child to lay out the place-value cards. Then ask him to find the hundreds, naming them in random order: 900, 700, 200, and so on.

Greater or less. Have the child take 6 blue tiles and 4 yellow tiles. Place the 6 blue tiles in a group and the 4 yellow tiles in another group on his dry erase board as shown below. Then ask the child: Which group has the greater number of tiles? [blue] Which group has the lesser number of tiles? [yellow] Have him write the correct symbol between them. [>]

   6 is greater than 4.

Ask the child: What is 10 + 4? [14] What is 10 + 8? [18] Continue by asking other 10 plus a number equations.

Write 39 + 6 = __ and ask the child to find the sum. [45]

Word problem. Ask the child to draw a part-whole circle set on his dry erase board. Then give him the following problem:

> Nine children are getting on a bus. Six children are already on the bus. How many more children must still get on the bus? [3]

Tell him to write the quantities he knows in the part-whole circle set. See the left figure on the next page.

EXPLANATIONS:

Lessons 131, 132, 134, 135, 137, and 139 are review and game lessons for the end of year assessments. If preferred, these lesson may be taught sequentially, then the assessments may be presented as a single final test.

The first concept is taught in lesson 29 and the second in lesson 30.

This concept is taught in lesson 47.

This concept is taught in lesson 26.

This concept is taught in lesson 86.

ACTIVITIES FOR TEACHING:	EXPLANATIONS:

Tell the child to solve the part-whole circle set and write the equation. See the right figure below.

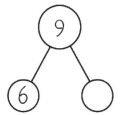

Writing the 10 minus a number equations. Ask the child to enter 10 on his abacus. Then tell him to move 1 bead a little ways away as shown below. Ask him to say the subtraction equation [10 minus 1 = 9] and to write it on his dry erase board as shown below.

This concept is taught in lesson 85.

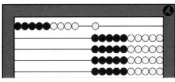

10 − 1 = 9.

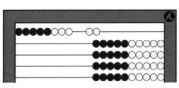

10 − 2 = 8.

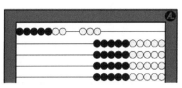

10 − 3 = 7.

```
1 0 - 1 = 9
1 0 - 2 = 8
1 0 - 3 = 7
1 0 - 4 = 6
1 0 - 5 = 5
1 0 - 6 = 4
1 0 - 7 = 3
1 0 - 8 = 2
1 0 - 9 = 1
1 0 - 1 0 = 0
```

The dry erase board showing 10 minus a number facts.

Four-digit addition. Give the child the place-value cards. Ask him to make and set aside the following numbers:

  8 thousand 6 hundred sixty-four
  3 hundred fifty-nine
  1 thousand seventeen
  5 thousand 8 hundred ninety-eight

Ask him to write the first two numbers in his math journal and then add them. Then ask him to write and add the last two numbers.

This concept is taught in lesson 72.

```
  8664         1017
+  359       + 5898
  9023         6915
```

© Activities for Learning, Inc. 2013

Lesson 132: Number and Operations in Base Ten Games

OBJECTIVES:
1. To review the number and operations in base ten topics

MATERIALS:
1. *Math Card Games* book
2. Place value cards
3. AL Abacus

ACTIVITIES FOR TEACHING:	EXPLANATIONS:
Can You Find game. Play the Can You Find game in the *Math Card Games* book, N43. Ask the child to spread out the hundreds, tens, and ones place-value cards. Say a number and ask the child to pick up, stack, and set aside the corresponding place-value cards. All the cards will be picked up at the conclusion of the game. Below are suggested numbers to say: 1. Can you find 400? 2. Can you find 43? 3. Can you find 104? 4. Can you find 57? 5. Can you find 629? 6. Can you find 760? 7. Can you find 215? 8. Can you find 998? 9. Can you find 371? 10. Can you find 502? 11. Can you find 86? 12. Can you find 830? ***Go to the Dump with Fifteens game.*** Play Go to the Dump with Fifteens, the advanced version of the game Go to the Dump from the *Math Cards Games* book, A3. Use the basic deck of cards but only the numbers from 5 to 10. The pairs are two cards whose numbers total 15. The remaining rules of the game are the same.	

ACTIVITIES FOR TEACHING:	EXPLANATIONS:

Addition War game. Play the game Addition War from the *Math Cards Games* book, A44. Use only the cards with numbers from 5 to 10. Let the child to use his abacus if needed. Tell the child he is to say the sums out loud before comparing them.

Corners™ Exercise game. The Corners™ Exercise is found in the *Math Card Games* book, A8. Tell the child to take 12 Corners™ cards and put them together to create the highest possible score.

Short Chain Solitaire game. Play Short Chain Solitaire, found in the *Math Card Games* book, A47.

LESSON 133: NUMBER & OPERATIONS IN BASE TEN ASSESSMENT

OBJECTIVES:
1. To assess the number and operations in base ten topics

MATERIALS:
1. End of Year Assessment 1 (found in the back of the child's *Worksheets*)

ACTIVITIES FOR TEACHING:

Assessment 1. Give the child the End of Year Assessment 1.

Problem 1. Tell the child to write the numbers 108 to 118 in the blanks of the worksheet.

Problems 2–4. Ask the child to find and circle the numbers to be read out loud:

   2. 978
   3. 237
   4. 786

Problems 5–8. Ask the child to put the correct symbol in the circles; greater than, less than, or equal:

   5. 7 + 8 ⊜ 8 + 7
   6. 1 + 90 ⊘ 19
   7. 200 ⊘ 50 + 50
   8. 100 + 1 ⊘ 110

Problems 9–15. Have the child solve the equations:

   9. 56 + 6 = **62**
   10. 57 + 7 = **64**
   11. 47 + 8 = **55**
   12. 88 + 9 = **97**
   13. 37 + 5 = **42**
   14. 85 + 8 = **93**
   15. 77 + 10 = **87**

Problem 16. Have the child read and solve the following problem and write the equation:

   Twenty-two children will ride the train at the zoo. Eleven children are already on the train. How many more children must still get on the train? [11]

EXPLANATIONS:

ACTIVITIES FOR TEACHING:

Problems 17–22. Have the child subtract:

17. 80 – 79 = **1**
18. 34 – 30 = **4**
19. 91 – 85 = **6**
20. 16 – 13 = **3**
21. 60 – 57 = **3**
22. 36 – 26 = **10**

Problems 23–26. Have the child add:

```
  1398        3149
+ 1406      + 7788
  2804       10937

  9385        2925
+   99      + 1464
  9484        4389
```

EXPLANATIONS:

---

1. Write the numbers 108 through 118 in the blanks below.

108 109 110 111 112 113 114 115 116 117 118

2–4. Find and circle the numbers that are said.

9087   980   (978)   987
 372 2037 2307   (237)
(786) 687 7086 7860

5–8. Write <, >, or = in the circles.

| 7 + 8 = 8 + 7 |
| 1 + 90 > 19 |
| 200 > 50 + 50 |
| 100 + 1 > 110 |

9–15. Add.

56 + 6 = 62	37 + 5 = 42
57 + 7 = 64	85 + 8 = 93
47 + 8 = 55	77 + 10 = 87
88 + 9 = 97	

16. Solve the following problem and write the equation.

Twenty-two children will ride the train at the zoo. Eleven children are already on the train. How many more children must still get on the train?

11 + 11 = 22

17–22. Subtract.

80 – 79 = 1	16 – 13 = 3
34 – 30 = 4	60 – 57 = 3
91 – 85 = 6	36 – 26 = 10

23–26. Add.

```
  1398        3149
+ 1406      + 7788
  2804       10937

  9385        2925
+   99      + 1464
  9484        4389
```

Lesson 134: Operations & Algebraic Thinking Review

OBJECTIVES:
1. To review the operations and algebraic thinking topics

MATERIALS:
1. Dry erase board

ACTIVITIES FOR TEACHING:	EXPLANATIONS:
Review. Ask the child: When you add, what do you call the answer? [sum] When you subtract, what do you call the answer? [difference]	
Problem 1. Read to the following problem to the child:	This concept is taught in lesson 94.
Mikayla has a book with 36 pages and Nathan has a book with 50 pages. Whose book has more pages and how many more? [Nathan, 14 more pages]	
Draw a part-whole circle set and ask: Which number goes in the whole-circle? [50] What number goes in a part-circle? [36] See the left figure below. Ask: Whose book has more pages? [Nathan] How many more? [14] Ask the child to write the equation.	

$$50 - 36 = \underline{14} \text{ or } 36 + \underline{14} = 50$$

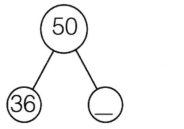 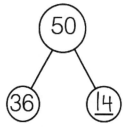

Problem 2. Read the problem to the child.

Jamie walked 13 blocks. Kim walked 3 blocks farther. How far did Kim walk?

Draw a part-whole circle set. Ask him: Is 13 a part or a whole? [a part] Is 3 a part or a whole? [a part] Ask him to fill in the part-whole circle set. See the left figure below. Also ask him to write the equation. Ask: What did you find, a part or a whole? [a whole]

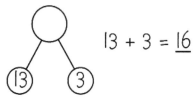

Finding the distance Kim walked.

ACTIVITIES FOR TEACHING:	EXPLANATIONS:
Making equations. Write: 5 __ 1 __ 6 Tell him to make an equation using +, –, and = signs. [5 _+_ 1 _=_ 6] Repeat for 3 __ 8 __ 5 [3 _=_ 8 _–_ 5]	This concept is taught in lesson 95.
Even and Odd. Ask the child to say whether the following numbers are even or odd: 32 [even] 63 [odd] 14 [even] 32 [even] 17 [odd] 89 [odd] 60 [even] 19 [odd]	This concept is taught in lesson 97.
Problems 3 and 4. Give the child the following problems to solve: A young child counted all the shoes in the family's mudroom. The child counted 17 shoes. Do you think the answer is correct if no shoes are missing? [no] There are 9 mittens in a box. Do you think there are any missing? [Yes, at least 1 mitten must be missing.]	

© Activities for Learning, Inc. 2013

Lesson 135: Operations & Algebraic Thinking Games

OBJECTIVES:
1. To review the operations and algebraic thinking topics

MATERIALS:
1. *Math Card Games* book
2. Dry erase board

ACTIVITIES FOR TEACHING:	EXPLANATIONS:
Subtraction Memory game. Play the Subtraction Memory game, found in the *Math Card Games* book, S6. Use a 9 card for the number being subtracted. Play the game again with 8 as the number being subtracted. **Harder Difference War game.** Play the Harder Difference War game from the *Math Card Games* book, S13. **Zero Corners™ game.** Play the Zero Corners™ game, from the *Math Card Games* book, S9. Use the starting scores given in the game instructions. **Harder Difference War game.** Play the Peace Variation of the Harder Difference War game from the *Math Card Games* book, S13. For the Peace Variation, the player with the lower difference takes the cards. **Change from Twenty-Five Cents game.** The game, Change from Twenty-Five Cents, is played like Change from Fifty Cents found in the *Math Card Games* book, M12. 	

RightStart™ Mathematics Level B Second Edition © Activities for Learning, Inc. 2013

ACTIVITIES FOR TEACHING:

EXPLANATIONS:

Make the Amount game. Play the game Make the Amount from the *Math Card Games* book, M10. The players can keep score with tally marks on the dry erase board.

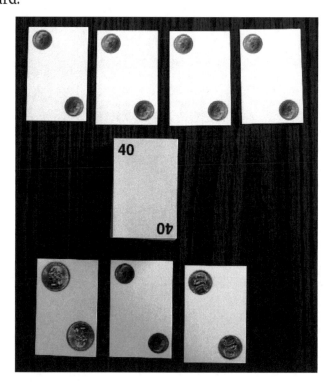

Make Sixteen Cents game. Play the Make Sixteen Cents game found in the *Math Card Games* book, M6.

Lesson 136: Operations & Algebraic Thinking Assessment

OBJECTIVES:
1. To assess the operations and algebraic thinking topics

MATERIALS:
1. End of Year Assessment 2

ACTIVITIES FOR TEACHING: | **EXPLANATIONS:**

Assessment 2. Give the child the End of Year Assessment 2.

Problems 1–2. Ask the child to circle the correct answer to the following questions:
  1. When you add, what do you call the answer? [sum]
  2. When you subtract, what do you call the answer? [difference]

Problems 3–4. Have the child read and solve the following problems:
  3. Matt has a book with 43 pages and Emily has a book with 61 pages. Whose book has more pages and how many more? [Emily, 18 more pages]
  4. Kevin walked 23 blocks. Penny walked 8 blocks farther. How far did Penny walk? [31]

Problems 5–9. Have the child complete the equations:
  5. $\underline{4} + 3 = 7$
  6. $2 = 10 - \underline{8}$
  7. $3 + \underline{3} = 7 - 1$
  8. $16 = 10 + \underline{3} + 3$ or $16 - 10 = 3 + \underline{3}$
  9. $8 + \underline{0} = 9 - 1$ or $8 - \underline{0} = 9 - 1$

Problems 10–17. Ask the child to write whether the following numbers are even or odd:
  36 [even]   83 [odd]   14 [even]   22 [even]
  57 [odd]   99 [odd]   40 [even]   19 [odd]

RightStart™ Mathematics Level B Second Edition © Activities for Learning, Inc. 2013

ACTIVITIES FOR TEACHING:

EXPLANATIONS:

1. (Sum)   Difference   Equation

2. Sum   (Difference)   Equation

3–4. Solve the following problems.

Matt has a book with 43 pages and Emily has a book with 61 pages. Whose book has more pages and how many more?

<u>Emily, 18 more pages.</u>

Kevin walked 23 blocks. Penny walked 8 blocks farther. How far did Penny walk?

<u>31 blocks</u>

5–9. Complete the following equations.

| 4 + 3 = 7 |
| 2 = 10 − 8 |
| 3 + 3 = 7 − 1 |
| 16 = 10 + 3 + 3 |
| 8 + 0 = 9 − 1 |

10–17. Write whether the following numbers are even or odd.

36 <u>even</u>   83 <u>odd</u>   14 <u>even</u>   22 <u>even</u>

57 <u>odd</u>   99 <u>odd</u>   40 <u>even</u>   19 <u>odd</u>

© Activities for Learning, Inc. 2013

Lesson 137: Measurement and Data Review and Game

OBJECTIVES:
1. To review the measurement and data topics

MATERIALS:
1. Centimeter cubes
2. One set of tangrams
3. Tiles
4. AL Abacus, optional

ACTIVITIES FOR TEACHING:	EXPLANATIONS:
Centimeters. Give the centimeter cubes and tangrams to the child. Ask him to measure the longest side of the large triangle in centimeters as shown below in the left figure. Ask: How many centimeters long is it? [10 cm]	This concept is taught in lesson 104.

Next ask him to measure the side of the large triangle. [7 cm] See the right figure. Repeat for the other side. [7 cm]

Longest side is 10 cm.

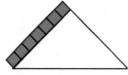
Side is 7 cm.

Measuring tangrams. Ask: Which shape has $3\frac{1}{2}$ cm on all side? [square] Which shape has two sides measuring $3\frac{1}{2}$ cm and two sides measuring 5 cm? [parallelogram] Which shape has one side measuring 5 cm and two sides measuring $3\frac{1}{2}$ cm? [small triangle] See figures below.

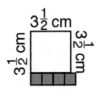
Square.

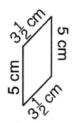
Parallelogram.

Small triangle.

Inches. Give the child the tiles. Review that the edge of a tile is 1 inch long. Tell him to measure the longest side of the large triangle. [4 in.] See figure below.

This concept is taught in lesson 106.

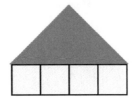
Measuring in inches with tiles.

RightStart™ Mathematics Level B Second Edition © Activities for Learning, Inc. 2013

ACTIVITIES FOR TEACHING:

Find all the sides of the tangram pieces that measure 2 in. [6 sides]

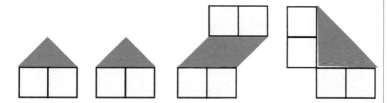

Comparing inches and centimeters. Ask the child: How many centimeters is 4 inches? [10 cm] Encourage him to use his tiles and centimeter cubes to help him find the answer. Ask: How many centimeters in 2 inches? [5 cm]

Measuring the abacus. Review that what we measure with is called a *unit*. Ask the child to solve the following problems:

> Doug measured a side of a plastic AL Abacus and found it was almost 10. What were Doug's units, centimeters or inches? [inches] Which side did he measure? [the longer side]

Continue with:

> Derika measured the length of 10 AL Abacus beads. She found it was 10. What were Derika's units, centimeters or inches? [centimeters]

I Spy game. Tell the child you are going to look at the tangram pieces and say, "I spy with my little eye..."

> . . . a side of a triangle that is 10 cm long. [longest side of the largest triangle]

> . . . a side of a shape that is 4 inches long. [longest side of the largest triangle]

> . . . a side of a shape that is 1 inch long. [a tile]

> . . . a side of a triangle that is 7 cm long. [longest side of the medium triangle or short side of the largest triangle]

EXPLANATIONS:

© Activities for Learning, Inc. 2013

Lesson 138: Measurement and Data Assessment

OBJECTIVES:
1. To assess the measurement and data topics

MATERIALS:
1. End of Year Assessment 3
2. Centimeter cubes
3. One set of tangrams
4. Tiles

ACTIVITIES FOR TEACHING:	EXPLANATIONS:
Assessment 3. Give the child the End of Year Assessment 3. **Problems 1–7.** Give the child tangrams and the centimeter cubes. Tell him to measure the sides of the tangrams using the centimeter cubes. Write the lengths for the pieces on his worksheet. 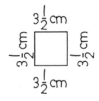  **Problems 8–9.** Solve the following problem on the worksheet: Jason measured a side of a plastic AL Abacus and found it was 19. What were Jason's units, centimeters or inches? [centimeters] Continue with: Jessica measured the length of 10 AL Abacus beads. She found it was 4. What were Jessica's units, centimeters or inches? [inches]	

RightStart™ Mathematics Level B Second Edition © Activities for Learning, Inc. 2013

ACTIVITIES FOR TEACHING:	EXPLANATIONS:

Problems 10–11.

10. How many centimeters is 4 inches? [10 cm]

11. How many centimeters in 2 inches? [5 cm]

Problem 12. Give the tiles to the child. Tell him to measure the longest side of the large tangram triangle. Write the answer on the worksheet. [4 in. or 10 cm]

 4 inches

Problems 13–19. Ask the child to find and circle all the sides of the tangram pieces that measure 2 inches [6 sides]

6 sides

© Activities for Learning, Inc. 2013

Lesson 139: Geometry Review and Games

OBJECTIVES:
1. To review the geometry topics

MATERIALS:
1. One set of tangrams
2. Geoboard
3. Geometry solids
4. **A brown paper bag**

ACTIVITIES FOR TEACHING:	EXPLANATIONS:
Triangles. Hold up a large triangle from the tangrams. Ask: Is this a quadrilateral? [no] Why not? [It doesn't have four sides.] Ask: What is it? [triangle] What is special about this triangle? [It has a right angle.] A right triangle.	This concept is taught in Lesson 25.
Right triangles. Tell the child to spread out his seven tangram pieces. Ask him: How many of the pieces are right triangles? [5] How many right angles are there in all the pieces? [9, 5 in triangles and 4 in square]	
Two right angles. Tell the child to place his two large right triangles next to each other as shown below. Ask him: What happens to the right angles? [They turned into a straight line.] What is the new shape? [another right triangle]	
 **Two right angles together make a straight line.**	
Dividing a circle into halves and fourths. Tell the child to use the a circle side of his geoboard. Then tell him to place a rubber band around one fourth of the circle. See the left figure on the next page. Tell him to do another quarter next to his first quarter. See the second figure on the next page. Ask: What is another name for two quarters or two fourths? [one half]	This concept is taught in Lesson 102.

ACTIVITIES FOR TEACHING:

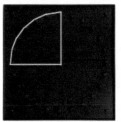  

One fourth, or one quarter, of a circle. Two fourths, or one half, of a circle. Four fourths, or one whole circle.

EXPLANATIONS:

Have the child make two more fourths to complete the circle. See the third figure above. Ask: How many right angles do you see at the center of the circle? [4]

Prisms. Give the geometry solids to the child. Ask: How many solids have curved faces or sides? [5] Tell him to set those aside. Then tell him to find and set aside the pyramid, the figure whose sides meet at a point.

Say: Prisms have congruent figures at each end. Ask the child to find the prism with triangles at each end. Ask: Do you see parallel lines on the triangular prism? [yes] Do you see perpendicular lines? [yes]

Ask: What congruent shape is at both ends? [square] Tell him to find three prisms with rectangles at each end.

Stereognostic game. Start with about six to eight solids in the bag. The child feels each solid, says its name, and shows it.

Ask: Which figure is round all over? [sphere] Which have circles on a face? [cylinder, hemisphere, and cone]

I Spy game. Tell the child you are going to look at all the solids and say: "I spy with my little eye. . ."

   . . . a solid that has two triangles. [triangular prism]

   . . . a solid that has no straight lines. [sphere, hemisphere, cylinders]

   . . . a prism with all the faces the same. [cube]

   . . . a solid with a circle at one end and a point at the other end. [cone]

This concept is taught in Lesson 109.

© Activities for Learning, Inc. 2013

Lesson 140: Geometry Assessment

OBJECTIVES:
1. To assess the geometry topics

MATERIALS:
1. End of Year Assessment 4
2. One set of tangrams
3. Geometry solids

ACTIVITIES FOR TEACHING:

Assessment 4. Give the child the End of Year Assessment 4.

Problems 1–3. Point to the large triangle from the tangrams. Ask the child to answer the following questions:

1. Is this a quadrilateral? [no]
2. What is it called? [a triangle]
3. Does it have any parallel lines? [no]

A right triangle.

Problems 4–10. Tell the child to look at the seven tangram pieces on his worksheet. Ask him to answer the following questions:

4. How many of the pieces are right triangles? [5]
5. How many right angles are there in all the pieces? [9, 5 in the triangles and 4 in the square]
6. How many pieces are rectangles? [1]
7. How many triangles are there? [5]
8. How many pieces are parallelograms? [2]
9. How many pieces have parallel lines? [2]
10. How many pieces have perpendicular lines? [6]

Problems 11–16. Tell the child to look at the geometry solids and answer the following questions:

11. How many solids are prisms? [6]
12. How many solids are pyramids? [1]
13. Do the prisms have parallel lines? [yes]
14. Do the prisms have perpendicular lines? [yes]
15. What shape are the sides of the pyramid? [triangle]
16. How many solids are cylinders? [2]

EXPLANATIONS:

ACTIVITIES FOR TEACHING:

Problems 17–22. Tell the child to:

17. Draw a line under the circle that is divided in half.

18. Draw a line under circle that is divided into fourths.

19. How many quarters are in a whole? [4]
20. How many quarters in a half? [2]
21. What is another word for quarter? [fourth]
22. How many right angles do you see at the center of the circle? [4]

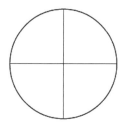

EXPLANATIONS:

© Activities for Learning, Inc. 2013

Congratulations!

Your child has completed RightStart™ Mathematics Level B and is now ready for Level C Second Edition.

Certificates of completion are in the back of the child's worksheets.

To move on to RightStart™ Mathematics Level C Second Edition, all you need is the Level C Book Bundle. This can be purchased at RightStartMath.com or by calling 888-272-3291.

APPENDIX

Assessment Checklist 1

Name	Can show with fingers			Can recognize on the AL Abacus			Can enter on the AL Abacus					
	2	5	7	3	6	9	8-ten 6	92	5-ten 3	47	1-ten 8	12

RECTANGLES

Flat Hundreds Squares

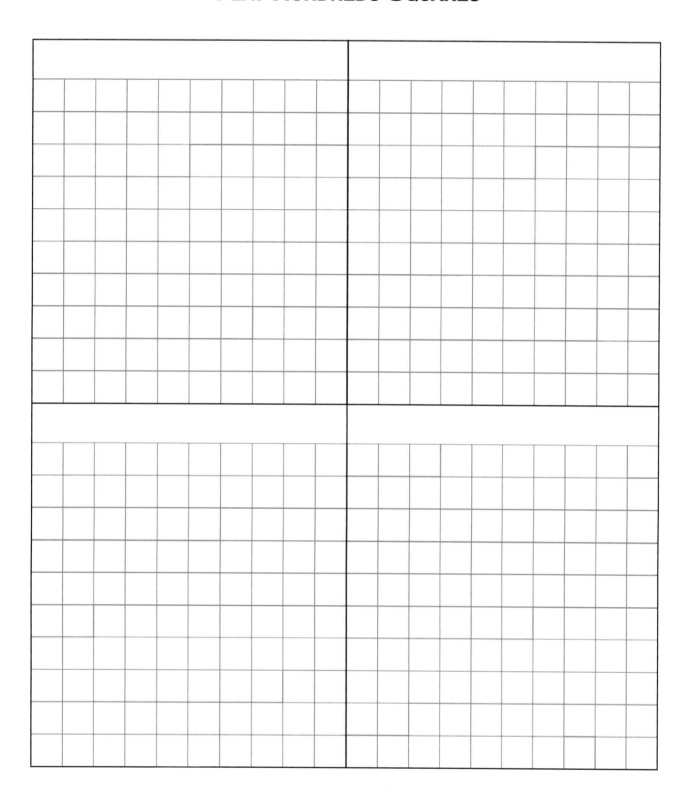

Appendix page 5

THE COTTER TENS FRACTAL

Fractals are a new branch of mathematics only a few decades old. There are two types of fractals, regular and random. Scientists use random fractals for computer modeling in order to study some of nature's irregular patterns and structures. Regular fractals, also called geometric fractals, consist of larger structures that are identical to the smaller structure.

The Tens Fractal, a regular fractal starts with ten small equilateral triangles arranged in the pattern of a larger equilateral triangle, the ten triangle. Ten of these ten triangles arranged in the same pattern forms the hundred triangle. And ten of the hundred triangles in the same pattern forms the thousand triangle, the Cotter Tens Fractal.

One purpose of building this fractal is to help the children visualize and experience the repeating tens structure of our number system. Another purpose is integrating mathematics and art.

This Cotter Tens Fractal was built by

_____

Ones Triangles for Cotter Tens Fractal

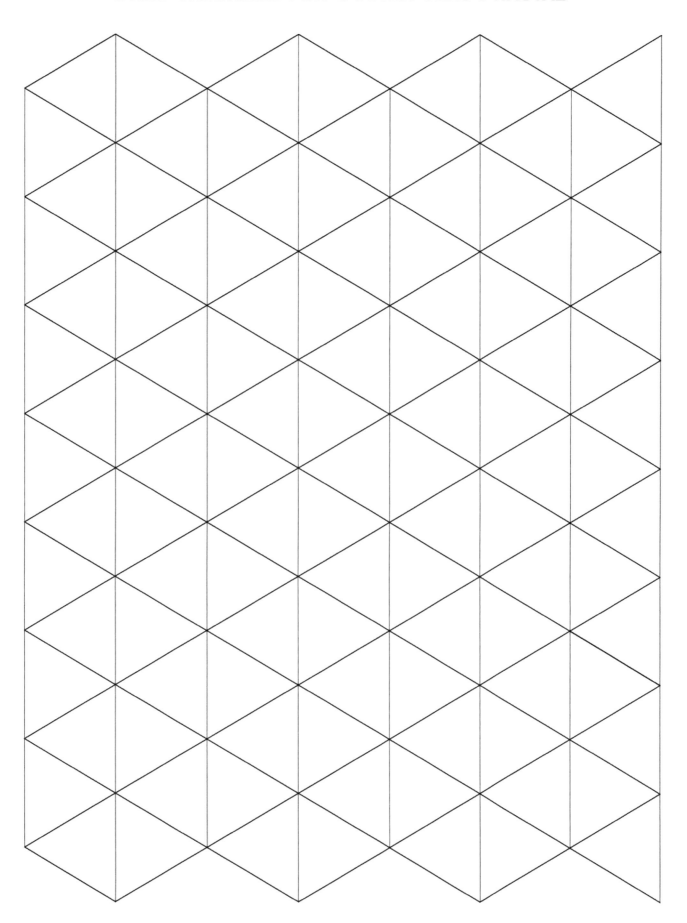

TENS TRIANGLE OUTLINES FOR COTTER TENS FRACTAL

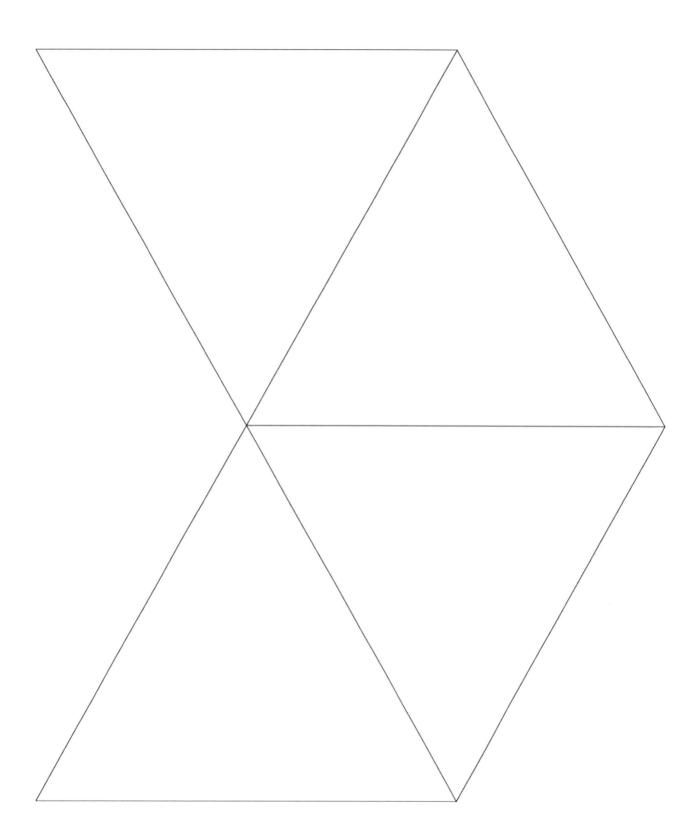

Appendix page 8

Thirty Days has September

Lyrics by Joan A. Cotter

Composed by Rosine Hermodson-Olsen
Arranged by Barbara Ask

Clock without Numbers

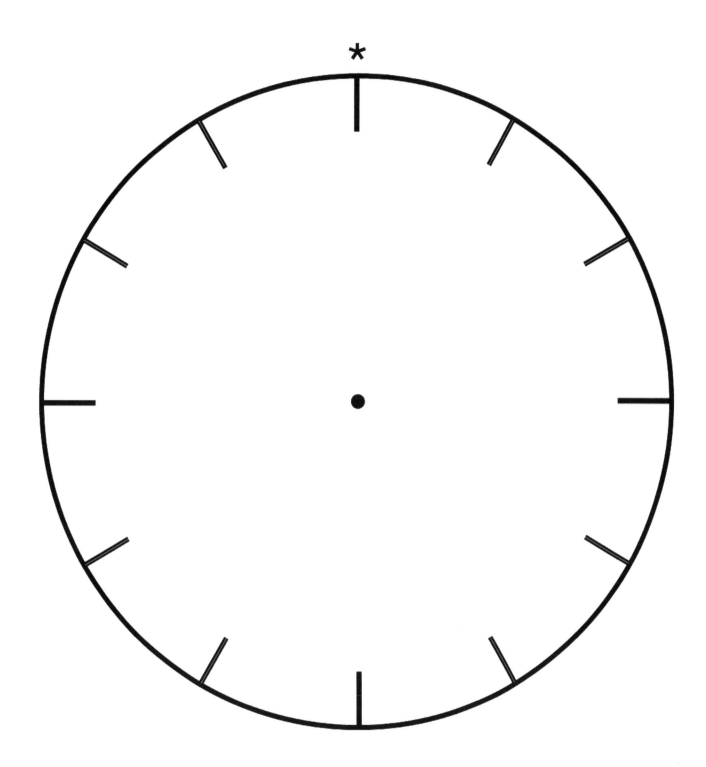

Clock with Minutes

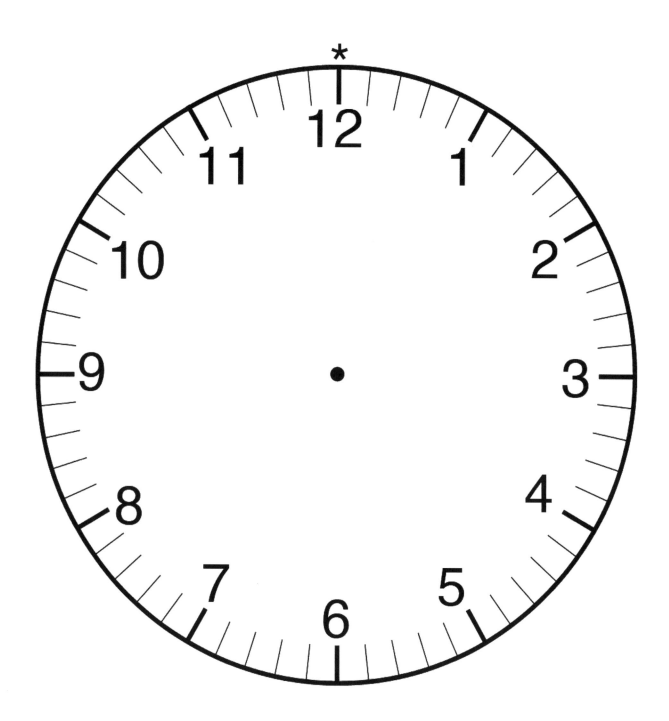